B.S. Lehman

3/91

THE MAKING
OF A PUBLIC MAN

The Making of a Public Man

A MEMOIR

BY

Sol M. Linowitz

LITTLE, BROWN AND COMPANY · BOSTON · TORONTO

FIRST EDITION

Library of Congress Cataloging-in-Publication Data

Linowitz, Sol M., 1913–
    The making of a public man.

    Includes index.
    1. Linowitz, Sol M., 1913–   . 2. Lawyers—United
States—Biography.   3. Statesmen—United States—
Biography. I. Title.
KF373.L533A35   1985   349.73′092′4 [B]   85-15899
ISBN 0-316-52689-4   347.300924 [B]

DESIGNED BY DEDE CUMMINGS

*Published simultaneously in Canada
by Little, Brown & Company (Canada) Limited*

PRINTED IN THE UNITED STATES OF AMERICA

*To Toni, who made
it all worthwhile*

It is required of a man that he should share the passion and action of his time at peril of being judged not to have lived.

—*Justice Oliver Wendell Holmes, Jr.*

Foreword

SEVERAL YEARS AGO, while I was visiting Yale University as a Chubb Fellow, a student asked me a question: "If you could run the reel of your life back, would you still make the same choices you did?"

In a way, this book tries to answer that question.

I have, certainly, no regrets. As a lawyer, I have had an exciting practice in corporate and international law; as a businessman, I have helped found and develop a great American company; as a diplomat, I have represented my country in important negotiations.

But I cannot claim that I planned it that way. My career evolved as it went along — by serendipity, if you will, rather than according to a prepared plan of action.

Much of my good fortune has been just that; I have been lucky. Lucky to be able to devote my life to things that interested me, lucky in my wife and family, lucky in the friends who were always there.

Running the reel back, I am more certain than ever about the answer I gave the young student: "I made the right choices — and it was a lot of fun making them."

Acknowledgments

THIS BOOK OWES much to the help and encouragement of Martin Mayer. Martin and I have been friends since 1966, when he wrote an article about me for the *New York Times Magazine*. In later years he was among a growing group — including my wife and our four daughters, some friends, and even a few publishers — who urged me to write my memoirs. I always said no, for the same three reasons: (1) I didn't think my story was all that interesting; (2) I couldn't make the time commitment; (3) there's always tomorrow.

Then, in 1982–1983, I accepted Columbia University's proposal to engage in a number of tape-recorded interviews for its admirable Oral History Project. Out of that came almost a thousand pages of recollections and reflections, based in large part on my experiences since coming to Washington in October 1966. Some years earlier I had written about a hundred pages on the story of my earlier years, especially the two decades with Xerox. As I read over all this material, I began to consider the possibility of a book, and I asked Martin if he would look at it and give me his opinion.

He did, and told me that he thought there were the makings of a book in those many pages. He was then completing the work on three books of his own that would be published in one academic year: *The Diplomats*, a subject we had discussed together on numerous occasions; *The Met*, a centennial history of the Metropolitan Opera House; and *The Money Bazaars*. I told him I didn't see how I could find the time to organize, coordinate, and shape my mass of material, and he said, incredibly, that he had some free time and would commit it to help me with my book — provided that I would make the necessary commitment myself. He did, and I did, and the book came into being. Martin knows how grateful I am for his assistance and guidance and — above all — his friendship.

My special thanks also go to my former colleagues Ambassador Ambler H. Moss, Andrew Marks, and Kenneth Sparks, and to Robert Banks, General Counsel of the Xerox Corporation, for going over various chapters and giving me the benefit of their suggestions and corrections.

My editor, Roger Donald of Little, Brown, was thoughtful as well as perceptive in his comments, suggestions, and criticisms.

My wife, Toni, prodded, cajoled, encouraged — and occasionally threatened — to keep me at the book, and my daughters, Anne, June, Jan, and Ronni, even promised to read it. To all of them, my love and gratitude for making me do it.

Contents

PART I

Introduction: The Government Years

1

The Transition

MY WIFE, TONI, and I had just arrived in Nice for a weekend of rest and relaxation between two weeks of business meetings in London. We were walking on the beach when the hotel concierge came running up to us, red-faced and breathless. "Monsieur, monsieur," he shouted. "We have been trying to find you. The White House is calling!" "Who in the White House?" I asked. He came to a sudden stop. "Monsieur," he replied icily, "When the White House calls, one does not ask who is calling."[1]

It was Bill Moyers, President Lyndon Johnson's assistant, and his message was brief: "The President wants you back as soon as possible. He plans to announce tomorrow." I began to explain that I was in the midst of some very difficult and important negotiations in London when Moyers interrupted me: "I'm afraid you don't understand. The President wants you back *now*." And that was that.

This was October 1966. I was then fifty-two years old, and chairman of the executive committee of the Xerox Corporation, chairman of the board of Xerox International, and a senior partner in a large Rochester, New York, law firm. I telephoned Joe Wilson, president of Xerox and my closest friend, to tell him that the time had come to release the statement we had prepared in advance to announce that I

---

[1] I recalled this conversation many years later when I learned that President Carter's Attorney General, Griffin Bell, told that "the White House is calling," had admirably responded, "I don't talk to buildings."

was resigning my positions with the company. I also called my law partners in Rochester to tell them to announce my departure from our firm. Toni and I packed our bags and flew out that afternoon so we could be back the next day when the President told a press conference that Llewellyn Thompson would be taking a second tour in Moscow as ambassador to the Soviet Union; Ellsworth Bunker had accepted an assignment as ambassador-at-large; and Sol M. Linowitz was leaving Xerox for a new joint appointment as ambassador to the Organization of American States and U.S. Representative to the Inter-American Committee of the Alliance for Progress.

Throughout my business and professional career, I had taken considerable time for public causes and for efforts to establish public-private partnerships, and I had worked for the government before. During and just after World War II I had been an assistant general counsel of the Office of Price Administration and then a naval officer doing legal work for the Navy Department. But Moyers's phone call ushered me into a different world, a world of ceremonies in the Oval Office and pictures on the front page of the *New York Times*. When we returned to Rochester, cameramen and reporters were camped around our house awaiting my arrival, full of questions I had not the faintest notion how to answer.

My plan was to take a kind of sabbatical, fulfilling what I had long considered to be an obligation of the successful professional or businessman: to devote a period of his life to the service of his country. I would be away from Rochester, I thought, no more than two years; then, I expected, I would return to Xerox and to the practice of law. But even friends who knew that I had been thinking about government service were surprised that the announced post was ambassador to the OAS, and so were a number of my acquaintances in Washington. Those on the White House staff who knew that President Johnson had offered me several other positions — including Secretary of Commerce — wondered why I would take *this* one. On one occasion during his Dominican Republic adventure, Lyndon Johnson had been overheard expressing an opinion of the Organization of American States: "They couldn't pour warm spit out of a boot if the instructions were written on the heel." My predecessor as OAS ambassador, Ellsworth Bunker, told me quite frankly that he had found the post rather unrewarding: "You don't," he said, "make policy here."

One of the reasons for that, it seemed to me, was that the United

States did not really have a Latin American policy. It was an area of the world that presidents preferred to ignore. Americans thought of the continent to their south as a homogeneous blob and did not understand that these were sovereign countries with their own histories, traditions, and economic circumstances. I had traveled to some of the cities of South America in the years just before I went to the OAS, setting up Xerox subsidiaries, and I knew that crossing a border on that continent could mean changing centuries. We shared a hemisphere with these people; they, too, were "Americans"; yet we had consistently relegated them to the backwash of history. I thought that here in our neighborhood the United States should be investing its best resources of political attention, economic aid, and human understanding, and I wanted to try to help.

And there was President Johnson himself. When he really wanted something from you, it was almost impossible to deny him. He was a man of endless contradictions: he could be ruthless, yet intuitively sensitive to what everyone around him was thinking; coarse, yet highly sophisticated about what made people tick; cruel, yet capable of great tenderness, especially toward poor and disadvantaged people. He was confusing, enchanting, offensive — sometimes all at once — and he knew it. If you went to a family dinner at his ranch, you saw him eat like someone who had never learned table manners, while his wise and sensitive Lady Bird winced and looked away. If you went to a state dinner at the White House, however, you saw a gracious President fully aware of all the niceties of protocol. He used his personality recklessly, but some part of him always knew what he was doing.

I remember one occasion early in 1967, when Johnson was trying to get Congress to make commitments in support of a Latin American Common Market that the countries were expected to negotiate during a forthcoming summit conference of American hemisphere presidents — the first such conference ever — at Punta del Este in Uruguay. Johnson was upset because he could not get Congress to authorize any funds. He called to his office the leaders of the foreign relations committees of both houses of Congress and growled at them: "You don't want to support your President. You don't care about your President. Hell, then I won't go to the meeting." He looked over at Secretary of State Rusk and said, "Dean, let's you and me call a press conference, and tell 'em the President won't go, can't go, can't get the support of the Congress." He seemed so unhappy and hangdog that William Mailliard, a Republican Congressman from California, was touched. He went over and put his arm around Johnson's shoulder. "We don't want to hurt you, Mr. President," he said. "We want to help you." Johnson replied, "Well, I hope so. I sure hope so." I was standing on the other side of him, so I could see that as he said it he winked at Rusk — a wink that clearly meant "It's working." It did work on Mailliard; he was quite helpful in the House. By then, however, the President was feuding with Senate Foreign Relations Committee chairman William Fulbright, who had developed antibodies to the Johnson charm, and the authorization failed.

During the years before joining his administration, I had developed an easy and congenial relationship with President Johnson. He knew that I liked him, that I was not intimidated by him, and that I was not looking for anything from him. As time went on, he involved me in various group meetings at the White House. I would receive a wire or a phone call from Bill Moyers or Jack Valenti, his assistants: the President would like you to join a group of business leaders for a discussion of the budget, or a meeting of leaders in higher education to talk about some proposals for federal aid, or to participate in some other session with him. These were usually small groups, and sometimes as the meeting ended the President would take my arm and say, "Come into my office for a minute, I want to talk to you." Then it could be anything — the subject of the previous meeting, a bill pending in Congress, a newspaper headline about business leaders attacking Johnson, even the Vietnam War.

It was often just a matter of his talking *at* me. He discovered early that I respected his confidence and never told the press or anyone on the outside what we had talked about. On April 27, 1965, he wrote me a letter, asking me to send him my "candid comments, suggestions and observations about what we are doing — and what we should be doing — to prepare for the challenges facing this country at home and in the world. It means much for me to keep a fresh perspective in this office, and I don't know anyone whose counsel I would rather have." I was pleased but surprised, and I asked someone at the White House how many other such letters the President had sent. The word came back that mine was the only one.

That was a time when I was seeing a good deal of Johnson. In 1964, at his urging, I had taken the lead to form (and chair) the National Committee for International Development, "to promote

public understanding of how United States programs of foreign assistance help to foster a stable, free, and peaceful world." This was a
very distinguished group indeed: the vice-chairman was General
Alfred Gruenther, and the other members included Arthur Dean,
Lewis Douglas, Marriner Eccles, Milton Eisenhower, John Gardner,
James Gavin, Clark Kerr, Stanley Marcus, Walter Reuther, and
David Sarnoff. At the same time, as a trustee of Cornell University
and Hamilton College, I was also working with the White House on
legislation to help higher education, another matter close to Lyndon Johnson's heart. I began hearing from him that I "ought to
come down here and work in the government." I said that I would if
it were the right post, one in which I felt I could really make a contribution, and he would brush off the subject he had raised himself
by saying, "Oh, I don't believe you want to take a job anyway;
you're just talking."[2] Then in the summer of 1966, the President
asked me to come to the White House.

Johnson took me to his little room off the Oval Office, and told me
there were three posts in the State Department he was going to have
to fill: Under Secretary, Under Secretary for Economic Affairs, and
Ambassador to the Organization of American States. Did I have an
interest in any of those, and if so, which? I said all three of those
positions might be of interest to me, and I would be glad to consider
any of them if he wanted me to do so. During the next weeks I had a
number of conversations with Bill Moyers and Walt Rostow, and it
became increasingly clear to me that of the three I preferred the
OAS. The idea of undertaking an administrative responsibility, of
running some part of the State Department, did not excite me. But
at the OAS perhaps I could make my own contribution in an area
that urgently needed attention and commitment.

What may have brought Johnson to this more direct approach
was my relationship with the Kennedy family. Not long after President Kennedy's death, the family and the government agreed that
the best memorial to him would be the performing arts center already being planned for Washington. Johnson, who knew that I was
a violinist, appointed me to the board of trustees of the Kennedy
Center, and the other trustees elected me a vice-chairman. The cen-

---

[2] Every so often, however, one of his people would call to sound me out on whether I might
be interested in a position: the Agency for International Development? The Peace Corps?
The Office of Economic Opportunity? Secretary of Commerce? I thought carefully about
each and decided that none of them was the right niche for me.

ter was something the Kennedy family cared about deeply, and I
came to know them on a social as well as a working basis.

Early in 1966 Senator Robert Kennedy decided that Sol Linowitz
would be the best Democratic candidate for Governor of New York
against Nelson Rockefeller. I was, he pointed out, "liberal and Jewish but also an upstater and a businessman" — in Bobby's view, the
ideal combination. I began to hear rumors that I was interested,
which was itself a remarkable experience, as I knew for a fact that I
was not the source of the rumors. Suddenly I learned that James
Perkins, president of Cornell, had urged that I be given the nomination. There was an article in the *New York Times Magazine* about
me, pegged to the possibility that I might be running for Governor,
then another long article in *Life*. Joseph Alsop wrote one of his nationally syndicated columns on my anticipated gubernatorial candidacy, headed "Why Not Linowitz?" I appeared on "Meet the Press"
to be asked the question: would I be a candidate for Governor?
Bobby assured me that if I said yes, he was ready to move, but all I
felt I could say was that if the nomination were offered, I would
have to consider it — and that was, understandably, not enough.

It was after I had made clear that I would not accept Kennedy's
invitation that the President approached me more directly and more
personally to take a job in his administration. The three State Department positions had been linked in his mind from the beginning:
George Ball (an early dissident on Vietnam) was quietly leaving the
Department to return to private life, and Johnson apparently
wanted to move Bunker into a position from which he could be assigned to the embassy in Saigon. Johnson sat at his desk, moving
pieces of paper on it as though he were filling boxes; he said he
wanted to put my name on one of them.

It was part of my understanding from the start that if I took the
OAS post it would be expanded to include the Alliance for Progress
representation, then part of the duties of Walt Rostow, the President's national security adviser. (Giving this sort of line responsibility to the security adviser would seem strange today, but it should
be remembered that Rostow's academic specialty was develop-
mental economics.) I had run into aspects of the Alliance for
Progress during my weeks in Latin America on Xerox business, and
I had become an admirer.

A venture from the earliest, most idealistic days of the Kennedy
administration, the Alliance was a serious effort to create an inter-

American partnership for the development of Latin America and to bring to this hemisphere some of the lessons learned in the success of the Marshall Plan. Latin America was, of course, very different from Europe. In Europe the task had been to rebuild an economy, and in Latin America there was all too little to rebuild; any program had to start from the ground up. But the most important lesson of our European experience applied here, too: that economic aid works best when the recipients make their own plans for using it and provide most of the resources themselves. In fact, although few Americans realized it, four-fifths of the resources committed to Alliance for Progress programs came from the countries of Latin America. Politically, the Alliance had been the first major initiative of an American president in Latin America since Roosevelt's Good Neighbor Policy. On my visits to Latin America, I had felt the enthusiasm of governments and businessmen alike for the opportunities that had been opened up by this unique collaboration of recipient governments, international lending agencies, and the U.S. foreign-aid program.

Rostow was especially encouraging. He greatly admired CIAP, the inter-American committee of experts, a nine-member group of whom only one was from the United States. This council would receive a country's documentation for its economic plan, hear the planning and economics experts of the country present their projects and their budgets, then make recommendations on allocating aid funds. It was, Rostow said, a wonderfully imaginative approach to managing the problems of economic development. He was giving up his seat on that committee only because he could not get to the meetings — Presidents do not like to be told that their national security adviser is unavailable because he is at some foreign-aid conference. Rostow offered me avuncular congratulations on my new responsibilities: the job would broaden my horizons, he said, and give me the opportunity to participate in one of the most important experiments of our time.

The general and somewhat unfair belief was that the Alliance for Progress was failing. Its economic promise had been a growth rate of 2.5 percent per capita per year, and with the Latin population growing at a rate of 3 percent per year that was an impossible target. Corruption, petty nationalist quarrels, and the persistence of a hog-the-wealth attitude in the ruling oligarchies compounded the discouragement. In four countries — Argentina, Brazil, Ecuador, and

Honduras — military coups had recently overthrown elected governments. The Alliance was only five years old, however; its problems were, I thought, signs of growing pains rather than portents of systemic collapse.

The position Johnson offered combined my two continuing international interests — the United Nations (for the OAS is a regional organization within the United Nations) and economic assistance programs. I had already done some work for the government on United Nations matters. A few years earlier, in the Kennedy administration, I had been chairman of a State Department advisory committee on international organizations that conducted a well-received and I think useful study of our relations with the United Nations for Adlai Stevenson as our ambassador to the United Nations and Harlan Cleveland as Assistant Secretary for International Organizations. And I had reason to hope that Latin American affairs would command a growing share of the President's time and attention. In the spring of 1966, during a visit to Mexico, Johnson had given general approval to the idea of a meeting of all hemispheric Presidents (except, of course, Castro) to revivify the Alliance for Progress. The original proponent of the suggestion, President Arturo Illia of Argentina, had since been overthrown by his military, but the general approval continued. Whoever took over at OAS would have the important job of bringing about such a meeting.

Because of his experiences with Mexican children as a young teacher in Texas, Johnson thought he had a special feeling for Latins. He did have, beyond doubt, a special friendship with President Gustavo Díaz Ordaz of Mexico, although they could communicate only through an interpreter. He had a film that had been taken of his first visit to Mexico City, brilliantly organized by Díaz. It showed great crowds of excited Mexicans mobbing the Johnson procession as it came through the city. He liked to show the film to visitors at his ranch — it took about twenty minutes. Then he would slap his leg and say, "You know what President Díaz Ordaz said to me? He said, 'I only got but a million people, and you got 'em all.' " It would put him in a good mood for the whole evening.

Johnson had felt unjustly treated by the Latins at the time of the Dominican intervention. (They had felt even more unjustly treated by him, of course; the United States had gone in unilaterally and then demanded OAS approval for its actions.) The man he was taking out of the OAS post, Ellsworth Bunker, had handled that for him and earned his gratitude for life. It was a measure of how much he thought of Bunker that he would soon send him to South Vietnam as proconsul (the word "ambassador" did not begin to cover the duties Ellsworth Bunker would undertake in Saigon). Whatever the President might have said in the past about the OAS, to be Ellsworth Bunker's replacement was no mean honor in Lyndon Johnson's eyes.

When Moyers called to say that the President definitely wanted to offer me the post, I said I would like to talk it over with some people directly in touch with the situation — people like Lincoln Gordon, an academic economist (later president of The Johns Hopkins University), who was then Assistant Secretary for American Republic Affairs. I had met Gordon the year before, when he was ambassador to Brazil, and I was visiting that country on Xerox business. That was out of the question, Moyers said: Johnson didn't allow people he was appointing to put him in a position where the offer was being discussed all over Washington. Then he called back and said the President would authorize my talking to *one* person, if he knew in advance who that person was. The next time I saw Johnson I told him the person I wished to consult was Douglas Dillon, who had been Under Secretary of State for Eisenhower and then Treasury Secretary for Kennedy, and for Johnson himself through the transition year. Johnson looked hard at me from under those eyebrows and agreed that I could talk with Dillon.

When I saw him in New York, Douglas Dillon told me he thought I should take the post, that it would be interesting. He then gave me one especially valuable piece of advice: "Never for a day let them forget that you can pick up your marbles and go home." I found myself acting on that advice very soon after I was sworn into office.

The autumn of 1966 was not a happy time for the President's foreign policies, and the foreign-aid bill was mired in Congress. The President asked me to reassemble the National Committee for International Development that I had chaired before coming to Washington, and add some others who might be useful in pushing the legislation through. The meeting was held in the Cabinet Room, with the President and Rusk and McNamara, who pointed up the importance of the aid bill from the perspectives of the State and Defense departments. I sat beside the President, who was in a surly mood. "We're in trouble," he said lugubriously. "We've got a hell of a job up there on the hill to get this bill through, and I don't know how we're going to do it. You know, sometimes you get one of these new ambassadors who comes in and thinks he knows his way around, and it doesn't work that way, and you don't make headway, and you don't know where you are." There was a lot more of that, always pointing back to the "new ambassador" who came down thinking he knew what ought to be done but didn't know, and made the situation worse. He never looked at me, but it was obvious whom he was talking about. At first, I was thunderstruck, and by the time he was done I was seething. I looked around the room at my old friends and acquaintances. David Rockefeller was studying the ceiling, avoiding my eyes. A few of the others looked embarrassed. One or two were smiling.

Johnson ended his gloomy tirade by saying: "So we particularly need your help again, because we've got this new ambassador who doesn't know how to handle things on the hill. I thank you for what you can do, and I appreciate it." As he got up to go, I got up with him and said, "Mr. President, I would like to see you." Now he looked at me for the first time, and he replied, "Come on in." So I walked with him into his office, and he said, "Sit down." I said, "No, sir. I don't have to sit down, Mr. President. What I have to tell you, I can tell you standing up. I hope you understand, sir, that if anything like this happens again, you have my resignation."

Johnson looked up at me in some consternation, and said, "What the hell are you talking about?" I told him that he had just embarrassed and demeaned me in front of the people with whom I would have to work, and had impaired my effectiveness so greatly that I didn't know whether I could still hope to do what I had come down to do. He stared hard at me and said, "Hell, boy, you're getting all upset about nothing. Where are those fellows now?"

I knew they had gone to a follow-up meeting in what was then called the Fish Room (now the Roosevelt Room). Johnson rose and said, "Come on, let's go." He guided me to the Fish Room and opened the door. When the group saw him, they all rose to their feet. He said, "Sit down," and put his arm around my shoulder. "I came here to tell you just one thing," he said. "This is one of the best goddamned appointments I ever made. I want you to know: this is one of the best fellows I ever appointed to any job, anywhere, and I want to be sure you understand that." Then he departed, leaving me in the room.

It was, I learned later, a vintage Lyndon Johnson performance with a new recruit on his team. Hubert Humphrey described the process to Merle Miller: "After he got you all bruised up, he put his arms around you and gave you a bear hug and told you that you were the greatest man that ever lived. And he'd get you almost to believe it for a half an hour or so." The interesting thing is that if you stood up to him, you could apparently win his respect and regard. In any event, I never had that sort of problem with Johnson again. I saw him do some devastating things to other people, but after that episode he always dealt graciously with me, while he was in the White House and thereafter.

The President sent my nomination to the Senate on October 6, 1966. I had both New York Senators — Robert Kennedy and Jacob Javits — strongly behind me, and I was friendly with Senator William Fulbright, chairman of the Foreign Relations Committee, whom I had come to know some years earlier when I was president of the Rochester City Club and he gave a talk in the club's lecture series. The hearings on my nomination were perfunctory ("It's about time we got you down here," Fulbright said), and I was confirmed one week later. I took my oath on November 9, in ceremonies presided over by Dean Rusk.

I had known Rusk in the context of my UN study and in connection with the annual push for the foreign-aid bill, but we had never talked about my coming to OAS, or about any subject related to Latin America. The first words Rusk said to me before the ceremony were that he had been trying to call to tell me how pleased he was about my appointment. At the swearing-in ritual, he said, "We combed the whole country for the best man for this job. . . ." He looked at me, smiling, when he used the word "we."

My job at the beginning was to concentrate on a single purpose: arranging Johnson's summit conference. As the OAS ambassador, I was in charge of working out what the United States might hope to achieve in such a meeting. Together with Lincoln Gordon, I was responsible for getting in touch with the Latin presidents and judging their receptivity to the idea.

The first of these responsibilities involved a series of meetings in my new State Department office — quite a large office, which the Department considered appropriate for the only U.S. ambassador assigned to represent his country in Washington. A sizable group attended, from Treasury, Commerce, Defense, Agriculture, and various White House fiefdoms as well as the State Department itself. Everyone agreed that we should not undertake a summit meeting unless we knew with some precision what was going to come out of it. The State Department had been collecting suggestions for a summit agenda from its ambassadors in the field and from old Latin American hands such as Adolf A. Berle and Milton Eisenhower. The accumulated quantity of paper to be read was awesome. Once we had hammered out within the U.S. government the kind of agreements we believed should come out of the meeting, Gordon and I divided up the work of visiting the presidents to determine how receptive they would be to a summit meeting and to our ideas for the outcome.

All this had to be done in a great hurry; the time reserved on the President's schedule was April, less than five months away. I had to establish relationships with my fellow ambassadors to the OAS and the staff of the organization and keep them informed of our plans. Without their support we would have had a far tougher time winning the necessary cooperation from their governments. My time was further compressed because I felt I should take intensive Spanish instruction.[3]

Fortunately, there were no major disagreements within the U. S. government about what were later promulgated as the eight points of Punta del Este. We wanted to push the Latins toward a Common Market that would allow them to become major players in the world economy, a result none of them (not even Brazil, twenty years ago) could hope to achieve on its own. We wanted U.S. aid directed primarily toward education as the key investment in the future and toward agriculture as the most pressing immediate need. In agriculture, we thought the goal had to be modernization of the living conditions of the rural population and a rise in food prices, which were

[3] I stopped my language lessons for a strange reason: it developed that I had something of a talent for Spanish pronunciation. Hearing my few words, the Latin ambassadors would assume that they could speak Spanish to me. I told Abe Fortas about my problem, and he suggested that I quit the lessons and rely openly and always on interpreters. You'll never be as good at their language as they are, he said, and once they think they can, they'll speak to you only in Spanish and keep you at a disadvantage. Later a few of the ambassadors told me they had not really been deceived, because they watched me during the formal meetings and saw that I was always listening to the simultaneous translation through the earphones. On my travels, I often used interpreters supplied by my hosts, and met some interesting people. I was especially impressed with the young man who interpreted for me at my meeting with the President of Uruguay, and then courteously escorted me to my limousine. Only after I had left the country did I learn he was Hector Luisi, the new Foreign Minister.

controlled at a low level all over the continent, to stimulate farm production. We were eager to encourage multinational projects like the Andean Highway, to develop regional economic infrastructure. We wanted to see the Latin economies orient themselves as much as possible to exporting. We stressed the need to bring science and technology to all of Latin America, and to improve health conditions throughout the continent. And we wanted them to work out and enforce on themselves a restraint throughout the Latin community that would prevent the fearful waste of resources (some part of which, after all, were our contributions) on "unnecessary military expenditures" — the purchase of what we called "prestige" instruments of war: supersonic aircraft, missiles, warships of cruiser size or larger, heavy tanks.

This last goal, as I quickly learned in my conversations with the ambassadors, was deeply resented as an intrusion on national sovereignty. A few of the presidents were quite supportive — Carlos Lleras Restrepo of Colombia and Eduardo Frei of Chile were even more ardent on the subject than I was — but for most of them our insistence on arms control seemed yet another example of Yanqui incomprehension, a failure to understand that the nations of Latin America were not all alike, and had their quarrels with each other. Once, in the Alliance for Progress context, I told a delegation from one of the smaller countries that when they told me they planned to purchase twelve advanced fighter aircraft it was as though they had said they were planning to build four castles on the hills near their borders, for $10 million each. If we were helping them with their construction funding, we would have a right to question whether building four castles was an intelligent use of that money. Similarly, it was within our rights to question their use of scarce foreign exchange for war planes. The argument was not well received.

During my attempts to persuade the various Latin presidents to include weapons restraint on the agenda for Punta del Este, I received confirmation of my belief that in diplomacy, as in business, personal relations can sometimes make all the difference. President Fernando Belaunde of Peru was strongly opposed to including weapons restrictions on the summit agenda. He had recently launched a major modernization program for his military, mostly to ensure that they remained happy with his elected government, but partly, too, because Peru had long-standing border disputes with its neighbors, especially Chile and Bolivia. He had threatened that Peru might not attend the summit meeting if its agenda included this intrusion on national sovereignty.

Belaunde's representative at the United Nations was then his uncle, Victor Belaunde, a distinguished diplomat with whom he was very close. On the day set for my discussion with him in Lima, his uncle died in New York. I immediately suggested to the State Department that it would be a thoughtful and greatly appreciated gesture for President Johnson to order Air Force One to go to New York, pick up the body, and bring it to Lima, together with any members of the family in New York who wished to accompany it. This would be seen not only as a kindness but as a statement of respect for a man who had been one of the outstanding statesmen at the United Nations.

After the State Department said it could not be done, I called Walt Rostow in the White House, who also doubted the feasibility of the suggestion — it had never been done before, he said — but indicated he would talk to Johnson. I suggested that perhaps I could talk with Johnson myself, and I did, briefly. The President liked the idea, but was noncommittal. Then I got a call back from Rostow to the U.S. embassy in Lima: Johnson had ordered up the aircraft. When I met with Belaunde that afternoon and told him what the President was doing, he burst into tears. Before our interview ended, he agreed to come to Punta del Este, even though the agenda retained the item on military expenditures.

On many of my trips I made time to change into a sports shirt and slacks and wander with an interpreter down to the barrios and favelas, the shantytowns where the poor lived around the big cities. The deprivation was horrifying — but the vitality of these people was dazzling, and their hopes were an inspiration. It was hard for them to believe that the person visiting their slum was an ambassador from the United States. I was impressed at how positively they reacted, and I thought the reason was the Alliance for Progress. Upon entering one of these shacks, you might find a picture of John F. Kennedy on the wall, sometimes with a candle lit below it, and often a single book, a child's textbook, and on the flyleaf would be stamped "Alianza."

In general, working through an interpreter was slow but not difficult. Every so often there would be confusion. My favorite came in a group meeting with Central American presidents, during the first of my trips to explore the possibility of a summit. One of the presidents politely said he had heard that before entering diplomacy I had been in business as the chairman of a company called Xerox. He had never heard of it: what was it? I explained what the company did, and my interpreter translated the explanation into Spanish. The group was obviously awestruck; they looked at me with new interest and increased respect, and began talking with each other in great animation and apparent incredulity. Concerned, I asked the interpreter to tell me exactly what he had told them. He replied, "I told them just what you said, that Xerox is a company that has invented a new method of reproduction."

One had to be careful not to offend a Latin president's sensibilities. Lincoln Gordon and I divided the labor of visiting the Latin countries to consult the presidents; on our last swing he was to visit Brazil, Argentina, and Venezuela, and I was to travel to Colombia, Uruguay, Chile, and Peru. Then we were going to meet in Mexico City before flying together to Texas to report to Johnson. On arrival in Montevideo, I got a frantic call from Washington. General Alfredo Stroessner, President of Paraguay, was furious that he was not being consulted, and I should make a detour to Asunción to see him. Our military attaché in Uruguay provided a rather battered C-47 (in civilian life, a DC-3) to take me to Paraguay, and after a six-hour, extremely uncomfortable flight I was greeted at the Asunción airport by a spit-and-polish military guard and a vast motorcycle escort that took me to the presidential palace, where Stroessner was affability itself, his central point being that the democracies of the world had to stick together.

I told the Paraguayan dictator that the word "democracy" seemed to mean different things in his country and in mine. He asked me to expand on that comment, which I did. The interpreter grew nervous, and his foot began moving back and forth. Suddenly Stroessner barked a rebuke (*"El pie"* — the foot), and for the rest of the conversation it was as though the foot had been nailed to the floor. I was told later that Stroessner had found our discussion "very interesting," and had taken up the subject with his cabinet. What was meant by that I did not then and don't now understand. The leaders of the official Partido Colorado party gave a dinner in my honor at which a toast was offered to "that great American President Rutherford B. Hayes." I spent the night in an almost frighteningly clean hotel and returned to Montevideo in the wretched C-47. Stroessner sent to the airport a gift of some Paraguayan lace and an

invitation to come back some time to hunt jaguars with him. I found
the invitation resistible.

When Gordon and I met in Mexico City, we agreed that our visits
had been fruitful, and the summit meeting would work. Johnson
wanted to be convinced, and we were now in a position to convince
him. We called him at the ranch, and he told us he wanted to see us
the next day. We flew to San Antonio that afternoon, checked into
our hotel, and went out to dinner. When we returned to the hotel, a
message was waiting that Johnson had decided to see us that night
and was sending a helicopter to Bergstrom Air Force Base to take us
to the ranch. We repacked, hustled to the base, and touched down at
the ranch landing strip about midnight.

A station wagon was waiting, driven by what appeared to be a
farmhand in a red jacket and stocking cap. Gordon and I went to the
car and stood beside it, waiting for the Air Force personnel to un-
load our luggage and stow it in the wagon. The driver remained
motionless in his seat. Then I opened the door to the passenger
seats, and the driver turned around and said, "Hello, Sol." It was the
President, who had driven out to the airstrip himself.

The conversation started in the living room, but after a couple of
hours Johnson got up and led us to a bedroom, where he undressed
and stretched out naked on a massage table. "Mate!" he called, and a
naval orderly came in and began pounding him, while he asked us a
string of questions: did the Latins really *want* to have a meeting,
what sort of real agreements could we get out of it, how would he be
treated on such a visit, should he make a tour of several countries or
just go down for a meeting, what did we think of the Presidents we
had met, how would they handle themselves at a summit? The in-
terrogation went on until well after three in the morning, at which
point Johnson, dressed now in pajamas, put his nose up to me and
said, very forcefully, "You two go back to San Antonio tomorrow
and hold a press conference. Tell 'em you spoke six hours with the
President, and that I'm going to do this because you convinced me
these fellows want us to do it. Tell 'em what these people told you
on your trip, and tell 'em I'm interested in it." So later that morning,
on the President's instructions, Lincoln Gordon and I officially announced U.S. support for the summit.

This did not put an end to preliminary sparring. The best facilities for this sort of conference were in Lima and at Viña del Mar in
Chile, but Chile and Peru were on such bad terms with so many of

their neighbors (including each other) that neither could be a successful host. We settled for Punta del Este in Uruguay, a resort town already grown a little seedy, but suitable for the occasion because it was at a meeting there that the terms of the Alliance for Progress had initially been worked out. There were difficulties about the date: the very fact that the United States wanted April 12–14 meant that others had to object. President René Barrientos of Bolivia said he would not attend because the agenda didn't include an item assuring Bolivia's access to the sea. The President of El Salvador said he would not attend unless there was an agenda item on maintaining the price of coffee. Colombia was furious at the International Monetary Fund and the United States because the IMF was insisting on a currency devaluation before it would approve a loan (eventually, the loan was made without the devaluation). As part of the preliminaries, President Frei of Chile was supposed to make a visit to the United States — and his Senate passed a resolution forbidding him to leave the country, which not only ruled out the U.S. trip but made his attendance at the summit unlikely.

We plowed ahead. In mid-February I accompanied Rusk to Buenos Aires for the preliminary meeting of Western Hemisphere foreign ministers. This meeting lasted a full week. (Rusk, badgered by Vietnam, mounting tensions in the Middle East, and the still-secret proposals for what became the Johnson-Kosygin meeting in Glassboro two months after Punta del Este, had to leave halfway through; Bunker came down to head our delegation in the final days.) The new source of disruption here was a demand by the military government of Argentina that the OAS set up a defense committee in which military men would coordinate the defense of the hemisphere; this was finally voted down, eleven to six, with the United States abstaining. Foreign Minister Juracy-Magalhaes of Brazil, a learned veteran of such affairs, found a wording of the need to control sophisticated weapons that was vague enough to permit Peru to accept it — but too vague, in the end, to accomplish anything. The achievement of the Buenos Aires meeting was a fairly solid agreement that the Latin American states would undertake the formation of a Common Market, and that if they did so, the United States would assist. "If you walk boldly along that path," Johnson would say two months later at Punta del Este, "we will be beside you."

Much of the next two months was spent on the effort to give the

President the authority he would need to commit the United States at Punta del Este. He sent to Congress a plan to raise by $1.5 billion the U.S. contributions to the Alliance for Progress over the succeeding five years, and asked for a congressional resolution backing Latin American efforts to create a Common Market. Meanwhile, we explored what he could do without new legislation or appropriations. Since 1960, American aid had been "tied" to the purchase of U.S. goods and services, by an executive order dating back to the Eisenhower administration. We examined the possibility that Johnson could include a Latin American Common Market within our boundaries for this purpose, so that Latin as well as U.S. products could be purchased with aid funds. Neither Congress nor the Treasury was in a mood to be helpful, however. (Not long after Punta del Este, in fact, Treasury Secretary Henry Fowler complained at the annual meeting of the Inter-American Development Bank that too much of the money the bank was lending was being spent outside the United States.) The only resolution the Senate Foreign Relations Committee was prepared to report was so generalized and watery that someone at the White House described it as "worse than useless," greatly offending Fulbright. Johnson had to go to the summit meeting virtually empty-handed.

Having committed, he played out the string. The summit was under OAS auspices, and he decided he would warm up the ambassadors. San Antonio was having a major fair (they called it the "Hemisfair"), and Johnson invited all the Latin American ambassadors and representatives to the OAS to go as his guests, flying down to Texas with their wives on the President's plane and then joining him afterward at a giant barbecue at the ranch. He decided that his gift to them would be a Texas sombrero for each, and the State Department called all the embassies and missions to learn the head sizes of those going to the fair. Then one of the ambassadors was quoted in the *Washington Post* as saying that Johnson wanted to make the Latins look foolish, and the sombreros disappeared. We never knew where they went; he never gave any of them to anyone. But the President was in his element at the barbecue. He was at home, he was the host, he knew his protocol obligations, but he could meet them in a relaxed way. It brought out the best in him. When you took him away from home, some of the bravado disappeared.

While flying down to Montevideo for the summit meeting, the

President had an anxiety attack. I was in the back of his plane, and I had just crept into my berth at one o'clock in the morning when an aide came for me and said the President wanted to see me. Johnson was sitting behind his desk on the plane, his robe hanging loosely on him, his chin in his hand, that hangdog look around his eyes. He motioned me to sit down, and then leaned forward, got very close to me, and said, "What the hell are we going down here for?" I said, "Sir?" And he repeated, "What the hell are we doing this for?" For about an hour, then, I undertook to lecture the President of the United States on why it was important for this meeting to go forward, the details of the agreement that was going to be announced at the end, the value of meeting the other Presidents in the hemisphere and having them meet him. Finally, he was satisfied and I could go back to my bunk and get some sleep.

I was not as confident as I had sounded. This was the late 1960s. The United States had only recently put marines in Santo Domingo, and we were bombing North Vietnam. There was all but certain to be some sort of student protest in Uruguay. We knew what was going to come out of the Punta del Este meeting, but we could not be sure of what the other Presidents would put into it. Some, perhaps many, might be tempted to make themselves heroes on their own national broadcast media by attacking Johnson and the United States, on camera, in this international meeting. Nor could we be absolutely certain (although I was reasonably confident) that the Latin Presidents would respond positively to the force of nature that was Lyndon Johnson in action. He was to meet most of them individually in the château that had been set aside for him at the resort. One of the main reasons for Punta del Este had been to subject him to them — and them to him — in just this way. Now that it was about to happen, no one could certify their mood or his.

Once we got to Uruguay, however, nearly everything worked as planned. The local security forces kept the rather small number of student protesters behind barricades at the airport. (Uruguay was then — as it is again — a functioning democracy, and protests were legal; both the police and the demonstrators behaved themselves.) All the Presidents were flown off in helicopters to Punta del Este, where the accommodations were comfortable. I had a worried moment at the first reception, given by the OAS, when I saw Johnson standing alone, huge (much taller than the tallest of the other Presidents) and looking lost in a corner of the room. But before I could get to him, the ever-alert Rusk had brought Frei to talk with Johnson. After the greetings, Johnson made a joke about how both of them were having trouble with their Senates, which was — and was intended to be — a gesture of equality between them. Frei was pleased, and the two men hit it off, greatly improving Johnson's confidence that he would be able to handle the situation.[4]

It may actually have been an advantage to Johnson at Punta del Este that the Congress had sent him off without promises to make. Latin Americans tend to believe that the President of the United States is all-powerful. Johnson could and did say to them that he wasn't. He would do all he could to help, but he could not write checks unless Congress would sign them, which meant that they had to help him make the case. Rather to their own surprise, the Latin Presidents found themselves with a certain *sympathy* for Johnson. He responded to the sympathy, and the result was, for the rest of his term, a new warmth in the relations between the Latin governments and the Colossus of the North.

There was only one awkward moment. President Otto Arosemena of Ecuador, a military dictator asserting a populist image, delivered a diatribe against the United States as an aggressive, predatory, exploitative power that was denuding Latin America of its natural resources and commodities production at dishonestly low prices. We had a continuing dispute with Ecuador about that nation's attempt to impose a two-hundred mile exclusive fishing zone in the Pacific, but the immediate cause of Arosemena's rage was something that did not become public knowledge until after his speech. The Alliance for Progress had cut Ecuador's aid allotment by 30 percent because its government had refused to reform the nation's tax structure and increase the tax receipts pledged to match Alliance contributions. Sitting behind Johnson, I could see his neck muscles working as he listened to the translation of Arosemena's speech, and I passed Dean Rusk a note to suggest that we hurry to prepare some effective reply. Rusk turned to me and shook his head, and passed me a note in return: let the other Latins do it, he wrote. And they did, especially Frei and Belaunde. Of course, Ecuadorean radio and television carried only Arosemena's speech, not the replies.

---

[4] He handled Frei with special grace. Having been informed that the Chilean's son was in Punta del Este, he had an extra place set at table for his lunch with Frei. After we had all seated ourselves, an aide came to Johnson's place and he left the room. He returned escorting young Frei, to his father's delight.

The Punta del Este communiqué included a twenty-three page "action program," which did not produce a great deal of action. It is sad to think that the target date for the full accomplishment of a Latin American Common Market was 1985, and today there probably could not even be an agreement to get started. Some progress was made toward commodity agreements to guarantee the Latins minimum prices, and over the years we did open our markets somewhat more to Latin manufactures and even some agricultural products we grow ourselves. In a way, President Reagan's 1982 Caribbean Basin Initiative, eliminating tariffs on imports from these island states, derives from the Punta del Este agreements. Restraint on arms purchases, however, died that same year, when we ourselves sold F-4s to the Peruvians because we could not dissuade them from ordering French Mirages or the French from agreeing to sell — and both the Treasury and the Defense departments felt strongly that we would rather have Peru buying its weapons from us.

From the beginning the Punta del Este agreements had their opponents. Even before the conference ended, Senator Salvador Allende of Chile made a speech to a student group at the University of Montevideo denouncing the agreements in terms not unlike Arosemena's. Later in the year a House committee would criticize the action program for not placing enough emphasis on social reform, and Wayne Morse's Senate subcommittee would complain about the failure to stress political change. Another House committee caused a flap by insisting that the General Accounting Office have the right to audit the Inter-American Development Bank, or else the House would reject the entire foreign-aid program. A former Assistant Secretary for American Republic Affairs testified that the whole program was hopeless unless something could be done to stop corruption.

I always thought it was significant that the year 1967, the year of Punta del Este, was the first in more than twenty years that no government was overturned by force in the Americas. One has to be careful not to press claims that jump from effect to cause, but I would argue that one reason for this year of peace was that the summit and its action program gave people a new sense of hope, of belief that working together might get things done.

The United States did little to move the action program along. Soon after Punta del Este, the Treasury and the Council of Economic Advisers forced Johnson to seek higher taxes to pay for the combination of the Vietnam War and the Great Society. Neither the President nor Congress was in a mood to increase the budget deficit by making the U.S. contributions that might have given us the leverage to improve both national and international economic planning within Latin America.

Less than two years after Punta del Este, Richard Nixon became President. The Alliance for Progress was identified with Kennedy, the Latin American Common Market with Johnson. Nixon himself had been humiliated on a trip to South America when he was Vice-President. The person he sent on a fact-finding mission to Latin America not long after his inauguration was Nelson Rockefeller, in whose presence all his insecurities rose and made him uncomfortable. To the extent that he thought about Latin America at all, President Nixon saw it as a place where he could reward those he perceived as friends and punish those he perceived as enemies. But the essence of Punta del Este, the source of the excitement the Latins felt, was the cooperative effort, the American willingness to say to the Latins, "We are in this *with* you." (It was an excitement that still echoes: when I was in Argentina in 1984 I called for another summit meeting in the spirit of Punta del Este, and President Alfonsin quickly endorsed the suggestion.) Richard Nixon did not convey this sense of comradeship, and in the absence of a shared ambition for the hemisphere, the agreements themselves became meaningless.

My time at the OAS left no institutional residue. I was *in* the State Department but definitely not *of* the State Department. When I traveled to visit the Latin American presidents, I carried with me a big black loose-leaf book, labeled "secret," that told me about the people I was to meet, the Department's estimates of their strengths and weaknesses, and our policies with regard to their countries. I had instructions, but I considered myself empowered to modify them; I was visiting on behalf of the President, not of the bureau. I never "cleared" any speech I made with the State Department, and nobody ever told me I should. I liked and admired Dean Rusk and got along with him very well. We occasionally had lunch together during the twenty-six months I served the Johnson administration, and after he left office. But I saw Johnson more often than I saw Rusk.

Lincoln Gordon announced his forthcoming resignation as assistant secretary after I had been OAS ambassador for less than ten weeks, and he was not particularly concerned about defending the bureaucratic customs of the department. We had a friendly relationship, and I made it my business to talk with him about what I was doing, but he didn't try to give me orders. The situation I found when I came to the OAS post was a difficult one, and I had to handle it my way. I had my own agenda, my reasons for accepting the post. Besides, I didn't know I was doing anything unusual. I had much the same easy, warm relationship with Gordon's successor, Covey Oliver, a University of Pennsylvania law professor and former ambassador to Colombia — and, later, with the Nixon appointee, Charles Meyer, a former Sears executive. Among the foreign-service officers in the bureau, I may well have been regarded as a loose cannon.

At the OAS itself, I was saddled with the legacy of the Dominican intervention. The organization had been hurt and the Latins felt betrayed, demeaned, resentful, and distrustful. For years we had ignored the OAS except when we thought it might serve our purposes, and the Latins believed that would always be our approach. Bunker had not been able to do much to mollify them, because he had to spend so much time in Santo Domingo. Then, of course, I had no time to ease into office. From the moment I arrived, I was traveling around to set up Punta del Este.

I gained some credibility from my colleagues' knowledge that I had been in charge of establishing the Xerox joint ventures in Mexico, Venezuela, and Brazil. These were well regarded. As a matter of policy, we had made local people real partners in those businesses, training managers and technicians on the spot and in courses we established for them in Rochester. Moreover, we had been good corporate citizens, helping the local schools and community institutions wherever we opened an operation.

From the beginning of my time as an ambassador, I tried to be completely candid with my colleagues. I found that they invariably respected my confidences, and we developed a mutual trust that persists to this day. I sympathized with their feeling that we had long taken Latin Americans for granted, patronized them, and noticed them mostly when we were annoyed because they had strayed off our reservation. What they wanted more than anything else, I thought, was to be taken seriously, have their countries taken seriously, and have their dignity respected. There were various ways that we could show we respected their dignity. I remember a conversation with Dean Rusk on the airplane flying down to Buenos Aires for the foreign-ministers' meeting that would firm up the plans for the summit at Punta del Este. Rusk asked me what I thought he should talk about in his presentation to the Latins. I said, "Vietnam." That was the subject uppermost in his mind, so he would talk about it easily. And the Latins would be pleased that he was soliciting their advice on the central issue in American foreign relations. He did talk about Vietnam, and they responded with sympathy and understanding.

My worst moment with Latin American colleagues came in the summer of 1968, when at the request of the State Department I took a group of about twenty-five ambassadors to the Democratic National Convention in Chicago. They saw the confrontation between Mayor Richard Daley and Senator Abraham Ribicoff, the demonstrators in the street, and the police clubbing them. They were baffled, bewildered, and disappointed. "Does this always happen?" they asked. "And we've never heard?" It is a vivid memory, for me and for them. On the rare occasions when I meet the men who were with me that week in Chicago, even today, they bring it up.

Just as I needed good personal relations at the OAS, I felt I needed them on Capitol Hill. Johnson had been having trouble with Fulbright, and with Wayne Morse, who was chairman of the Latin American subcommittee. I adopted a custom of a once-a-month meeting in Morse's office — he called it a "coffee hour" — for members of his subcommittee and others on the Foreign Relations Committee. I would speak frankly, in confidence, and I developed close relationships. Our exchanges were always candid, and as a result we all had a more comfortable time in the hearing rooms during my formal appearances before the committee.

At the beginning, I certainly had no feeling that I was working in a backwater or lacked influence on national policy. My first five months were bound up in the planning for Punta del Este, which was a major event in the year for Lyndon Johnson. I was deeply involved in planning what the President would do and say there, and few things are more important in Washington than influencing the text of a President's speech.

Bunker had said that the OAS post did not make policy, but sometimes I found that I did — even inadvertently. A few weeks before Punta del Este, I gave a talk at the Overseas Press Club in

New York and spoke of our "special friendship" for the Latin American democracies, and our "all-out support for constitutional democracy" south of our borders. The Alliance for Progress, I said, "will stand or fall on the capacity of the progressive democratic governments, parties, and leaders of Latin America."

I did not think I had said anything especially striking. The preamble of the communiqué issued by the meeting that launched the Alliance for Progress in 1961 proclaimed a belief that men can best realize their aspirations through representative democracy. Even Richard Nixon, when Vice-President, had spoken of an "abrazo" for the leaders of the democracies and a "handshake" for the military leaders. (By 1967 Nixon had changed his mind. Not long after Punta del Este, he made a visit to Rio, where he delighted the Brazilian military junta by saying that U.S. policy had gone wrong in trying to export political democracy to South America, where it was "unworkable.") But the New York and Washington papers played my speech prominently, and early the next morning I had a call from Walt Rostow, at home. "I don't think the President's very happy with you this morning," he said in his soft, professorial tone.

"Why?" I asked.

"That speech you gave yesterday. Do you know that the President ever said anything about our having a special friendship for the democracies down there?"

"I didn't say the President had said it."

"Yes," Rostow said patiently, "but the impression is that you wouldn't say it unless it was policy. Do you know that this is the President's policy?"

"I assumed it was," I said.

Even in a phone call, I could see him shaking his head. "The President has never said that," he said, and hung up.

A few days later the President made a speech, and as part of his discussion of what we hoped to accomplish at Punta del Este he *did* speak of a "special relationship" with the Latin democracies. In my own small way, I had made policy.[5]

There were also occasions when one had to toe the line and candor was impossible. I recall, for example, a speech I had to make

[5] This sort of policy tends to be fragile. After he had met the presidents at Punta del Este, Johnson had a lunch at his château for about ten of us in the U.S. delegation. He asked us which of the men we'd seen we would most want to have on our side if there were a real challenge and a need for support. Rusk, Gordon, Rostow, and I all had suggestions, but Johnson waved us off. "Costa Silva," he said finally. "That fella from Brazil. When he looks you in the eye and he tells you he's with you, you know he means it."

shortly after we decided to sell the F-4s to Peru, in which I defended the Peruvians and stressed that the Latin Americans spent less on arms as a proportion of gross national product than any other regional group in the world. And my time at the OAS was, of course, the time when the President and Rusk were overwhelmed by Vietnam. He knew of my misgivings and I recollect once saying to Johnson that I thought the war was going badly, and he angrily replied, "I don't want you to talk to me about this subject." What I remember best are several occasions when the subject was being discussed in my presence, and because I said nothing on either side Johnson apparently felt he could make me a convert. He clutched me by the arm and worked me over as though it were important to him that I assure him he was right.

My relations with the State Department were correct, but not warm. I was not impressed with the Department's efficiency. During the days when I headed the Advisory Committee on International Organizations, I had seen something of the International Organizations Bureau and discussed its problems with Harlan Cleveland's deputies, Richard Gardner and Joseph Sisco, but I had never gone into the entrails of the Department. Now I found myself with an office there, and with all those cables in that impenetrable print being put on my desk every morning. Having devoted roughly twenty years of my life to making it easier for organizations to drown in paper — in an unguarded moment I had told *Life* magazine that Xerox might have made a greater contribution to mankind if it had developed a new way to burn everything rather than to copy it — I could scarcely object on grounds of quantity. But there was no developed system for taking account of what the paper said, or for disposing of the problems raised.

Time and again in the State Department I talked to people who had prepared careful memos, hoping someone would say, "Send it upstairs." Then the memo would be sent upstairs, and they would never get an answer. Six weeks later, the author of a memo might start inquiring timidly, "Does anybody have an answer to my memo?" There were so many documents labeled "Urgent" or "Secret" that I developed my own technique for getting my views quickly to the attention of the people I thought should know them: I wrote letters by hand and sent them unclassified. That was so shockingly different that the recipients would read my letters immediately.

I learned to my dismay that at the State Department virtually any assignment could be disrupted on five minutes' notice. I found it happening in my own office. If I said that I'd like to discuss something with A, twelve people would show up five minutes later for a meeting.

There was no tickler file of the kind that is commonplace in business, no system for reminding people of the deadlines on work, because the decision as to what was urgent was made anew every day. I was incredulous when I found there were no dictating machines in the Department; it was simply assumed that secretaries would remain at work as long as their boss might wish to give them dictation.

I was never captured by the hours at the State Department, which seemed to me part of the competitive masochism of Washington. I was deeply impressed and often touched by the quality and commitment of the foreign-service officers, who, when asked in their country's interest, would work a schedule no businessman would dare exact from employees in the private sector. Unfortunately, many of them also worked that impossible schedule when no one asked. People at State appeared to believe that the way to get ahead was to show that they worked longer hours than other people. I thought that the dedicated and tireless foreign-service officers who came in at seven in the morning and stayed till ten at night (as many did) were proving not their fervor for their job but the Department's disorganization. I saw to it that I got out by seven o'clock, or earlier, every evening.

Of course, in the OAS post, I had an endless social schedule. There were more than twenty Latin American embassies, and if you went to the Honduran reception but not the Nicaraguan, the Chilean but not the Bolivian, there was trouble. Latins love entertaining, and their hours are their hours. The days and nights were grueling, but they opened up vistas we had not seen in Rochester, and I found I enjoyed the job and the life. In the second year I also had a considerable perquisite. Peter Lisagor of the *Chicago Daily News* happened to be passing by the Pan American Union (home of the OAS) after one of the meetings and saw the limousines picking up the ambassadors one by one, while I stood out on Seventeenth Street trying to hail a cab. He thought this amusing and wrote a column about it. Rusk saw the column and didn't think it was amusing. He personally ordered the Department's management to supply me with a car and driver, which I kept for the remainder of my term. I am told that at twelve noon on the day my resignation became effective, the car was reassigned to the Department pool and my successor never saw it. Given the politics of the State Department, as I realized only later, it was not trivial that I was given a car and driver.

Once Punta del Este was behind us, I spent considerable time working on Alliance for Progress matters. The institutional frame was CIAP (the Spanish acronym for Inter-American Committee of the Alliance for Progress), led by a resourceful Colombian, Carlos Sanz de Santamaría. This was not a committee of diplomats; except for myself, all the members were economists, former finance ministers, and the like. I was the only person who wore both the OAS and the CIAP hats. Attending the meetings were representatives of the World Bank, the International Monetary Fund, the Inter-American Development Bank, and the UN Development Program. The Economics, Planning, and Finance ministers of all the countries of Latin America came to make presentations before this group. In my last year, at my suggestion, the United States also made a presentation, about our budgetary plans and projections for 1969, to reduce the Latins' feeling that we sat in judgment on everyone else but never allowed our own policies to be questioned.

CIAP recommended the allocation of loan and grant funds for all the countries in the hemisphere. Before meetings I would get thick reports — analyses of the economy of the nation making the application, what its people thought they could do for themselves, and what help they thought they needed. My bright and extremely capable assistant, Ambler Moss, a multilingual foreign-service officer who later studied law and joined me in private practice (and a decade later became my right hand in the Panama negotiations), would read the material and give me a summary, which usually included the suggestion that I might want to read certain sections of the presentations. (If they were in Spanish, someone would have done a translation.) Then the panel would meet with the ministers from the country involved and discuss in detail whether what was being offered and asked was realistic, and how well this country's program compared with others'. It was an exciting example of cooperation in the hemisphere, a platform on which other things could have been built, especially if the proposed Common Market had come into existence. Within the context of these meetings, it was sometimes possible to discuss subjects otherwise taboo, such as arms expenditures and population control.

Rostow had even higher hopes. One day I and all the other OAS ambassadors received a hurry-up invitation to a meeting at the White House. We milled around in the East Room, wondering what it was about. There was a map of the Americas at the front of the room. Suddenly Johnson came in with Rostow, said Rostow had an extremely important message for us, and sat down in the front row. Rostow took a pointer and began tracing boundaries on the map. What was needed in Latin America if there was to be successful economic integration, he said, was "physical integration." Economic development was being impeded because the continent was "too divided." He spoke for the better part of an hour, and the Latins showed their bewilderment at the geography lesson. When it was over, Johnson and Rostow, pleased with this extension of the classroom into the White House, left the room. For weeks thereafter we received calls from Latin ambassadors who wanted to know how to go about applying for the U.S. aid money that Rostow must have been talking about. There was, of course, no money.

Shortly after my departure, CIAP closed down. It is a significant measure of the change in the relations between the United States and Latin America when Nixon succeeded Johnson that the work of CIAP had fascinated Walt Rostow as national security adviser, whereas his successor, Henry Kissinger, never mentions the institution (or the Alliance for Progress) in either volume of his memoirs. Indeed, he mentions the OAS itself only in referring to the violations of its resolutions by Chile under the Allende government.

A certain amount of my time necessarily went to putting out fires. In 1968 Venezuela captured some armed Cubans who had landed on its shores to stimulate revolutionary activity, and asked the OAS for a formal investigation. At the request of the organization, I was one of the investigators sent down to interview the prisoners and look at the evidence. Fidel Castro was not then the Communist-establishment figure he later became. He had diplomatic relations only with Mexico among the states of the hemisphere (the OAS had called on all member nations not to have relations with Cuba), he was openly promoting revolution everywhere, and he was bitterly and publicly critical of the Soviet Union for its efforts to improve its relations with what he called the Fascist governments in the hemisphere. In Venezuela I spoke with the Cuban prisoners (through an interpreter) and examined the cargo of arms they had been shepherding. I had no doubt that the Venezuelan charge was proved, but I also pointed out when I reported our conclusions to the OAS that the invaders had been caught, there was no real revolutionary threat to Venezuela, and it was important not to overreact.

In 1968 both Peru and Panama suffered overthrow of elected governments by the military. We were among the last nations in the hemisphere to recognize the juntas that took power, and in our statement of recognition we urged the restoration of democratic government as quickly as possible. In Peru the left-wing junta that ousted Belaunde expropriated the International Petroleum Corporation, an Exxon subsidiary, in a way that appeared to trigger the Hickenlooper amendment denying American aid to any nation that seized the property of U.S. nationals without compensation. I spent long days on the Hill working (unsuccessfully) to dissuade Congress from rash reactions. Other hours on the Hill were less satisfying. By fiscal 1969 the U.S. appropriation for aid through the Alliance was down to $336.5 million, a severe cut from the $508 million that had been made available in 1967, and the smallest total since the program began in 1961.

Lyndon Johnson had said we would persevere. We did not. The week before my resignation as ambassador to the OAS took effect, I told the House Foreign Affairs Subcommittee on Inter-American Affairs: "The most devastating thing you can do to a human being is to raise expectations and then frustrate them. We have helped to raise expectations in the hemisphere. We have helped to fulfill some of the hopes. But the overwhelming majority of them have not been fulfilled. . . . The future of international peace and security depends in large measure on what we are able to achieve together here in the Americas. . . . We cannot build the kind of hemisphere that is so vital to all of us by bargain basement tactics."

On March 31, 1968, I flew with Vice-President Hubert Humphrey and his wife, Muriel, to Mexico City for the signing of the treaty of Tlatelalco, in which most of the nations of Latin America renounced the possession of nuclear weapons in perpetuity. Johnson was to make a speech that night on the Vietnam War, and Humphrey told me the President had come out to his suburban house in the morning ("Muriel was still in her bathrobe") to read him the text. "You'll like it when you hear it," Humphrey said. Johnson, in his memoirs, says he told Humphrey then that he was going to announce he was not a candidate for reelection, but there was no indication on the plane that Humphrey knew. We played cards and talked of many things, but not of the 1968 elections or Lyndon Johnson's plans.

After the signing of the treaty there was a dinner in Humphrey's honor given by our ambassador, Fulton Freeman.[6] At eight o'clock Humphrey, Wayne Morse, Freeman, and I left the reception to go into a side room where there was a radio on which we could hear the President's speech. Just before the broadcast began, Humphrey was called to the phone; I was told later that it was Johnson's aide and friend Marvin Watson, telling him to make sure he heard the whole speech, right to the end. When the President seemed to end his speech, with his hopes that Hanoi would react positively to his announcement of a bombing halt, Freeman reached over to turn off the radio, and Humphrey stopped him. Then came Johnson's announcement that he would not seek reelection, and Humphrey burst into tears. He quickly wrote out a statement for the press traveling with us, saying that he was overwhelmed and would have no comment. I sat beside Muriel Humphrey at dinner, and she gave no indication that she had known what Johnson was going to do.

When we flew back to Washington the next evening, Humphrey kept to himself in a corner of the plane until we neared Andrews Air Force Base. We were sitting together when word came from the cockpit that there was a crowd assembled at the base waving Humphrey-for-President banners. "Oh, my God," Humphrey said. "Don't let them do that. Johnson will hate it." When we got there, the crowd had shrunk — but, to Humphrey's dismay, they were still carrying banners.

Johnson's decision not to run again had no effect on my plans: I had promised him two years, and had always expected to return to Rochester at the end of 1968. Oddly, it was the election of Nixon that extended my stay in government, because Nixon chose William P. Rogers to be his Secretary of State, and Bill Rogers was an old friend of mine from Cornell Law School. He asked me to continue at OAS and CIAP until he had time to think through what he wanted to do with those posts, and I agreed. Toni and I were still living in Washington, and I was still working for the government when Chester Carlson, the inventor of xerography, died, and we

[6] Freeman and I had a special bond: we were both musicians. He played bass. On a previous visit to Mexico, for a U.S. Chamber of Commerce function, I had joined him and the orchestra that played for dancing at the party in a rendition of some old popular tunes, provoking some stories in the Mexican papers about "diplomats in harmony."

went to Rochester for a memorial service and spent the day there. On the plane returning to Washington, Toni suddenly turned to me and asked, "Are you sure you really want to go back?" I replied, "I was afraid to ask you." Rochester was a comfortable life, a good life, and the Xerox Corporation I had helped to build was one of the most exciting businesses in America — but insensibly, never having thought about it, we had put that life behind us.

PART II

The Xerox Years

2

Joe and I

I FIRST MET Joe Wilson, with whom my life would be so closely intertwined, in the summer of 1946 at the home of Frederick Muhlhauser, a Rochester businessman who was then president of the City Club. Muhlhauser had formed a committee to plan the club's program for the 1946–1947 year, and had asked me to join it. Among the others on the committee were some of Rochester's most prominent citizens, including William S. Vaughn, who later became chairman of Eastman Kodak, Rochester's dominant force in both business and civic affairs. The City Club program consisted of an outstanding lecture series, one of the nation's most popular and influential efforts in adult education. From six hundred to a thousand people came to each of the sixteen to twenty Saturday lunches sponsored by the City Club at the Rochester Chamber of Commerce, and there were few political figures, businessmen, or diplomats in the United States who would not accept an invitation to participate. A few years later, when I was president of the club, the list of speakers I introduced included Vice-President Alben Barkley; Senators Hubert Humphrey, Paul Douglas, Estes Kefauver, and Leverett Saltonstall; Eleanor Roosevelt; and editor Norman Cousins. Joe and I were being initiated, perhaps not into a rite, but certainly into a responsibility.

Someone may have sensed that Joe and I would like each other. We were roughly the same age — I was thirty-two, Joe thirty-seven — and married and busily producing the baby-boom generation (Toni and I would have four children, Peggy and Joe would have five). We both cared for music, we both liked a good story, we both read a lot and enjoyed talking about books. We were both concerned about national and international affairs, on which our views were close enough to encourage dialogue and different enough to make the conversations interesting. (Ten years later we would write parallel columns one day in the *Rochester Times-Union,* Joe on why he was supporting Eisenhower, I on why I was supporting Stevenson.) We shared a humanities background and humanities interests, which is amusing in retrospect, considering that we would make our careers and our fortunes in the exploitation of a scientific discovery. Neither of us could do anything with his hands. Once at a party some friends staged a contest to determine which of us could get a nail hammered into a plank with the fewest blows. We both had a lot of trouble getting the nail started — it kept falling out of the plank.

Joe was a slight man with pink cheeks, very dark hair, and a remarkably youthful appearance. He had a large but shy smile that could be called forth in many different ways. He was a man who sought and enjoyed solitude, but it was also characteristic of him that he wanted companions — companions for walks in the woods, companions at work, companions in travel. Eventually, I would fit into all those categories. Crucial to the friendship that grew between us was that Toni and Peggy shared interests and vivacity; we all enjoyed spending time with each other. Still, it must have been a great surprise to most of those who had known us that Joe and I would become each other's best friend and closest ally through the long wars that had to be fought to create the Xerox Corporation. We could scarcely have come from more disparate backgrounds.

By the 1940s the Wilsons were Rochester aristocracy. Joe's grandfather ("Joseph C.," like Joe) had been mayor of the city. His father, Joseph R. (always "J. R."), had been among the founders, and for many of its thirty-odd years the president, of a publicly held corporation, the Haloid Company. A producer of photographic papers and machines (the name grew from the "silver halide" process that was the key to photographic development on film), Haloid lived somewhat precariously in Kodak's shadow, but it was one of the city's twenty or so largest employers. J. R. was a gentleman of the old school, courtly, dignified, impressive, and articulate. The sun rose and set for him in his son Joe. He never understood what we later did with his company, and never really tried to understand. At board meetings he would say, "If Joe tells me it's so, that's all I need."

At thirty-seven, Joe had just succeeded to the title of president of Haloid after two years as vice-president and general manager, and the better part of a decade as a member of the board. With the exception of two years at the Harvard Business School, he had spent all his life in Rochester. J. R., who was an alumnus of the University of Rochester, had persuaded Joe to stay home for his undergraduate years by giving him a convertible, and Joe had worked in the family business during summer vacations. As a multiple father and a key employee of a company that was a major supplier of photographic equipment to the Air Force, Joe had been exempted from military service during the war.

In fact, Haloid and J. R. Wilson had lived through a difficult time in the company's early years, and again during World War II. Early in its existence, the company had been forced to seek support and direction from Gilbert E. Mosher, a local entrepreneur who had sold his own small camera company to Kodak and had money and time to invest. Mosher had become president of Haloid and had set it on a course of product development through research that produced a photographic paper called Haloid Record, which sustained the company through the Depression and was still a major source of profit in the 1940s. But Mosher was essentially an absentee executive, who would visit occasionally, talk money matters, and run his hand over shelves to see that everything was being dusted properly. In 1936 Mosher turned over the presidency of Haloid to J. R. Wilson (from whom he had taken it more than twenty years before) and retired to Florida, although he kept the title of chairman of the board of what was by then a publicly held company.

As the war approached, Mosher decided to sell the company and take his profits (his chosen purchaser, oddly, was General Aniline and Film, a German-owned company that soon would be seized by the U.S. government under its war powers). The Wilsons managed to block Mosher's sale by mobilizing Rochester businessmen who held stock in the company and didn't wish to see its direction assumed by foreigners. During the war years, however, Haloid had operated in an anomalous state, with rival boards of directors claiming to control the company and both sides afraid to sue because a court case might have collapsed the enterprise. With the chairman far away in Florida, the Wilsons had been able to manage Haloid's day-to-day affairs and gain control of the board, but the fight had been difficult and its outcome had long been uncertain.

Whatever his corporate difficulties had been, however, by the time I met Joe he was an heir to social and business leadership in the city of Rochester, and beside him I was an outsider. I was from Trenton, New Jersey, where my father, who had recently died, had been a hard-working wholesale fruit dealer, whose business had never recovered from the shock of the Great Depression. Joe was a dedicated Republican; I was a committed Democrat. Joe was an un-churched Presbyterian with a Catholic wife; Toni and I were observing (although not Orthodox) Jews, in a city where the Jewish population was sizable but not yet fully "acceptable" in some of the best circles.

My presence in Rochester was essentially an accident. The oldest of my parents' four sons, I had gone from Trenton High School to Hamilton College in upstate New York because my English teacher, a Hamilton graduate, thought I would be happiest at this small liberal arts college. He persuaded me to accept Hamilton's offer of a $250 scholarship, even though the University of Virginia had offered a considerably larger grant and the money was important. I was one of only two Jews in my Hamilton class — we were assigned to share a room — and the other dropped out after a single term. The college then made a more sophisticated judgment, and assigned me to room with George Waters, a Mormon and a prodigious worker. Although I was the first Jew he had ever known and he was the first Mormon I had ever known, we became close friends. He graduated as Valedictorian and I was Salutatorian, delivering the commencement oration in Latin. My mother, who had never been to a college graduation before, made her first visit to Hamilton for this occasion. She was overjoyed by my success and delighted by my prominence on the program. She told me she thought I spoke very well but was hard to understand.

I waited on tables at Commons and then in a fraternity house; I had a job in the library funded by the National Youth Administration; I borrowed money from the bursar; I sold Christmas cards. My parents desperately wanted to help me, and every so often my father would somehow find twenty dollars that he would slip into my hand when I was home for a school break, not allowing me to talk about it. Once, I remember, my mother was very concerned about my financial condition. To stop her worrying, I took the last twenty-six dollars I had in the world that week and wired her flowers for Mother's Day. It worked. She decided that if I had enough money for that purpose, my finances must be in much better shape than she had realized.

Later I was paid to read to Elihu Root, who had chosen to spend his last years on the Hamilton campus (I was also paid to give violin lessons to his grandson). He was the college's most distinguished alumnus, a former Senator, Secretary of War, and Secretary of State in time off from a career as one of New York's most successful corporate lawyers. One day he suddenly interrupted my reading to peer at me and ask, "What are you going to do when you leave Hamilton?" I told him I had given thought to studying law or to becoming a rabbi. He paused only briefly. "Become a lawyer," he said. "I have found that a lawyer needs twice as much religion as a minister or rabbi."

Hamilton was a very beautiful, highly traditional college, with the sort of liberal arts program now unfortunately almost extinct, including a large number of required courses. The school was all-male, with compulsory chapel every weekday and compulsory church on Sunday. The experience of sitting through so many church services made me think in a different way about being Jewish. I had to become a representative of my religion on campus. My classmates asked me what the Jews believed, and what Jewish holidays were about, and I had to have answers. Often their questions sent me scurrying to the library for information about Judaism. At no other time in my life have I known so much about being a Jew, or been so conscious of it, but I did not feel isolated or set apart. In my last year, for example, because of my academic standing — even though I was Jewish — I was given the honor and duty of taking attendance at chapel and church. It was taken for granted that I would not be invited to join a fraternity, but I would not have had enough money to afford it anyway, which meant that I didn't think about it enough to resent it as much as I otherwise might have. One should note that things have changed: today a significant percentage of the student body is Jewish and Hamilton has an active Hillel Society.

My social life was limited at Hamilton, but I was very busy. I got home for the holidays because a French teacher, an immensely tall, thin aesthete, was from Princeton and drove me to and from New

Jersey; our conversations on those occasions, about life and literature, art and music, became part of my education. I was able to participate in various campus activities, including the one I cared about
most: the Charlatans, the school's dramatic society, which occasionally was directed by Alexander Woollcott, drama critic of *The New
Yorker* and a ferociously loyal Hamilton alumnus. I received a
memorable review for my portrayal of Banquo in *Macbeth:* "Sol
Linowitz," the critic for the *Utica Observer-Dispatch* wrote, "gave
a convincing, if somewhat nasal, performance." I also found time to
practice my violin and play in the Utica Symphony.

I majored in German and qualified to teach the language in high
school. It now seems a strange choice for someone as conscious of
his Jewishness as I had become at Hamilton, in the age when Hitler
was consolidating his power in Germany. But all that seemed very
far from Clinton, New York — indeed, very far from America. Governor Herbert Lehman came to speak to us, and in telling us about
the world we were about to enter he did not find it necessary to
mention Hitler or Mussolini.

I considered taking a job as a German teacher at Ithaca High
School, but when I went to Ithaca it was to interview at Cornell
Law School, where I was offered a scholarship and another National
Youth Administration job. I found a place where I could afford to
stay, plus a restaurant where I could get my meals in return for my
services as a waiter. That summer I also found a new kind of employment to help me pay my bills: my high school friend Henry
Rose and I organized the Lynn-Rose Orchestra, a five-piece group
that pleased the management of the New Irvington Hotel in Belmar,
New Jersey. The next year I led my own band under an abbreviated
name, Chick Lynn and His Orchestra, playing not only in Belmar
but also in Asbury Park and even Atlantic City.

I was deeply confused during my first weeks at law school, for I
found it hard to see the relevance of what we were expected to learn;
but eventually I did well at Cornell. In fact, I became editor-in-chief
of the *Cornell Law Quarterly* and graduated first in my class.
Among the friends I made at law school were several who later rose
to great prominence, including Senator Edmund Muskie, then a
shy, slow-talking, modest, likable, and very nonpolitical fellow, and
William P. Rogers, a gracious and witty colleague on the *Law
Quarterly*, who became Eisenhower's Attorney General and
Nixon's Secretary of State. But the most significant social contact I

made at Cornell was a girl in a green satin dress, whom I met at a fraternity dance that a friend had persuaded me would be more interesting than yet another hour with the books. Toni Zimmerman was studying bacteriology, not law, but after a while I persuaded her that she could do her reading as easily in the law library as in the college library — and in the offices of the *Law Quarterly* as easily as in her room. Our dates consisted of walks around the campus, through the gorge, or around Lake Beebe, for I had absolutely no money, but she put up with it. And although I did not admit it at the time, Rochester's proximity to Cornell — especially by comparison with New York City — was an important reason why I went to work for the Rochester firm of Sutherland and Sutherland instead of one of the great Wall Street law firms.

There were three Sutherlands, not two: Judge Arthur E. Sutherland, who had been a New York Supreme Court judge (New York calls its trial courts the "Supreme Court"; what other states term the "Supreme Court" is known in New York as the "Court of Appeals"), and his two sons, Andrew and Arthur, Jr. They needed a young lawyer to help in an expanding practice. A friend of Judge Sutherland's, Judge Harley N. Crosby of the Appellate Division, was the father of a girl at the law school whom I had been tutoring in some of her courses. She introduced me to him, and I became very fond of this sensitive, gentle, wise man. When he asked me to talk with Judge Sutherland on his visit to Cornell, I of course agreed, although I said I had no intention of going to work in Rochester.

The Judge asked me to visit Sutherland and Sutherland, and to meet his sons, and I did. I was delighted with them. They were just like Tutt and Mr. Tutt in the popular stories Arthur Train wrote about a fictional law firm in the *Saturday Evening Post*. Andrew was a devoted trout fisherman who rolled his own cigarettes and told long, droll stories. Underneath, he was a shrewd trial lawyer who found imaginative ways to undercut an opponent's case. His brother, Arthur, had been a law clerk to Supreme Court Justice Oliver Wendell Holmes, Jr. He was the more cultured Tutt — a man who read for pleasure in Latin and French, and spoke a carefully precise English. Arthur also played the guitar and sang, and when I visited his home he found a violin so I could play along. (Later he would satisfy his academic inclinations by becoming a professor, first at Cornell Law School and then at Harvard Law

School.) They offered me a job at twenty-five dollars a week, and I accepted. Before doing so, I said to Judge Sutherland, "I want to be sure you understand that I'm Jewish." He replied, "I hope you won't hold it against us that we aren't."

During my first year in Rochester I lived at the Jewish Young Men's and Women's Association, and made friends. Among the others at the JY, as it was universally known, was a young lawyer named Henry Denker, who was in Rochester to sell other lawyers the services of a Tax Research Institute (later the Research Institute of America) run by his friend Leo Cherne. We shared an interest in the theatre; we actually wrote a play together. This was the first time Henry had attempted anything of this sort, and he seemed to like doing it, although our play was never presented. A couple of years after leaving Rochester, he turned playwright for both Broadway and radio. He wrote the radio script for Fulton Oursler's *The Greatest Story Ever Told,* and liked to comment on the fact that this popular presentation of the life of Jesus had been written by a nice Jewish boy from New York.

I met a bachelor with a car who was looking for company and was happy to drive me down for weekends at Cornell, where Toni would find dates for him. There was a theatre group at the JY, and I acted in several plays. I also became active in the men's club of the Temple Berith Kodish, the Reform Temple, and performed in the pageant with which the temple marked its centennial. Among the roles I played was that of the rabbi of the Hebrew Temple in Newport, Rhode Island, who in August 1790 received the famous letter from George Washington acclaiming the freedom of religion on the new continent. Thirty-seven years after this performance, I would serve as national chairman of the Committee for the Bicentennial formed by the Synagogue Council of America and read the Washington letter again at a daylong observance at Touro Synagogue in Newport, with Vice-President Nelson Rockefeller among the listeners.

Toni and I were married three months after her graduation in June 1939, and settled into what would these days be called the status of the young, upwardly mobile professional. Toni was able to find a job in a doctor's office where she could use her training as a bacteriologist, but after a few months she decided that what she really wanted to do was paint. She worked at it systematically, and soon was showing both paintings and sculptures in regional exhibitions, and selling some (as she still does). I practiced law, enjoying the company of the Sutherlands and learning the practicalities of the profession. We joined the Conservative Beth El synagogue and became active in that community. When I look back at our friends and the people we saw socially in those early years, I find that there were the Sutherlands and George Williams (who was in the class after mine at Cornell) from the law firm, and virtually all the rest were Jews — the Sturmans, the Goldmans, the Schwartzes. We were at home in Rochester, but not yet in all of Rochester.

My twenty-eighth birthday turned out to be Pearl Harbor Day, and I immediately applied to the Air Force and the Navy for a commission. As a married man, I was classified 3-A, and I couldn't get anyone interested in my application. I began to make inquiries about positions in Washington bureaus that I knew were hiring lawyers, and one day I received a letter from Nathaniel Nathanson, associate general counsel for the Office of Price Administration, asking me if I would be interested in a position with the OPA as chief of the rent control review branch. The job, it turned out, paid fifty-six hundred dollars a year, which was about half again as much as I was then making in Rochester. And it seemed something I could do that would be a contribution to the war effort. Sutherland and Sutherland gave me a leave of absence, and I went to work for the OPA, in one of those hotbox "temporary" buildings in Washington, in the summer of 1942. Toni and I lived in apartments in Arlington, and our first daughters, Anne and June, were born there.

The OPA was an adventure, full of people with stars in their eyes, doing work that really was part of the war effort. We were engulfed in this exciting — but also stultifying, because of the climate — atmosphere of Washington in the summer. I was twenty-eight years old and I had a large staff of lawyers working for me — many of them much older than I was. We were making law all the time: What is due process in setting rentals? What is a fair rent? Is a rent freeze a valid and constitutional way for the government to proceed? It was all new, highly dramatic, and very uncertain, with little precedent to guide us. And every city and town was different, because the pressures of the war caused rents to shoot up faster in some areas than in others. There were questions of comparability: Could we freeze different rents for similar properties in the same area? There had to be a way for landlords to protest, to appeal, first through administrative process and then, if they wished, to a court. A special federal appeals court, known as the

United States Emergency Court of Appeals, had been constituted for this purpose. My office handled those cases.

The administrator of the OPA was Leon Henderson, a brilliant, mercurial economist with a gift for publicity that boomeranged on him in later life. Another, rather different economist at the OPA was John Kenneth Galbraith, a giant stork of a man, already very strong-minded, eager to argue his own ideas as an economist and to exploit his individual, droll wit. Ben W. Heinemann, a gifted Chicago lawyer, headed the legal staff that handled appeals against price controls; later he became Chairman of the Chicago and Northwestern Railroad (and turned it into the conglomerate Northwestern Industries). Among the others I saw fairly often were Chester Bowles, founder of the advertising agency Benton and Bowles, later Governor of Connecticut and an Under Secretary of State and ambassador to India for John F. Kennedy; and David Ginsburg, the OPA's brilliant general counsel.

I met some of the leaders of my profession while at the OPA. In the key case of *Stanley Taylor v. United States*, a challenge to the entire structure of federal rent control that went to the Supreme Court, I had the chance to work with Paul Freund, later Solicitor General and an eminent professor of constitutional law. The Emergency Court of Appeals that heard price and rent control cases generally met in the city where the case originated, and we lawyers would travel with the court. I especially remember one trip to Seattle, by train — for it was felt that air travel should be restricted to people who had real need of speed in wartime — when I shared a sleeper with Associate General Counsel Nathanson and relaxed with the judges of the court: Fred Vinson (who later became Chief Justice of the United States); Albert Maris, Chief Judge of the Federal Circuit Court of Appeals in Philadelphia; Calvert Magruder, Judge of the Circuit Court in Massachusetts; and Bolitha Laws of the District of Columbia Circuit Court. We were careful to avoid even the appearance of impropriety — I can remember Nathanson, who had been a law professor at Northwestern and was very punctilious, closing the door on our roomette and waiting to leave it until after one of the judges had walked by. We were several days on a train with them, and in the end the propinquity was meaningful as well as exciting. We would sometimes have a drink with the judges at the end of the day, and talk about the scenery and the train — anything but the cases. In later years I might see the Chief Justice or one of the others at a legal convention or a social occasion, and it was always, "Hello, Sol" in the way of people who have shared a memorable experience. (I should note that the rent control regulations were sustained: we won all our cases.)

I continued looking for a way to get into the armed services, and finally through a friend found a vacancy in the office of the General Counsel of the Navy Department. I then learned that a knee injury I had suffered at Hamilton, which the Navy doctors declared "organic" in nature, had made me ineligible for service. I appealed. A second doctor carefully examined my other knee and determined that I was able to qualify, and I became an ensign in the Navy. My eyesight was not good enough for sea duty, and my orders restricted me to office jobs. The General Counsel was H. Struve Hensel, later Assistant Secretary of Defense for Eisenhower, and later still my correspondent in Washington on work I needed done for Xerox. (On my departure from the Organization of American States in 1969 it was Hensel, then a partner in Coudert Brothers, who first invited me to join the firm, where I have remained ever since.) Among the others I met during my time at the Navy Department was a young assistant to Under Secretary James V. Forrestal named Adlai E. Stevenson.

A good deal of my work for the Navy involved the renegotiation of contracts with various government suppliers, and I represented the department in hearings before several government agencies. I especially remember one case before the Interstate Commerce Commission, an attempt by the Navy to get lower rates from the railroads on shipments to Hanford, Washington. The railroads insisted that they were entitled to premium payments, although they did not know what the shipments were, because all the traffic went to Hanford and nothing came out. When I inquired about the shipments as part of the preparation of my case, I was told that I should simply say I could not divulge the contents for national security reasons. Armed with this formidable defense, I made my case and — to my surprise — won it. Only after the first atom bomb had been dropped did I learn that the material going to Hanford was uranium.

By 1945 I had been promoted to lieutenant senior grade, and was told that if I waited for my release time to come up instead of applying for earlier discharge (the war being over) I would be able to leave as lieutenant commander. Instead, I received an urgent call

from Chester Bowles, who had become Administrator of the OPA.
The New York City landlords had successfully challenged the rent
control regulations. If the decision stood, rent control might be
crippled. The OPA had won a stay pending rehearing before the
Emergency Court, and Bowles wanted me to return to the OPA as
assistant general counsel to reargue the case. He felt it was important enough to justify my immediate release from the Navy, and he
went to President Harry Truman, who sent Forrestal a letter requesting that the Navy put me on reserve status.

This case had become a cause célèbre in New York, and when I
arrived to argue at the rehearing I was met by cameras and reporters
who besieged me with questions. The chief attorney on the other
side was Charles Evans Hughes, Jr., who sat in the courtroom sur-
rounded by about a dozen colleagues, while I was alone at the government table. The image of David and Goliath was irresistible to
the press, and made me, briefly, something of a public figure in New
York State. The publicity engendered by this case (which we won)
may well have been one reason why I was offered the Democratic
nomination for Congress when I returned to Rochester a few
months later.

Several interesting government posts were offered to me in Washington after the war, but Toni and I had decided long before that we
wished to return to Rochester. George Williams, my colleague and
friend from the office who had also gone into the Navy, sent me a
letter after a visit home to see his ailing father, warning me that
there wasn't going to be much of a law practice left at the Sutherland and Sutherland office. The judge was an official referee of the
Supreme Court; Arthur, Jr., had become a major (later a colonel) in
the Army and would not be returning to Rochester (he became a
law teacher instead); and Andrew, who no longer cared all that
much about practicing law, had retained only a few, not very significant, clients. When I got back I found it was even worse than
George had described. George and I talked it over between ourselves and then with Andrew, who was willing to help out to the
extent that his other plans permitted. We changed the name of the
firm to Sutherland, Linowitz and Williams (although we didn't
print new letterheads for a while, because we were saving money),
and set about rebuilding the practice. Toni and I and the girls lived
for a year in an apartment, then took the plunge and bought our first
house, for $12,500, with a $10,000 mortgage and $2,500 borrowed
from Toni's Aunt Rose.

Although I think I would always have wished to be as active as possible in civic and public affairs, I got in the habit of it in Rochester in those days simply because I had the energy and the time; there wasn't much law practice to absorb me. With some friends, I worked on starting a new radio station to give the city a public voice with a point of view different from that of the local Gannett newspapers. I contemplated the possibility of running for office, and was actually offered the Democratic nomination for Congress. I decided that before accepting it I wanted to talk with Kenneth Keating, who would be the Republican nominee, to see whether I really wanted to fight him. When I met with Keating, and found that we agreed on many more issues than we disagreed on, I told my Democratic friends that I did not wish to run against him. (Twenty years later, when Robert Kennedy was urging me to run for Governor, I followed the same course, meeting at length with Nelson Rockefeller and deciding that I had no reason to wish him to lose.)

I became an early supporter and later the president of the Rochester Association for the United Nations, a cause dear to the heart of Mrs. Harper Sibley, the widow of the former president of the U.S. Chamber of Commerce and our introduction to Rochester high society. The UN was popular in Rochester — the year of my presidency, the Rochester Association had a larger membership than any similar organization anywhere else in the United States. Two dozen Rochester civic groups supported a one-day conference on the prospects for world peace, which I chaired in December 1948. Through this conference I met a number of interesting and important people, some of whom became good friends. Among them was Dr. J. Robert Oppenheimer, who spoke at the meeting. He later asked me for some rather peripheral help when he ran into problems with his clearance at the Atomic Energy Commission; and Toni and I were occasionally guests of the Oppenheimers on visits to Princeton when he was head of the Institute for Advanced Study. Those were often sad occasions, for he was ill, embroiled in the politics of the Institute, and out of touch, he felt, with the greater world. But there were always flashes of that personal, histrionic fire.

Joe Wilson was active in the Rochester UN Association, too. It was an interest we shared, and kept. Nearly two decades later, in 1964, a series of programs about the United Nations was sponsored by the Xerox Corporation on national television, generating a John Birch Society campaign against the company — questions at stockholder meetings; huge bundles of letters (sometimes the whole bundle consisted of the same letter with different signatures) dumped into our mail room. Joe and I were taken aback, especially by the number of letters that came from professional people, usually doctors, expressing their dismay at our support for "the Communist UN." Eventually we shrugged it off as something that came with the territory.

On another front of civic activity, we both became involved in the Chamber of Commerce, of which we would each eventually become president. When Joe was president of the City Club, I was the program committee chairman. Two years later, I was elected president of the City Club myself and — somewhat inadvertently — became a public figure in Rochester. From 1949 through the mid-1950s, in fact, I was probably better known to my neighbors, and to people I might meet on the street, than I would ever be again.

The reason was the power of television, still quite new — so new that Rochester had only one station, WHAM-TV, an NBC affiliate owned by Stromberg-Carlson. They had done a program on the world peace forum, and I had appeared on it as moderator of the discussion. There was no doubt that the exposure on television had contributed to the extraordinary attendance at the meeting. (We had sold out the several thousand seats in the Eastman Theatre for the evening discussion, with lines of people hoping to get in extending around the block.) When I became president of the City Club, I suggested that WHAM-TV might be interested in offering a program that would present our speakers, giving greater currency to what they had to say while promoting our lunches. Each Saturday morning, I took our luncheon speaker to the studio, and we did a fifteen-minute interview on film, to be telecast the next Monday evening as a regular feature called "The City Club Corner." When the City Club speakers season ended, William Fay, president of WHAM, suggested that we develop a discussion program independent of the City Club and somewhat more ambitious.

From that suggestion grew a program we called "The Court of Public Opinion," which brought national figures — Governors, Senators, cabinet members, ambassadors — to the WHAM-TV studios to discuss significant world or national issues with two or three thoughtful local people, schoolteachers, businessmen, doctors, or lawyers. I served as moderator, setting the stage at the beginning by introducing the participants and outlining four or five of the more important and controversial aspects of our subject. Then at the end a couple of minutes would be reserved for me to summarize what the participants had said and indicate what had seemed to me their areas of agreement and disagreement. This was a formidable and sometimes nerve-racking assignment — the show was, of course, done live — but my summary soon became the trademark of the program, and I was not able to drop it.

The program was aired at half past seven on Saturday evenings, and it quickly developed an extraordinary audience. I was told that it had the highest ratings in the United States for any program of its kind. I was not misled, however, for I realized why the ratings were so impressive: the program appeared just before Sid Caesar's "Show of Shows," and anybody who tuned in early for Sid Caesar found himself watching us. We were sponsored almost from the beginning, either by the Rochester Gas and Electric Company or by the Union Trust Company of Rochester, on a public-service basis with institutional commercials. Before each program I prepared a brochure to be sent by the sponsor to all the schools and universities in the area announcing the topic and the participants, and suggesting reading material for people who might wish to continue with their own discussion at home or in school after the program was over. A number of groups were formed to meet at homes or community centers to watch the program and hold discussions afterward. I remember a maid at a dinner party whispering to me that she and her friends had seen our program the night before and had been "up until one o'clock in the morning, arguing with it."

I had complete freedom in determining who would be invited to participate in the programs and the subject for discussion. Because the programs were done live, I could never see them myself, and at the beginning we did not have a television set, so Toni and the girls never saw them, either. Stromberg-Carlson, which manufactured television sets as well as owning WHAM, learned that we didn't have a set and sent us one. When I came home after the first program my daughters had seen, our bubbly June came rushing to the door and threw her arms around me. "I loved it, Daddy," she shouted, "except for two things: the way you looked and the way you talked."

I benefited from the time I had spent in Washington. I knew things and — most important from the City Club program committee's point of view — I knew people who were faraway figures and rather exotic, even to the leaders of Rochester. This was, of course, still before jet aircraft and casual travel. My friends at the Chamber of Commerce were not very sympathetic to price or rent control, but the fact that I had been a participant in administering such programs gave me a status different from any I might have had if I had simply remained in Rochester and practiced law. It was not generally known that Toni and I were having a financial struggle. Sutherland and Sutherland had been a well-established and well-regarded law firm in Rochester, and the legal profession was not then as gossipy as it has since become; the fact that the firm was having difficulty was known to only a handful of our intimates.

Joe Wilson knew, as I knew about his concerns for the future of Haloid. Our friendship ripened through the fall and winter of 1946. We got into the habit of taking walks together on weekends, often in Mendon Ponds or around the reservoir, talking about everything — politics, literature, business, personal matters. Frequently, the four of us had Saturday dinner together. Soon, Joe and I began what became a habitual Sunday morning walk. While Peggy and the Wilson children went to church, Joe would drive over to our house and pick me up, and we would go off together to walk and talk.

In later years, much to the horror of the management consultants Joe occasionally called in to advise him, those Sunday walks became central to the management process of a large and growing company. Joe would come on Sunday with a folded sheet of paper containing a list he had dictated to his secretary of the things he wanted us to talk about before he made his decisions. When we had finished discussing an item, he would take his pencil and cross it off the list. Then, as no one knew for years, he would keep his lists, which later reappeared, disconcertingly, in the discovery proceedings for the antitrust case brought against Xerox by SCM Corporation. It would have seemed strange to both of us that anyone but ourselves would ever know about or take an interest in these casual meanderings among our essentially poetic dreams and hopes.

After I joined the Haloid board in 1951 there were occasional executive committee meetings (at the Rochester Club, as there was no appropriate place for such meetings in the spare and run-down offices of the old Haloid Company), but Joe liked to conduct business by memorandum. At the same time, however, he wanted to be sure he had thoroughly thought through and talked through a decision before he acted. Joe was a great enthusiast, and he knew he could be captivated by a person or idea he had just encountered. Often I played devil's advocate on our Sunday walks, challenging his assumptions and predilections, pressing him to measure his soaring hopes against earthbound probabilities. After a while, colleagues at Haloid, wishing to call a matter to Joe's attention, would telephone me on a Friday afternoon to discuss their problem and to ask me to bring it up Sunday while walking in the woods with Joe. John Dessauer, our enterprising German-born director of research, was particularly accomplished at this. He would call on Friday to say, "You will want to take up with Joe this issue" — and often I did.

With the passage of time, Joe's path and mine crossed more often and in more places. We saw each other frequently at the City Club, the meetings of the Board of Trustees of the University, the Chamber of Commerce, the Rochester Philharmonic (where both of us were subscribers and on the board), and the United Nations Association. We also served together on the boards of the Rochester Savings Bank and Superba Cravats. And, of course, we saw each other more often on Haloid and later Xerox business as I became first a vice-president, then general counsel, later chairman of the executive committee, and finally chairman of the board, while continuing to practice law. In a fundamental sense we were partners. Years later, after Joe's death, I had to testify in the antitrust suit brought by SCM against Xerox. Counsel cross-examining me kept trying to read something sinister or conspiratorial into the way Joe and I operated jointly, during walks in the woods and on social occasions, outside the formal corporate structure. There was no way to explain it to him — indeed, there had been no way to explain it at the time to the occasionally bewildered staff at Xerox — other than to say, "Joe was my best friend." He was, and I miss him still.

In the first months after my return to Rochester, I had no business connection with Haloid. The company's law firm was Nixon, Hargrave and Devans, the largest in Rochester, and also counsel to Eastman Kodak. Early on, however, Joe began talking to me about his hopes for and worries about the future of Haloid. Its strength was the quality of its coated paper, especially for what was then the rather messy and time-consuming business of making photocopies. The superiority of Haloid Record paper helped the company sell its Rectigraph photocopying cameras to both the government (especially the military) and private industry. But Haloid had been standing still, and it was standing next to an elephant in the form of Eastman Kodak. Should the elephant roll over — should Eastman's

laboratories develop something better than halide-coated paper for
photocopying — Haloid would simply be squashed and hardly anyone would notice.

Joe felt a need to move ahead technologically, and to restructure
his personnel, move younger people into more responsible positions
and older people to retirement. While still a vice-president, he had
acquired an exclusive license for a patent on the more rapid pro-
cessing of photographic materials, and he had a partnership arrangement with a company called Microtronics in New York City to
create what they would call a FotoFlo camera for the continuous
creation of microfilm records. In 1946 he was in consultation with
his friend Charles Glavin of the First Boston Corporation on the
possibility of new financing for Haloid, and shortly after Thanksgiving a special meeting of Haloid stockholders approved a $1 mil-
lion issue of preferred stock with a 4 percent dividend, which Glavin
had presold as a private offering to a group of four insurance companies.

I heard about all this on our walks, as he heard about my law firm
and our struggles to restore it to its prewar prosperity. He was
pleased to learn that Superba Cravats had become one of my clients.
Some weeks later, I heard from Muhlhauser that Joe had been inquiring about the legal work I was doing for Superba, and toward
the end of the year I got a call from Joe asking for an appointment to
come into the office. He started by telling me that Haloid's counsel
was, as I knew, Nixon, Hargrave. I stopped him and told him that
we were friends, our friendship had nothing to do with business,
and I didn't even want to talk to him about his business. After
brushing that aside, he told me that there was a single piece of work,
a "one-shot," that he did not wish to take to Nixon, Hargrave, because it might also be of interest to Eastman Kodak and give his regular counsel a conflict of interest.

That piece of work, he said, involved drawing up an agreement
by which Haloid would acquire a license on a new process for copying that had been patented by an inventor in New York. The rights
to the patents were controlled by the Battelle Memorial Institute in
Columbus, Ohio. A charitable foundation established in the will of a
Columbus businessman named Gordon Battelle, the Institute had
pioneered the concept of contract research, making deals with both
the government and private firms to conduct scientific studies and
develop products from patents. John Dessauer, the Haloid director

of research whom Joe had charged with searching for new products, had read a description of the new copying process in a monthly bulletin published by, of all companies, Eastman Kodak. He had investigated its status and found it scientifically feasible — and an unsponsored orphan at Battelle. In his typical methodical way, Joe had checked with his friends at Microtronics, who had interviewed the inventor, a patent attorney named Chester F. Carlson, and agreed with Dessauer that "electrophotography," as it was then called, was both an original and an interesting idea, although still far from practical application.

Carlson had followed up on this interview and arranged for Ernest Taubes, Microtronics's chief engineer, to visit Battelle. Joe himself had gone to Columbus in May, when he had met with a man named John Crout, vice-president of the Institute and head of a Development Corporation Battelle had established to insulate the foundation from the tax consequences and other legal liabilities associated with commercial product development. From that day on, Joe knew that he wanted electrophotography for Haloid; from our earliest talks on the subject he described the Carlson invention to me as "a revolutionary development," although he also warned me that it was "in a very primitive state." Battelle and Carlson were still hoping to interest some larger corporation that could make greater contributions than could be expected from this little photocopying materials manufacturer in Rochester. Battelle, after all, was a major research laboratory, and not the least of Joe's reasons for wishing to secure the license on electrophotography was his admiration for the facilities he saw in Columbus. The strategy of leveraging Haloid's assets through much larger operations, crucial to the subsequent development of Xerox, was present in Joe's mind from the beginning. Battelle hung back, assuring Joe that Haloid would have "first consideration" when the time came to award licenses.

Joe returned to Columbus in the summer and again in October, when he met Carlson, whom he described in a letter to his father as a modest and capable man with a fertile imagination. Carlson's anxious desire to see *some* commercial company pick up a license on his patents may have tipped the scale with Battelle, which agreed to give Haloid a short-term license, with renewal options, for certain uses of electrophotography. In return, Haloid would make a cash contribution to the research at Battelle and do some work on the process in its own laboratories. Joe was returning to Columbus yet again, this time to put the option into the form of a legal agreement, and for that he needed a lawyer. This was the "one-shot" for Sutherland, Linowitz and Williams. It was implied, perhaps, that while my firm could not expect to receive additional legal assignments for Haloid, subsequent work relating to electrophotography might also be assigned to us.

I found it a joy, on all counts, to work with Joe. My files contain a letter from Joe in March 1949, complaining about the fees we were then charging him for the growing work on what we had begun to call xerography: they were too small. From then on, he wrote, he was going to add 20 percent to our bills as a signal of "how we feel concerning the service, brain power and energy we are receiving from Sutherland."

That first trip to Columbus remained in both our minds. It was abominable. We shared a compartment on a sleeper. Everything was dirty. The beds were bumpy and the roadbed worse, the heat didn't work and the train was bitterly cold, there was no dining car and we had to do without breakfast. We were stuck several hours in the snow, shivering in our overcoats and staring out the filthy windows. And what we found when we got to Battelle did not make me particularly cheerful or optimistic about the prospects for electrophotography. Joe had of course seen demonstrations of the process during his earlier visits to Battelle, but somehow he had been led to believe that Battelle had made major progress in the succeeding months. It seemed to me that he was looking at the demonstration the Battelle group now staged for us with almost the same innocence as I was. With some fanfare, our hosts at Battelle brought out a metal roller coated with some dark substance, a rag of cat's fur, a transparent plastic child's ruler with dark lines scratched in it, and a bright light. They rubbed the roller with the cat's fur. Then they shined the light through the ruler onto the roller, and some feeble off-white lines appeared on the dark surface.

I remember Joe leaning over to peer at the roller through his bifocals. "That's it," the Battelle scientist said.

"*That's it?*"

"Yes."

I thought even Joe's enthusiasm had dimmed, but it returned after the roller was dusted with dark powder through a handheld sifter and brushed clean and pressed onto a piece of paper — which thereupon displayed, in rather blurred form, the lines of the ruler.

There was a copying process here, and the scientists and engineers would one day make that process, and the company that controlled it, important in the world. We settled down to negotiate the last items in Haloid's agreement with Battelle: how much money, what rights Battelle would license, and how long the license would run.

For our initial $10,000, Battelle wished to give us only six months; we insisted on, and got, a year, with options to renew for $12,500 in 1948, $20,000 in 1949, $25,000 in 1950, and $35,000 in 1951. Battelle would spend this money for research on the fundamental process, and Haloid would do its own research on treated papers to improve the process; the two research staffs would work together in their respective areas of responsibility. Haloid would pay Battelle a royalty of 8 percent on any sales of products embodying the patented principles, once a certain sales volume was reached.

What Haloid was acquiring was strictly and solely the right to make copying machines to produce fewer than twenty copies of a document. Even in our later agreements, until we bought all the foundation's rights to the patents in 1956, some uses of electrophotography would not be included in the Haloid license. Battelle reserved for itself the use of electrophotography for "the recording and reproduction of fingerprints, for electron-microscope shadowgraphs, and for electronic writing." But the use Battelle was especially insistent upon retaining was "toy and model kits." Battelle clearly regarded everything else as speculative; xerography as a toy was, for Battelle, the one realistic prospect for profits.

This first agreement was limited and narrow. A year later, when it began to appear that significant business values might emerge from Carlson's process — and Joe decided that he should put before his board of directors for approval his plans to increase Haloid's expenditure on electrophotography in its own labs — Joe and I agreed that it was necessary to renegotiate the agreement and secure something much more comprehensive, detailed, and specific, which we did.

The human experience of that first trip to Columbus was a cement in our friendship. We found we could enjoy each other's company while working as well as while walking in the woods or dining with our wives. Nine years later we went together to Europe — a first trip for all of us — to look over possible partners in the manufacture and marketing of copiers abroad. We crossed the English Channel on the ferry, in one of those storms made famous in the novels and histories Joe and I had read so often, and Joe was hanging over the rail, wretchedly seasick. The ferry heaved and rolled, and Joe turned to me and flashed his still boyish grin. Through the howling wind I heard his yell: "It beats Columbus!"

3

Battelle and Carlson

THE STORY OF Chester Carlson should be told anew to every generation, for it is so splendid and bittersweet a parable of the American dream. Born in 1906 in Seattle to an immigrant Swedish barber, an only child, Chet watched his parents sicken with tuberculosis and his father bend in hopeless pain under the burden of spinal arthritis. The family wandered through California and even Mexico (where a cruel swindler had sold the senior Carlson title to a "farm" of dry mesquite on which nothing could be grown). From high school age, Chet supported his parents. Among those for whom he worked while in high school was a job printer, from whom he bought an old press that he used to print a magazine for amateur chemists and high school chemistry students. His mother died when he was seventeen, leaving him the task of nursing as well as supporting his father. He worked his way through junior college and then through the California Institute of Technology, emerging with a degree in physics in 1930 just as the Great Depression choked off employment chances for scientists. There were no jobs in California. An offer came from Bell Labs in New York. Chet's father seemed to be feeling better; with his encouragement, Chet came to New York.

He found bench work in Bell Labs uncongenial and transferred to the patent department, but AT&T was cutting back its patent development during the Depression and the job disappeared. After a brief stay with a small patent firm, Chet went to work for the patent department of P. R. Mallory and Company, an Indianapolis electronics and electrical engineering company that maintained a patent office in New York. Annoyed at his junior status, he began attending law school at night to qualify as a patent attorney. Because he could not afford textbooks, he worked in the library, taking copious notes. Both the slow photostat process he had to use to prepare applications for patents at his job and the nuisance of copying passages by hand from the law textbooks left Carlson with the conviction that the world needed an inexpensive, accurate, fast way to make copies of documents. In his book *My Years with Xerox*, John Dessauer relates a conversation between Chet and an associate at Mallory as they labored until midnight at the photostat machine:

"There must be a better way of making these copies!"

"Sure," his colleague agreed. "But nobody has ever found it."

"Maybe nobody has ever tried," Chet said.

Carlson began his search for a new way to make copies at the New York Public Library, of which he later became a benefactor. From his training as a physicist, he thought there should be a way to use photoelectric effects — changes wrought by light in materials that were "photoconductive" — to generate a kind of print. In the library he found that Paul Selenyi, a Hungarian physicist, had made pictures by dusting a surface on which the outlines of an image had been electrostatically charged.[1] Harold Clark, a physicist (and photography hobbyist) who left a professorship at Union College in 1949 to work for Haloid on the principles of what we had just begun to call xerography, once said that Carlson's intuitive combination of photoconductivity and electrostatics was among the great intellectual achievements of the 1930s. It was scientifically brilliant and extraordinarily original. The only problem was, Clark added, that it didn't work.

The first of Carlson's patents was dated 1937; it was a patent on an idea. He began trying to make a copying device based on his theory, working nights and weekends in the kitchen of his New York apartment. Legend has it that he met his wife when she came bang-

[1] Distribution requirements at Hamilton College required me to take a year of biology, a year of chemistry, and two years of college mathematics. Nobody required me to take physics, so I did not. A lawyer learns to sound authoritative about a number of subjects he understands only dimly. The discussions in these pages about the scientific end of the Xerox story should be regarded as a reflection of what has been told to me by knowledgeable people I have reason to trust, rather than as a statement of something I "know."

ing on his door to find out what the terrible smell was. His wife's mother owned a house in Astoria, in Queens, where there was a vacant apartment behind a beauty shop, and Carlson moved his experiments there. He was not an engineer, however; he could not put the pieces together. Early in 1938 he saw an ad in an electronics trade journal, from a German refugee engineer with a background in physics who was looking for work. Carlson's was the only reply Otto Kornei received to his ad, so he took the "job" Carlson could offer — a painfully small salary (a piece of what Carlson was making at Mallory), a "lab" in an apartment behind a beauty parlor in Queens, and a budget for materials that Kornei later told John Dessauer totaled ten dollars a month.

It was Kornei who made the zinc plate and coated it with sulfur as the photoconductive insulating element that could be charged sufficiently by rubbing it with a piece of cloth. And it was Kornei who stood beside Carlson in the kitchen in Queens on October 22, 1938, when Carlson wrote the numbers "10-22-38" and the word "Astoria" with a grease pencil on a glass plate, shined a floodlight through the glass onto a sulfur-coated zinc plate, scattered lycopodium powder onto the plate and blew it off — and saw the symbols he had written reproduced in the powder that stuck to the plate. It was fuzzy, and the print Carlson thereupon made by pressing paper on the plate was fuzzier still, but it was what Carlson's theory had predicted. He had proved his point.

And no one was interested. Kornei soon found a real job at IBM (many years later, after the breakthrough of the 914 copier had made Xerox one of the highest-priced stocks on the New York Stock Exchange, Carlson sent him a hundred shares as an unsolicited and entirely unexpected gift). Chet was left alone to improve his product as best he could, add to his collection of patents, and call fruitlessly for attention to what he had invented. He sent letters to IBM, A. B. Dick, RCA, and many others, describing his invention and soliciting an appointment to display it. Some never answered, some politely declined, a few invited Carlson to demonstrate his machine — and then after the demonstration (which rarely worked well) saw him to the door with the comment that they had no interest at this time but would of course call him if they changed their minds. Carlson grew monomaniacal about his invention, and spent all his salary working to improve and promote it. The spinal arthritis that had afflicted his father brought its special, painful curse upon him.

He felt he had no time. Then one day in 1944 Dr. Russell W. Dayton of the Battelle Memorial Institute came to P. R. Mallory to discuss some patents on entirely different subjects, and Carlson brought up his own invention. For the first time in six years of scrambling for attention, someone told Carlson that what he was saying sounded fascinating. Carlson showed Dayton some copies he had made with his process, and Dayton invited him to come to Columbus and present his invention to Battelle.

The arrangements Battelle made with Carlson gave the inventor little immediate reward for his labors and his dreams. Indeed, it was shortly after Battelle had taken on electrophotography that Carlson's wife, Janet, left him and filed for divorce: if this was success, she wanted none of it. Battelle became Carlson's exclusive agent under his patents, three of which, dated between 1942 and 1944, were central and superb. Frank Steinhilper, for many years the chief (originally only) patent counsel at Haloid and Xerox, said recently that if those patents had not expired, they would still cover every copier using electrostatic principles being made today. In return, the Institute offered to spend three thousand dollars on electrophotography research and pay Carlson an honorarium of a thousand dollars a year for as long as they retained the rights. Carlson would be entitled to 25 percent of all profits and royalties Battelle received from licensing the patents — except that at any time within five years of this 1944 agreement he could reimburse the Institute for its research expenses to date and raise his share of profits and royalties to 40 percent. It is a measure of Carlson's continuing confidence and courage that shortly before that option expired in 1949 — with xerography still in its cradle and not having earned a penny for anyone — he scrounged around among his friends and his second wife's family to borrow the seventeen thousand dollars he would need to reimburse Battelle and increase his share of the royalties to 40 percent. It was a good investment; in time, that additional 15 percent translated into about $7 million.

By then Carlson was living in Rochester and working at Haloid. ("He and I and a secretary," Steinhilper remembered, "shared an office big enough for one person.") He had never got on particularly well with the Battelle scientists. They were, he told Wilson, unfairly, not interested in fundamental research. The laboratory people in Columbus were tired of Carlson's sporadic appearances on his time off from his job at Mallory and the criticisms he would offer as he watched over their shoulders. Research on electrophotography was a very small part of Battelle's million-dollar budget. When Chet received the Edward Longstreth Medal of the Franklin Institute of Pennsylvania in 1953, it was Haloid and not Battelle that gave the celebratory lunch in his honor in Philadelphia.

The two top scientists at Haloid were vice-president John Dessauer, who was a highly competent chemical engineer still engaged mostly, and very successfully, in the creation and perfection of new coated papers that kept Haloid at the forefront of its traditional business, and Harold Clark, who had left his academic career and come to industrial research because of his fascination with the questions raised by Carlson's invention. (It was, he once said to me, using a term of high praise for a physicist, "an *elegant* thing.") Long before the outside world had heard Carlson's name, they considered Chet a genius and treated him with great respect. Of equal importance, Joe and I *liked* Chet. Haloid was a much more pleasant place to work and visit than Battelle. Chet came to visit us when he could make the time for the drive to Rochester and find the money for gas to put in his jalopy. After our first public demonstration of xerography, at a meeting of the American Optical Society in Detroit in 1948, Chet wrote Joe a letter: "The trip to Detroit was perfect from beginning to end, and I can truthfully say — you thought of everything. The more I see of you and your associates at The Haloid Company the happier I am to be associated with you rather than with any other group of persons with whom I am familiar."

Chet's "job" at Haloid grew out of a conversation with Joe one day the next year, when Chet stopped off in Rochester on a drive back from Columbus to New York. Chet was then forty-three, a tall, stooped, scholarly man already bowed under the burdens and fears of his inherited spinal arthritis. He saw time passing, with only ten more years on his basic patents, and relatively little of a commercial nature being accomplished. Meeting with Joe and Dessauer, he poured out suggestions for work to be done, and complaints that Battelle was not doing it. Joe said, on the spur of the moment, that if Chet wished to leave Mallory he would be delighted to give him a job as a "consultant" to Haloid at a salary of a thousand dollars a month. A few years later, when royalty monies began pouring in (as early as 1953, before any paper-copying product had been marketed, Chet's share of the payments to Battelle exceeded seventy-seven thousand dollars), Chet renegotiated his arrangements with Haloid. He cut down his time at the office to one day a week and his emolument to a derisory two hundred dollars a month, in return for which Haloid set up and supplied materials for a lab Chet started in his old farmhouse out on the edge of the suburbs. Questions then arose as to the ownership of xerography-related patents that grew out of the work Chet did in that lab.

I negotiated the arrangements with Chet and also did some personal legal work for him. With guidance from the Washington law firm of Hogan and Hartson, who were tax specialists, I helped him restructure his contract with Battelle so that his royalties, when they began coming in quantity, would be taxed as capital gains rather than as income. We also had considerable conversation and correspondence about new federal court decisions in the patent area, a subject on which he kept current. He was, after all, a patent lawyer (which I was not), and he had an inveterate suspicion of the thoroughness of the outside patent counsel I had retained to help Frank Steinhilper.

He was a prodder and a pusher, and for all his other-worldliness he could be demanding. He kept making the point that his basic patents were going to expire; we weren't doing enough about that, we weren't moving fast enough. (He called me on such things, and prodded me on the telephone. I told him to put it in writing because then Joe might take it more seriously.) At one point he offered to sacrifice some portion of his royalties to help pay the cost of added personnel in the Haloid patent department. I worked with him most closely on those matters in the context of the "patent commission" established inside Haloid in 1953, with me as chairman, to obtain patent protection for the products we hoped to make after Carlson's basic patents expired in 1959 and 1961.

Except in the patent law area, where he had a tendency to react emotionally to decisions that might be seen as reducing the protection of his inventions, Chet's great strength in our meetings was that he was usually right. We were understaffed in our patent department for years, and the research was forever running ahead of our capacity to protect it. Moreover, the tendency in our patent department, forced to pick and choose among inventions rising from the labs, was always to protect what might be needed in next year's commercial products rather than what might be crucial to the products we would not be developing for years to come. Yet it was precisely those future products that potential competitors would stress, hoping to supplant us in our own markets after our basic protection had expired. Like Joe, Chet preferred to discuss subjects one-on-one, or to put his ideas on paper, and he didn't speak often at the meetings. He was a gentle person and disliked face-to-face disputes of any kind, but he was very bright, and when he intervened it was to ask the most pertinent questions. He liked to say he operated by instinct — even to say that he had found his inventions by instinct. My strongest recollection of Chet in a business context is this slow, serious man thinking hard about what had just been said, then smiling a sweet half-smile and saying, "You may be right. But I don't think so."

No one spent much time with Chet socially. Years of deprivation and the daily pain of his arthritis had limited his capacity for casual companionship, and his second wife, Dorris, a beautiful and intelligent lady, was a devotee of Eastern religions, psychic phenomena, and spiritualism. Chet and I talked politics once in a while, however. He was a compassionate man of strongly liberal views. When he became rich — and he became very rich (John Dessauer has estimated that in the mid-1960s Chet's income from his stock and patents ran as high as $6 million a year) — he gave most of his money away. Robert Hutchins came from California to the memorial services for Chet in 1968 (as Toni and I came from Washington), and told us something nobody else had known before: for the previous five years Chet had been the largest single supporter of the Center for the Study of Democratic Institutions in Santa Barbara, contributing more than a million dollars a year. And, of course, asking nothing for it. Hutchins said Carlson was "the only saint I ever knew."

Chet died in New York of a heart attack he suffered in a movie theatre one afternoon. No one knew whether he had gone in because he wanted to see the film or because he had felt ill and needed a place to sit down. At the memorial services we learned of the last thing he did before entering the theatre. There had been a balloon seller on the street outside, filling his gaudy wares from a helium cylinder. Chet had bought a bunch of the balloons, stepped back, and then released them to fly high in the sky over the city. The balloon seller had asked him why he did that, and Chet replied, "I wanted to set them free."

Recently I had occasion to return to Rochester, and I discovered the new Chester F. Carlson YMCA, erected in 1983 by Dorris, "in memory of her husband's extraordinary life." On the entrance wall — presented, with charming pertinence, as a reproduction on steel of a page from his personal notebook, in his own handwriting — there is a list of instructions Chet had written to himself:

Pay Attention
Respect others' rights and feelings [underlining in the notebook]
Don't enter where I have no business
Voice modulated
No fuss
Self-discipline to build character
Love all
Avoid pleasure principle
Control of speech
Refuse unnecessary gifts
Abandon worldly ambitions
Contin. devotion to Brahman
Don't be a rubber stamp

We shall not see his like again.

With Battelle, our relations were neither so affectionate nor so trusting. There was, of course, a necessary tension between two research groups working on the same subject matter; they were bound to be vying with each other. There was also a certain conflict of interest on the allocation of contract research funds after the government (especially the military) took an interest in the development of electrophotography. Further problems arose when customers began paying for products that incorporated the Carlson patents. Haloid was not so much a manufacturer as an assembler in those days, and it seemed to us unfair that we (or our customers) should be asked to pay a royalty on the full price of an item largely assembled from parts that could be purchased off any number of shelves. It seemed to Battelle, on the other hand, that the only reason anybody was buying or leasing the item was the copying it would do, and that therefore royalty should be paid on every penny the customer paid to Haloid.

Beyond such individual disputes, Haloid had a continuing uneasiness in its relationship with Battelle — our sense that the foundation was not really proud of its joint venture with an insignificant little company like ours. We were conscious — perhaps too conscious — that Battelle, in discussing the Carlson patents with the government and with its other clients, and in its occasional public references to electrophotography, did not always mention Haloid. We knew we had not been allowed to bid for a license until Battelle (and Carlson) had knocked fruitlessly on every other conceivable door — electrical equipment companies, photography companies, duplicator companies. We also knew that Battelle was still soliciting licensing agreements elsewhere. We were constantly fighting to impress them and to persuade them that they were betting on the right horse.

Ultimately, the Xerox research effort became much larger than that at Battelle, and much more successful, although Battelle continued to make significant contributions. When John Dessauer and Harold Clark edited their classic text on xerography in 1965, only three of the twenty-three contributors were employees of Battelle, and all the rest were working in the Xerox labs. It was in the Xerox labs and shops that the ultimately triumphant copying machines were designed, breadboarded, and engineered for mass production, while Battelle did not succeed in its efforts to make a desktop copier, develop a color xerography product, or create devices for transmitting Xerox copies over telephone wires. The profits on the Xerox stock Battelle had acquired by selling us all rights to the Carlson patents were the major factor enabling the Institute to expand from the two hundred employees working in Columbus at the time the first Haloid contract was signed to its grandeur as a worldwide research organization with more than seven thousand employees.

Still, the fact remained that it was the researchers in Columbus who had made electrophotography into a viable process. Carlson's device could be nursed to make copies occasionally, but it was a dubious pig in an unlikely poke. One of the things that had convinced Dessauer and Wilson to seek the license for electrophotography had been a long report on Battelle's preliminary work on the process, a report in which one page — page 142 — had been duplicated by Carlson's methods. Wilson asked for more copies of page 142 for distribution to his board of directors, and Battelle was unable to replicate the results. Months passed before this one page could be duplicated successfully. Every step in the long, complicated Carlson process had to be done by hand, and any one of a number of missteps — some of which could not even be recognized as such —

could ruin the experiment. Within two years, Battelle's Applied Physics Laboratory had solved the problems. Harold Clark, later scientific director of Xerox and as loyal to his lab and his colleagues as a man could be, said recently that when he came to Haloid in 1949 there was much work to be done to understand scientifically why the Battelle materials were successful, and on the practical construction of a potentially commercial product — but all the vital improvements of the Carlson process had been made.

Carlson had used sulfur and anthracene as the photoconductive materials that would accept an electrostatic charge, but they created fuzzy images and were subject to fatigue: the plates could be used only a few times before they had to be cleansed and coated again. A young Battelle researcher named William E. Bixby found that selenium produced cleaner images and that a selenium-coated plate could be reused more often. (Among the more remarkable patents the Haloid-Battelle partnership secured was one on the use of selenium, a common element, in xerography. Since no one ever came up with a better photoconductive insulator, this patent became a bulwark of the Xerox competitive position after protection ended on Carlson's basic invention. The last significant contributions of Battelle research, before Xerox acquired ownership of the patents and the sheer size of the Xerox lab overwhelmed what was being done in Columbus, was the perfection of a coating, based on the cleanser Glass Wax, which made the selenium plate almost infinitely durable.) And it was Bixby, again, who discovered that with the selenium plate a dim light at the red end of the visible spectrum produced a much sharper reproduction than Carlson's floodlight.

Carlson had used a lycopodium powder as his "dry ink" and had sifted the powder by hand over the charged plate. Battelle developed a carbon powder that was more reliable and made darker prints. It also invented a far superior "cascade carrier" method by which the powder was delivered to the plates as a coating on a flow of tiny glass balls, which would then be returned to the powder bath and coated again for the next use. Carlson had charged his plates by rubbing them with a cloth or a piece of fur; Battelle (although in this instance only after following a suggestion from Carlson, who was visiting the lab) designed a system of "corona charging," by which a voltage was applied to a bank of sewing needles suspended over the plate and scanning it.

A year and a half after the first Haloid-Battelle contract, Battelle, with only a little help from Haloid, was ready to demonstrate a machine to the annual convention of the American Optical Society. Battelle paid two-thirds of the cost of making and shipping the machine, and Haloid's nonfinancial contribution was confined to verbal suggestions and the creation of a few backup parts in the Haloid shops, just in case. By happy coincidence, the date of the meeting was October 22, 1948, exactly a decade after Carlson's first successful experiment. The device shipped to Detroit for the demonstration was a monstrosity of four huge red boxes, requiring a person to operate the process in each box — but it worked. As we had claimed, it made paper copies in less than sixty seconds.

The business as well as the scientific press gave considerable publicity to Battelle's success in making what was still exactly one functioning copying machine on the principles of the Carlson patents. But at the end of its laudatory story, *Time* magazine added a paragraph that expressed the sort of uncertainty and depression that accompanied our every moment of joy and hope for the next dozen years. Although the Carlson machine was impressive, *Time* commented, it might already be obsolete: Addressograph-Multigraph was reported to have "perfected" a machine that would make faster, better copies, based on the "Huebner smoke printer" (a system that coated a cloud of ink onto an electrostatically charged plate, and looked rather promising — to Chet, among others — but never did produce a satisfactory copier).

Battelle had also contributed to this demonstration a new name for the Carlson process, which came out of a conversation between one of the Battelle researchers and a professor of classics at Ohio State University. The process was, the scientist said, looking for a useful simplification, a form of dry printing. "Xerography," the professor suggested, taking the Greek for dry and writing. Haloid needed a brand name for what it now assumed would soon be a commercial product. Joe and I had "Kodak" on our minds, with its nice balance of consonants fore and aft, and Joe chose the name "Xerox." It was a decision made during a walk in the woods.

Nearly a year after the American Optical Society demonstration, it cost Chet only seventeen thousand dollars to reimburse Battelle for its total expenditures of its own monies between 1944 and 1949. In the autumn of 1948, when xerography was first publicly demonstrated, Haloid's contribution to Battelle on our option still added up to less than twenty-five thousand dollars and our expenses on the process in our own labs were much less than that. The work that had been done clearly had cost much more — the rest of the money had come from contracts with the U.S. government.

This does not mean that the Truman administration, with some primitive gift for industrial policy, was picking winners. The reason for the support, I fear, was a rather unfortunate one. The Army Signal Corps was looking for ways to make reproductions of documents and pictures that would not be affected by residual radiation on the battlefield of the future. Joe had continuing contacts with the Signal Corps from Haloid's large sales of photocopying equipment and machines during World War II. He got in touch with his friends there to see if they would have any interest in supporting the research Battelle was doing on electrophotography. They did, and a demonstration was set up for them in Columbus in November 1947. The next month Joe took me with him when he went down to Fort Monmouth, New Jersey, to begin the tedious process of negotiating with the government. My function, of course, was to make the process even more tedious, to make sure that Haloid (and Battelle and Carlson) would not sacrifice patent rights in the course of securing government assistance, and that the company was not getting in over its head in its venture on these uncharted seas. Like the Columbus trip, this became part of the private saga Joe and I shared. Waiting with John Crout at Penn Station for the train to Monmouth, we became so engrossed in conversation that we missed the train. My advice, which Joe and John accepted, was that we should claim delay in New York because of important other business we had to do that day rather than admit negligence: it was better to look arrogant than stupid.

Eventually, the Signal Corps would put two hundred thousand dollars into the research at Battelle and Haloid, a sum roughly equal to half the profits of the Haloid Company in 1947. Later there were contracts from the Air Force and the Navy, and from several civilian departments of government. As late as the mid-1950s, more than half of Battelle's research expenditures on xerography were met by government grants. (And one of our first rentals, when we had a machine to rent, was to the CIA, itself then quite a new agency. "WHEREAS," the contract read, "The Central Intelligence Agency of The United States Government deems that, in the interest of national security, it is essential that appropriate equipment designed for accurate and speedy reproduction of material available in single copy only be obtained. . . .") Once that money started coming in, it became increasingly clear that contractual relations with Battelle had to be put on a broader and firmer footing than we had achieved in the rather limited document we had negotiated the year before.

The immediate question was the exact status of the Carlson patents themselves, which had never been adequately explored, and the relationship between Battelle and those patents. I wrote to Walter Derenberg, a highly regarded trademark expert (and an old friend from OPA days who had played piano to my violin), to ask for "information relating to companies and persons who may have from time to time made inquiry or an investigation in connection with these patents." He replied that he could not find any evidence that anyone had ever inquired, which squared with what Battelle and Carlson had told us. It was strange — many companies were attempting to develop copying machines: in the next few years, Minnesota Mining and Manufacturing would announce its Thermofax, and American Photocopy would produce its Autostat, and Eastman Kodak would begin to market Verifax. The Huebner process was publicized, A. B. Dick and Ditto and Addressograph-Multigraph were all working along, and we had suspicions about IBM. But the report from Washington was true. Dessauer gave his book on his years with Xerox the subtitle "The Billions Nobody Wanted." The Carlson patents had been ignored.

Although we had asked for it, we had not been shown the agreement between Battelle and Carlson prior to acquiring the first limited license. In giving the original option to Haloid, Battelle had identified itself as Carlson's "agent," but what did that mean? Agent for what? What rights were Battelle's to convey? Where exactly did Haloid stand? What royalties were we committed to pay on what sales? What were the risks? I noted with interest that Battelle had set up a separate Battelle Development Corporation, so that the Institute itself would be protected if it turned out that the Carlson patent infringed on someone else's rights. I recommended to Joe that he establish a separate Haloid Development Corporation, so that he would not be in a position of betting the company. But he decided that he wanted the losses on the development work as a deduction from Haloid's taxable income, and if he had set up a separate corporation he would have had to capitalize them.

The negotiations with Battelle dragged on through the winter of 1947–1948 and the succeeding spring, and then into the summer. The key question, the one we had to have answered to our satisfaction, was the extent of Battelle's commitment to Haloid. If we were going to make major investments of our own funds in this process, we had to have an exclusive license, an assurance that nobody could sneak up behind us with greater resources and overwhelm us with faster and bigger exploitation of the same patents. We needed relief from the provision in the license that we restrict ourselves to machines that would make no more than twenty copies (once we sold a machine, after all, there was no way we could restrain the purchaser from making more than twenty copies). Partly because of our growing contacts with Chet, and partly because we were caught up in a vision for the future of xerography, Joe and I were already making speeches about the use of xerography as a means of communication with beings on other planets. We had become increasingly convinced that the Carlson patents opened the door to something much larger than the mere improvement of photocopying, and we wanted to be in on that.

In the end, because even after the Signal Corps grant no one else was interested, Battelle agreed that it would no longer seek to find licensees other than Haloid. They retained the toy kits, fingerprint reproduction and electron-microscope shadowgraphs; Haloid won the exclusive license for everything else. In return, Haloid agreed that it would find at least three sublicensees in the following year to multiply the research effort on xerography, sharing the royalties with Battelle. We were now compelled by contract to follow the path we wished to be on. If xerography had the promise we believed it to have, Haloid and Battelle between them would never command sufficient resources to explore its potential. In outlining our licensing policy, I used to say, "We have to latch onto the laboratories of the great companies." Even if what they tried didn't work, we would have the side products — and especially the knowledge of what would *not* work, which is very expensive to find out.

The labyrinthine ways of that strategy are the material of chapter 4 of this book, but let it be noted now that we rarely found it easy to gain the attention of these large companies. In the end we had a long list of very important companies that had taken some sort of license to work on some aspect of xerography — RCA, General Electric, Western Electric, IBM, General Dynamics, Bell and Howell, even Kodak — but most of them did little work on the process, and getting their attention was a painful experience. As late as 1957, I sent out a bundle of 126 identical letters — "If your company is interested in discussing with Haloid a license for the application of xerography to your field, we would welcome your inquiry," signed "S. M. Linowitz, vice-president in charge of patents and development." When the reply was, "Don't call us, we'll call you," I sent another letter, very polite, hoping to hear from them again when they had found some use for xerography. When we did get appointments, Joe and I went calling, and waited anxious and insecure in the anterooms of the large companies in the hope that we might get a meeting with some vice-president — and we were grateful if we got a polite reception.

We did not offer a license to companies that wished to produce machines that would make copies on plain paper. Even if we had done so, it is by no means clear that we would have found anyone really interested. Nobody, including us, foresaw the size of the market for copiers. It was only after the process arrived that people felt they needed it. In later years, I liked to say that this was a case where invention was the mother of necessity. If any of the large companies had ever expressed the slightest interest in xerography, however, we never would have obtained the rights from Battelle. And if it weren't for the patent laws, we could never have kept them.

The 1948 negotiations with Battelle were my first experience working with Joe in a context where the precise terms of a deal were immensely important. It was an experience that would be repeated often in the next eighteen years. Joe was a great learner, and he enjoyed the process of finding out, of mastering the details. Then he wanted to make the deal, to go ahead and *do* it. A number of our licensing discussions started with Joe meeting someone and having a conversation. Then I would receive a memo, saying that this could be one of the most exciting things we've ever done; draw up a proposal. Then my function — we joked about it — was to slow him down.

Joe said that one of the important reasons he wanted me to be an officer of the company was that it would permit me to speak for Haloid or Xerox with far greater authority than I'd have coming into the picture as only an outside lawyer. This was especially useful in the early years of our negotiations with Battelle, when I was strengthened by my feeling that Clyde Williams (director of the Institute) and John Crout (the head of Battelle Development) were keenly, perhaps overly, aware of Joe's great eagerness and idealism. Crout once said to John Dessauer that Battelle had awarded its first license to little Haloid because he and Wilson seemed "hungry" for the process. Battelle's sense of that hunger was of course a bargaining tool in the Institute's hand.

It must be said that in the biggest single deal we made with Battelle — the purchase of all rights to the Carlson patents in 1956 — their offer delighted both me and Joe, although the contract turned out to be fantastically advantageous to them. They agreed to take the entire $3 million purchase price in the form of fifty thousand shares of Haloid-Xerox stock, permitting us to conserve the cash we would need in such quantities to start the manufacturing and marketing programs for our office copiers. Ten years later, the stock they acquired in that deal was by far Battelle's greatest asset, and Xerox was so cash-heavy it was looking about almost frantically for diversification opportunities.

In the end, none of us could resent the profits Battelle made on Xerox, for its contributions to the company went beyond the development of the materials and methods that made xerography practical. Battelle's scientists taught us that there was more to xerography than copying machines, which kept people like Joe and me excited and optimistic about the prospects despite repeated disappointments. And at one key moment, Battelle's vision may have saved the entire enterprise. After the demonstration to the Optical Society in 1948, and the enthusiastic reception, Joe authorized the construction of half a dozen enormous copiers like the one displayed in Detroit. We called it the Xerox Model A, and Dessauer's staff, guided by an engineer named Clyde Mayo, who would later prove to be a genius at copier design, built it by hand. We sent these expensive samples out to be tested by potential users, and they all came back with negative reports. The process was too complicated; it required too many people to do too many things, and to do them just right each time. The quality of the copies rarely was high, and often was so low that the results were useless. Multiple copies were impossible because the selenium plate faded, and at sixty seconds each they took too much time if the plate didn't fade. There were no suggestions of ways to improve the product: it was no good. Perhaps Battelle had known what it was doing when it reserved for itself the use of xerography in toys and toy kits. Of all the disheartening moments of those often discouraging early years, this was perhaps the worst.

One of the Xerox Model A's had been sent to Battelle for a separate evaluation. Lew Walkup, chief of Battelle's Applied Physics Laboratory, made his report by telephone. As it happened, the call came in the middle of a meeting in which Joe was trying to extract from Dessauer, Clark, and Mayo any ideas they had to remedy the failures of their machine. According to Dessauer, Walkup said, "Say, do you fellows know what you've got up there?" Wilson replied, "*What* have we got?" And Walkup said the Model A, whatever its defects as a copier, was a perfect machine for making paper master plates to be used in offset printing, especially with the then-popular Addressograph-Multigraph duplicator. The returned machines were packed up again and sent out to be tested as makers of master plates by such Addressograph-Multigraph users as Ford, Standard Oil, National Gypsum, and Bell Aircraft. Without exception, they reported back enthusiastically: the cost of making master paper plates for lithography was cut by almost 90 percent when the Xerox process was used instead of conventional methods, and the results were every bit as good.

Haloid had a product it could sell. We contracted with Todd Equipment Company, a Rochester manufacturer, to build the machines. By 1953 the revenues from the sale and lease of the Lith-Master, and the sale of the special papers, toners, and plates it required, had passed the $2 million mark. Although our expenditures on research and development would continue to exceed our xerography profits for another seven years, the success of the process in this one unexpected application was enough to sustain our faith and justify the laboratory costs to what had been a nervous board of directors. Without Battelle's ingenuity, we might never have known about the possibility of this success, and the Xerox story might never have been written.

4

Strengthening the Patents, Preserving the Company

CHESTER CARLSON HAD invented xerography in his effort to create a paper copier, and Joe Wilson had taken an option on the patents because Haloid was seeking to expand in the copying business. But Haloid was also a photographic equipment and supplies company, and Joe was intrigued by what might have become a new method for making photographs and prints. From the beginning he was fascinated by the possibility that electrophotography, which could use toners of any color, might become the process of choice for making color prints. It seemed important, too, that Carlson's process could develop black-and-white images faster than any process using light-sensitive treated paper. Among our larger research contracts during the Korean War was one from the Air Force for a xerographic camera that could produce faster and better aerial reconnaissance photographs. In the antitrust trial against Xerox in 1978, counsel for plaintiffs asked me whether Joe had not said to me in the early days that "the Carlson invention is the greatest advance in photography since the silver-halide process." The only reply I could make, more than thirty years after the supposed conversation, was that I had no recollection of his saying just that, but he certainly could have said it.

Photography and photocopying as an office tool were the "Haloid fields," to use a term of art we would later apply to others in the development of xerography. They were, at the start, the only fields we knew about. As late as our 1948 negotiations, when Battelle had been working on the process for more than three years, the question of possible uses of xerography for purposes unrelated to photography and paper copying simply did not arise. The rescue of the Xerox Model A by the discovery of its uses as a tool in lithography did not greatly change attitudes toward the potential uses of the process, because lithography was still a form of copying.

Once the process had been publicized, however, we began to get queries from companies that thought they might be able to solve some of their communication and even production problems through an adaptation of xerography or xeroprinting. To take an example with which I was closely involved in the early years (perhaps because my connections with Superba Cravats had given me some insight into the problems of printing cloth), there was a project for the use of xerography in textile finishing. United Merchants and Manufacturers, a giant in that field, came to Haloid with the suggestion that xerography might be modified for use in printing on a piece of cloth. Instead of pressing a piece of paper onto the electrostatically charged and coated plate, the UMM proposal would pass the roll of cloth between the "printing" plate and an oppositely charged plate that would pull the toner down onto the fabric. Different colors could be added on different passes through the machine, and the process would be more attractive and faster than conventional mechanical printing.

Our scientists and theirs were both excited about the prospects, and I met a number of times with executives at the highest levels of United. In 1952, after more than two years of negotiations, we agreed on a license for "xeroprinting onto cloth." UMM would promise to spend at least fifty thousand dollars a year on research in this "field," and would make available to Haloid, on a nonexclusive basis, any xerographic inventions that came out of its labs that might be useful for purposes other than printing on cloth. In 1955 there would be a fifty-thousand-dollar payment to Haloid as a license fee, and thereafter Haloid would receive a royalty of at least thirty-five thousand dollars a year against payments of one-half cent per yard on cloth to sell for fifty cents or less, three-quarters of a cent on cloth to sell for fifty cents to $1.25, and a penny on cloth to sell for more than $1.25 a yard. It was an intricate and hard negotiation, but we came to terms. And then nothing happened, because neither our people nor United's could get xerographic printing on cloth to work on a cost-effective basis.

One of the first, most exhilarating, and ultimately most disappointing approaches to Haloid came immediately after Joe had demonstrated the hand-tooled machine from the Optical Society event — an enormously awkward machine, known around Haloid as "the ox box" — in a segment of a local news show on WABC-TV in New York. Among those watching the show, it turned out, had been Thomas Watson, Jr., of IBM, who knew Joe (the Watsons had lived in Rochester while Thomas Watson, Sr., was selling first new, then used, cash registers to every storekeeper north of the Finger Lakes). Tom was fascinated by what he saw and had his people call Joe for a meeting to discuss how IBM could use xerography. Their first idea was for a very limited use — for machines to produce mailing labels. We were delighted with the thought that IBM would become involved with xerography, and negotiated enthusiastically with them from January to May 1949. Then the IBM representatives suddenly informed us that they had decided to use other techniques for the production of mailing labels and were no longer interested in licensing our patents.

In 1950 and 1951 we went to IBM with suggestions of ways they might use xerography. By then we knew that xerography might be valuable as a high-speed output device for the accounting machines that processed what were already being called "IBM cards." IBM did not have computers in those days, but its engineers had cobbled together a high-speed electric calculator that turned out information much faster than a typewriter could print it. Today there are laser printers that can churn out documents the size of this book in about a minute, but at that time output devices were typewriter keys on levers that could barely manage thirty pages an hour. The IBM scientists agreed that there might be some way to register information electrically on a Carlson plate, which then could be printed much more rapidly than a typewriter could bang on pages.

The question of what to do about licenses for IBM was one that agitated us throughout the decade of the 1950s and well into the 1960s. In 1951 IBM took a license on xerography, for applications limited to accounting and tabulating machines, the production of punch cards, and output devices for computing machinery. In 1954 they came to us with a request for an *exclusive* license to make — or, if we made it, to distribute — an automatic office copier. To Dessauer's distress, they showed a sketch of what they had in mind, which was virtually identical to the machine we were trying to develop ourselves; indeed, Dessauer maintained that they had simply followed the ideas we had discussed with them in previous meetings. By 1954, however, Haloid already had a profitable business in supplying xerographic supplies for use in our Standard A and Copyflo models, and was gearing up to produce supplies for a similar process RCA had patented.

Joe proposed that we take what we could get, which was the large market for supplies an IBM machine would create. James Birkenstock, who supervised the negotiations for IBM throughout the decade and beyond, stressed that this arrangement would be best for us. A superb negotiator with a transparently open countenance, he took an avuncular attitude toward Haloid. He was always impressed with the work we had done and the sacrifices we had made, and when he disagreed with our positions he often prefaced his argument with a phrase such as "I must tell you as a friend. . . ." In August 1954 we offered IBM a *nonexclusive* license to make and sell a xerographic duplicating machine, with a sizable royalty to Haloid, our now established grant-back clause, and an agreement that Haloid itself would not make a machine that imitated too closely what IBM might produce. The following April, they told us that they were interested in a license for a copier/duplicator only if it was exclusive — indeed, only if Haloid would commit itself never to go into that business itself. This, of course, we turned down. Birkenstock was quite disappointed, for our sake. "Do you have any idea," he asked, "of the infinite costs it's going to take for you to develop your own machine, the risks you'll have to run?" But we held our ground.

Toward the end of the decade, relations came to life again between IBM and Haloid Xerox, as the company was called between 1958 and 1961. The Haloid labs were, we felt, on the edge of designing a commercial copier. We now knew about the "infinite costs" and we knew we could use help in manufacturing and marketing our copier. We explored the possibility of a joint venture with IBM in which Haloid would contribute its patents and designs and the larger company would contribute its production facilities and marketing muscle. In the course of these negotiations, IBM sought again a license to make xerographic copiers under the IBM logo, and we refused. In fact, IBM urged us to consider adopting as our own a design its engineers had worked out for an intermediate-sized copier, between the size of our freestanding 914 and the later desktop 813. They were far from complimentary about our capacity to build the machine we planned; the IBM engineering staff warned that our production run machines would never make copies of the quality they had achieved with their hand-tooled models.

Joe appointed a Committee on Study Project Xerox 914-813, with Harold Clark as its chairman. The committee recommended strongly that Haloid Xerox go it alone with the office copiers, but Joe still liked the idea of a partnership with IBM and feared the size of the gamble — it really did mean betting the company — we would have to take if we went out into this market on our own. At the least, he wanted access to the IBM marketing and service organization and dreaded the expense of developing such a network from scratch, especially for an untried product.

Then the consulting firm of Arthur D. Little did a study for IBM on how many large copiers American business would wish to lease or buy, and the number was so small — a few thousand, at best — that IBM lost interest. Competition, Little said, was heating up in the copier field. The trend was to acquire desktop copiers so that people could simply use them at or near their own work stations, rather than maintain a separate copying room to which people would take their work. The large 914 was an anachronism before it was made, and our longer-term project for the desktop 813 was a bad risk because it would be too expensive. IBM authorized Little to present its findings to us at a special conference in Rochester. That was a grim day. Birkenstock strongly urged us, for our own good, to forget our rash project of making an automatic copier: "Are you *sure* that you wish to take this path?" But we had hired our own market research company, which was far less pessimistic than Little (although not, I must say, optimistic, either: this was one of those mountains we got over by faith).

Some years later, IBM would return to what was by then the Xerox Corporation, pressing us to license them to make a plain paper copier. This was 1963, after the unimaginable success of the copier Little had said would never find a market. Birkenstock announced that he was immensely impressed and pleased with our success, but we were now, he said sorrowfully, too big to retain our exclusive patent rights on such important products, however much we had spent creating them and however great the risks we had taken. He spoke of antitrust dangers and proposed that we avoid them by issuing a license to IBM. When I indicated that we had carefully examined the antitrust aspects and were not disturbed,

Birkenstock suggested that we would be wise to secure an outside opinion. I agreed, with an enthusiasm he seemed to find a trifle disconcerting. We engaged the Wall Street firm of Simpson, Thacher and Bartlett (and especially its senior partner Whitney North Seymour, a lawyer of excellent business judgment as well as legal distinction) to evaluate our position. Seymour's firm spent weeks visiting our patent department and more weeks in its own library, and finally advised us that we didn't have to license anyone to make a plain paper copying machine — and that if we did decide to issue such a license, we should do so to the world at large and not under any circumstances with any special benefit for IBM. Thereafter and to this day, Xerox and IBM were competitors.

Another license that loomed large in our thinking during the 1950s was one to General Electric, for the development of a xerographic process that would produce better, easier-to-read X-ray pictures. *Life* magazine found the process dramatic enough to warrant a full-page xeroradiographic picture of a hand. Battelle had done the first work on this system, discovering in 1949 that selenium-coated plates were even more sensitive to X rays than to visible light. We restricted the GE license to xeroradiography, and secured an agreement that any patents to grow out of GE's work would automatically be licensed back to Haloid and through Haloid to its other licensees, for possible use in fields other than X-ray reproduction.

For several years we lived in expectation of a GE breakthrough and a large new market for xeroradiography that would generate royalties and a possible product for Haloid. In the end, however, GE scientists were unable to find a xerographic process that did not require a much higher intensity of X rays than was generated in the old photographic-film system, and the dangers of increasing the power of the X-ray machine overwhelmed the benefits of the more easily read final print.

GE was also interested in computer printout, and at one point announced what it called "ferromagnetography." Dessauer and Harold Clark visited the GE labs and were shown "a rotating wheel with characters which are optically projected onto a xerographic drum." They thought GE and Haloid should move to get a patent on the process, but in the end it was decided that the system could not be manufactured at a practical price.

One of these licensees did produce four apparently significant products actually offered for sale, a source of considerable satisfaction to us. This was the license to Stromberg-Carlson, a Rochester company that was struggling unprofitably to compete against larger organizations in both the consumer electronics and industrial fields. (During the course of its work on xerography, Stromberg was acquired by General Dynamics, which made its chief executive, Bob Tate, a friend of Joe's and mine, all the more eager to demonstrate that what was now a division of a conglomerate could make a major contribution to its owner's product lines.) There was a Stromberg–Air Force project to create an electronic teleprinter with a xerographic output, and a Stromberg–ITT–Strategic Air Command project to build a projection system to magnify pictures taken by a xerographic camera. (The word for the latter was PROXI, for "Projection by Reflection Optics of Xerographic Images"; it worked because the selenium surface of the printing plate was shiny, and the places where the toner stuck were not.) Twenty-one units of this system were sold to the Signal Corps.

One of the Stromberg products was a computer-output device, for which Haloid built some of the parts. This involved a special cathode ray tube Stromberg called a "Charactron" that shined an electron beam through a kind of stencil cut with numbers and the characters of the alphabet. Stromberg's beam, like the one that illuminated television screens, could scan the stencil very quickly, printing at a rate of almost ten thousand letters or numbers per second, not far off the best speeds of today's laser printers. But the SC-5000, acclaimed in its promotion literature as "breaking the output-recording bottleneck," was massive, expensive, and not completely reliable. Still, we had hopes. We arranged to have the Haloid sales staff work with Stromberg on leasing it (we were to supply some parts and share the rentals as well as earn a royalty), and IBM toyed with it until 1958. One Xerox Charactron Computer Readout Printer was marketed, for a very special purpose: the generation of labels — "dick strips," as they were called, because A. B. Dick's products were practically synonymous with the business — that could be pasted onto magazines or advertising pieces for mailing.

Even more promising, and backed by government research, was a Stromberg device to transform the oscilloscope images of a radar screen to a continuous "flicker-free" flow of almost instantaneous paper copies, much easier to read in an air traffic control tower. The Air Force bought some of these SC-2000s, and the Federal Aviation Administration was more than interested, but the reliability demands were more severe than the Stromberg machine could meet at a plausible price.

As early as 1949, Sun Oil Company came to Haloid with a query about the possible use of xerography to produce a running record of results of seismological testing for oil, and toward the end of the decade our labs worked unsuccessfully with Schlumberger on the same problem. The oil drillers could not simply read their results from an oscilloscope, because the kind of analysis required was too detailed for the sort of transient data that flick across a screen. At the same time, it was an inconvenience for them to wait while a wet-process recording medium generated the necessary log. It seemed to us as well as to them the sort of thing xerography could do, but in the state of our art in the 1950s we could not make it a reality. Eventually, a small high-tech company called Century Electronics, which we licensed, did develop such a machine on xerographic principles, but it was too slow for the drillers' needs, and the creation of magnetic disc technology made the xerographic log obsolete.

There would be months when inquiries poured in, from big companies, small companies, academic labs. The Brookhaven Laboratories inquired about the use of xerography to make records of infrared spectroscopy. Bell and Howell took a license to explore the use of selenium plates in making prints of motion pictures. Technicolor wanted to do a fifty-fifty deal with Haloid, on Haloid's money, to develop a consumer product that would compete with Kodachrome, using xerography as the printing method. Haloid's established business was entirely black-and-white. Joe handled the negotiations with John Clark, Technicolor's number-two man: "Here comes a gigantic opportunity," he wrote me. He thought we should be prepared to offer Technicolor two-thirds of the joint venture, because its patents were worth more than ours. I did some checking on Technicolor and its founder-president, Herbert Kalmus, and found that far from Technicolor's challenging Kodak, Kodak was about to overwhelm Technicolor. "The significant thing," I wrote Joe, "is whether Technicolor is financially in a position to work with xerography." Dessauer thought there was a question of fit between Technicolor's inhibitory process and xerography. "If to [the problems of xerography]," he wrote, "are added the ones involving the technology of dyes and dye systems, of unbelievably precise mechanical registrations . . . , of control through electronic techniques . . . , the task may exceed the prudently applied resources, financial and technical, of Haloid." Reluctantly, Joe gave it up.

A company called UARCO took a license to make a xerographic printer to generate business forms. A Massachusetts company called Vectron took a license to build and market a xerographic printer "solely and specifically adapted to make enlargements in a non-continuous manner of individual frames": that is, for animated films. The wording was a kind of triumph for me, because I had fought to get away from scientific gobbledygook in our licenses. As early as 1952 I complained about the terms of the license our research department wished to issue to a company called Pneumatic Seals, which thought xerography might be a perfect means for imprinting messages on tea bags: "In the light of the uncertain and unlimited future for xerography in a number of fields, we should do everything possible to avoid granting to anyone rights beyond those we could clearly see at the time the license was granted." Write it in plain English, I urged, "licensing companies to produce *particular products* by xerography or xeroprinting rather than to operate in a broad technically defined field."

Perhaps the happiest, and certainly the most fruitful of these early arrangements with the nation's industrial giants was our relationship with the Western Electric subsidiary of AT&T. Western Electric wanted to use xerography to make a number of copies of the many blueprints and engineering drawings generated by the company's engineers. The first license to Western Electric was granted in 1949, and by 1950 the company had made a copier for its internal use that was perhaps the most reliable designed to that time. All the plans and drawings for it were made available to Haloid under terms of the Western Electric license, and they were helpful in the improvements we made to the Standard Model A that became the lithography master-maker. In 1953 Western Electric asked us to design and make a special copier to handle paper twenty-two inches wide, for them to buy rather than to lease (they paid fifty thousand dollars for it), and also requested a license to work on printing from microfilm — a field Haloid had made a high priority in its own lab. Both requests were granted. "Our moral obligation," Joe wrote me, "is very great, because of the work they did in the early stages."

In 1958 Western Electric was back with a proposal for a xerographic nonimpact printer to replace its established Teletype machine. The model was to be the "nonoptical approach . . . exemplified by the Haloid–Air Force Teleprinter," which was not yet in production. The minimum specification for speed was two hundred characters per second, or about nine pages of a double-spaced document per minute. Using a VHF (television frequency) radio link, we had made, in collaboration with RCA, a machine operating at about that speed for use by the Navy. The arrangement Western offered was a royalty-free exchange of licenses, with access for Haloid to Western Electric's patents in the area of long-distance communications. Joe wrote enthusiastically: "In general, the Teletype field is absolutely barred to Haloid. Therefore, anything we can get in this field is highly desirable. I would give Teletype all kinds of rights and privileges for this field in return for access to their patent structure on a reasonable basis, and what is more important, the development of a research relationship which might give us access to some of the top brains in the world in the field of communication and printing." Our relations with Western Electric were in fact significant in the 1963 creation of the Xerox LDX facsimile machine that operated over telephone wires and delivered reliable but at first rather slow copies at a distance.

Presenting this list of licensees in drumfire fashion, over the course of a few pages, doesn't reveal the perceptions and the realities of the people who were risking their company, and in many cases their personal futures (people took mortgages on their homes to buy stock Haloid issued as part of the plan to finance the work on xerography), on what remained the long shot that the Carlson patents would yield an important and profitable product. *The crucial fact is that fourteen years elapsed between the first license on the patents and the successful introduction of the Xerox 914.* The weeks when others seemed eager to join us in the work on xerography were followed by months when nothing happened, when the results from our own labs were discouraging and we heard nothing from the licensees for the good if unhappy reason that they had nothing to report. We sold licenses cheap in return for pledges to conduct research in the process and make the results available to us and to our other licensees — and the majority of our licensees treated their privilege as though it were worth exactly what they had paid for it.

If one pulled out of the calendar of the decade 1948–1957 the days when something actually *happened* at Haloid, the great majority of them would be days of disappointment. Joe and I used to say — only half-facetiously — that the primary reason we remained optimistic was that we had little scientific competence or technical training and therefore didn't know enough to understand how devastating some of the failures in the labs really were. It was not that xerography would not work; it was that the costs of the systems the scientists designed put the process out of the reach of possible commercial users. In 1958 I bought a new home in Rochester, and as part of the mortgage application to the bank I had to make a list of my assets. My recollection is that I did not even list my Haloid stock options, which would presently become by far the most valuable of my possessions, because I couldn't claim that they were worth very much.

The decade was not without accomplishment, of course, and not without income-generating xerographic products. The Lith-Master was improved and became an almost standard product for people who used lithographic printers that took paper plates. With support from the Air Force, our labs produced cameras that permitted xerography to reproduce not only lines but shadings, until virtually any photograph could generate an accurate xerographic image, which was an enormous advance. In 1953 we introduced the Copyflo, essentially a fast xerographic printer that made paper copies from microfilm. Three years later, an ingenious, wholly mechanical rigging of lights and mirrors enabled us to insert in effect an opaque projector so that the Copyflo could handle documents. Still, it was an enormous machine, big as a printing press, with a very small potential market and a very high price: the largest of the document-printing Copyflos sold for $130,000.

"Our early products," Harold Clark said, "were all monsters. We could make big, fast, steadily running machines, but that was all we could make." A simple problem like getting the xeroprinted paper off the selenium-coated plate or drum could be solved at that time only by pulling the paper through from one giant roller to another, and cutting it after printing. In addition to our relatively few customers, we sold some of these machines to ourselves, for use in storefront copying facilities we had opened in a dozen cities. This caused disputes between those in the company who were committed to xerography and the established Haloid sales staff, whose best customers for treated paper were the photocopiers and photofinishers with whom Haloid's xerographic copy shops would now be in direct competition. Then there was the week when we discovered that a machine we had sold to International Harvester was being used by a friend of that company to offer a copying service in competition with our Chicago copy shop — and that there was nothing we could do about it.

Worst of all, we lived in fear that one of the giant companies — either one we had licensed or another — would suddenly emerge from its laboratories with a copier based on principles other than those on which we had patents. It would be cheaper or faster and it would make better copies, and we would have put in all that time and money and have nothing to show for it. The contract officers who came calling on us in connection with our military research were constantly telling us that Kodak or Photostat or Bruning had something dramatic on the fire that they were about to make public. At the stockholders' annual meeting in 1954, Joe added to his opening statement an astonishing comment that on that very afternoon one of the companies we worried about was planning an announcement of a product that might "put us out of business."

It may have been RCA. Certainly, RCA caused us more problems than any other licensee. They had taken licenses on the Carlson patents in 1951, for purposes of computer output. They had also requested a license for work on printing microfilm enlargements, but since this was one of the fields Haloid wished to develop itself we were reluctant to agree. We had to face the fact that there was no way we could stop other people from doing whatever they wished in their labs with the published Carlson patents. And they could then hold close to their chests whatever improvements or devices they created in those labs, leaving us vulnerable to sudden and overwhelming attack when the relevant patents expired. We worked out an arrangement whereby RCA paid five thousand dollars a year for licenses to develop products in the field of electrical signal recording methods, and would use information in the public domain if it wished to attempt creation of a microfilm copier. RCA promised to share with us any progress its engineers made in designing a microfilm printer (this was before we had the Copyflo), at which time we would share ours with them.

Then came a bombshell. In early 1953 RCA informed us that it had developed a commercially feasible office copier using a xerographic process different from Carlson's. Their machine, they said, was not covered by any of the patents on the Carlson devices; the most we and Carlson could claim was a "methods" patent, which RCA thought would not stand up in court. Nevertheless, they were prepared to pay fifty thousand dollars for an unrestricted license to use the methods patent themselves and to convey its use to anyone who took a license on their system. In Carlson's view, what RCA wanted was "90 percent of the present strength of our patent position."

Joe was deeply upset. In a memo he wrote to himself in preparation for a meeting at RCA in April 1953, he pointed out that Haloid over the previous five years had spent some nine hundred thousand dollars — 20 percent of its total profits — for research in xerography; a comparable proportion of the RCA profits would have been $62 million. "We aimed at RCA [as a licensee]," he wrote, "for these reasons:

"a) its tremendous know-how in the related field of photoconductivity, which we wanted to tap,

"b) because its interests (or so we thought and were told) were not in the fields of copying, etc., where our major concentration was to be."

We had made a quite delicate deal with RCA in connection with microfilm copying, and they had unilaterally changed it. "The very thing we wanted them to collaborate with us on a year ago," Joe wrote, ". . . has been done. The only catch is that it isn't being made available to us." Joe then wrote me an anguished letter about the relationship with RCA: "Haloid's determination in the face of adversity is an obvious one, one that does not spell 'vulnerability,' but one which accounts for the fact that we are going to be tenacious and stubborn about our interests because we have hazarded so much to get where we are." I was even more disturbed, and angrier. RCA had changed negotiators in its meetings with us. I wrote of the executive vice-president who had now been assigned to handle the negotiations with us that he "is out to do a job of throwing weight around by offering a wholesale dose of bluster with just enough fact thrown in to kill the taste."

RCA's core system, which they eventually called Electrofax, did not involve a selenium-coated metallic printing plate or a cascaded toner carried on our tiny glass balls. Instead, RCA used a zinc-oxide-coated paper (which both of us soon called a "picnic plate," because it would be used only once and then discarded) that could be charged electrostatically and exposed to the document being reproduced. A very fine powder was then dusted onto the surface through a sieve. The powder was then brushed from the areas that had lost their electrostatic attraction through exposure to light, and the resulting reproduction was fixed onto the paper by heat. The obvious disadvantage of this system was that it would make only one copy from each exposure, whereas our selenium plate could continue printing as many copies as desired. It also required an expenditure for a heavy, rather unattractive piece of coated paper. But the paper was panchromatic — the user could copy originals from any color — whereas our selenium plate was still partial to originals in black-and-white. And there it was, in the RCA labs, and it worked. Moreover, RCA had applied for a patent on Electrofax without any indication that this process had any relation to the Carlson patents.

RCA supplied some sheets of the zinc-oxide paper, which were studied almost frantically by our scientists. If the paper were photo-emissive — if the zinc oxide worked as an emulsifier worked in photographic paper — then indeed we would have virtually no claim on royalties from the RCA machines. If, however, it was photoconductive, like the selenium coating, the basic Carlson patents could be held to apply. We held our breath as the paper was tested. It proved to be photoconductive. Nothing is certain in patent law, but in our judgment RCA's legal position, if it chose to proceed without our agreement, was untenable. There was some discussion within the company about just how good the RCA machine was, or was likely to become. Carlson thought it was second-rate by comparison with what we could build — and it turned out he was right. Joe and I considered it a ponderable threat.

Characteristically, Joe made a pro-and-con list of what would happen if we yielded to RCA; the pro side was much longer, and started with the sentence, "We gain goodwill and continuity of a relationship which is the most fruitful one we have yet had." RCA suggested that although Haloid could not receive royalties on Electrofax, it would, after all, have the inside track on manufacturing the zinc-oxide paper, which was (RCA implied) Haloid's proper business in this area. In May 1953, after an unhappy visit to RCA headquarters, Joe wrote me: "We're involved now in a poker game. . . . Haloid has much more to recoup from sales than it will ever get from royalties." He sent a memo around the company: "We must go into the business of supplying zinc-oxide coated paper. This is too big a thing for us to neglect for five minutes."

Dessauer and I were more skeptical. We put together highly specific lists of what Haloid really had to have in any agreement with

RCA. During the summer of 1953 a general understanding was reached on a deal that would give them the use of our "methods" patent in their own manufacture of Electrofax machines and give us a license to make such machines ourselves, both on a royalty-free basis. This was a considerable potential sacrifice for us, because it meant that we abandoned any prospect of suing RCA for patent infringement. On the other hand, it gave us the right to build our own machines using the RCA technology. (A few years later, I argued in the councils of the Xerox executive committee, of which I was then chairman, that we should have our own Electrofax copier in our stable of machines, partly as an insurance policy against the day when improvements in that process, and reductions in the cost of the zinc-oxide paper, might make it more desirable than our own. Wiser heads prevailed.)

RCA welcomed Dessauer and Carlson for a demonstration and exposition of the principles of the new process, and Joe wrote me: "RCA people were most cooperative with John Dessauer yesterday. . . . I would say that they have shown good faith, plus, in view of the fact that we haven't yet signed an agreement." To John Crout of Battelle, he wrote; "This negotiation has been a colorful and fascinating one. I must give you the bloody details some time. We are elated at its outcome because our relationship with RCA is closer and better than ever."

Then it turned out — almost predictably — that RCA's understanding of the agreement was different from ours. There was a problem with the terminology in our license — RCA refused to use the word "xerography," and insisted on "electrography." I went to New York to meet with RCA's counsel and wrote Joe that he "did not come prepared to present agreements which correctly represented what I understood you and [the RCA vice-president in charge] had felt to be a meeting of the minds. Once more there has either been bad communications within RCA or else there is involved here a somewhat less naive method of operations which makes me a little uncomfortable."

Eventually, RCA backed away from its more aggressive demands, and the licenses (including one for "xerography") were exchanged. Joe retained his optimism about our relations with RCA, and in April 1954, when the company placed a hurry-up order for twenty-five thousand feet of zinc-oxide paper, he approved filling the order without any agreement on price on the grounds that it would place

RCA "in our debt . . . the more we can tie them up with moral obligations, the better." After I warned him that such an arrangement could raise antitrust questions of collusion between RCA and Haloid — making supplies available at a price to be negotiated later was clearly not an arm's-length transaction — Joe agreed that we ought to find out how much they would pay before we shipped the merchandise.

Later, RCA would make its Electrofax patents available to a number of office-copier makers, including SCM, Bruning, APECO, Savin, and Dennison. We were now in a quandary, for under our contracts RCA didn't have the right to sublicense our patents. By permitting production of Electrofax machines by third parties to go entirely unchallenged, we risked the possible loss of our own hard-won patent protection. But we did not wish to have to sue, or to give the RCA licensees an excuse to sue us. I carefully drafted letters suggesting to all those who were building machines based on the RCA designs that they should "look carefully" at the patents covering xerography and certain improvements to the Carlson designs that we and Battelle had developed. Thus we would keep our options open to move at a time of our own choosing. Eventually, despite our planning, one of the RCA licensees did seek a declaratory judgment to bar us from suing Electrofax makers for patent infringement. We countersued, and the RCA licensees took licenses from us, too. By then, the superiority of the reusable selenium plate and the plain paper copy had become apparent. Not until 1984, however, did Xerox dispose of the last lawsuit deriving from our original challenge to RCA's licensees to "consider carefully" the patent situation surrounding the development of Electrofax.

The strategy Haloid followed in the 1950s was intricate and balanced carefully between our need to gain outside support for the development of xerography and our need to maintain the protection of our patents and our corporate integrity. The outside support was important in itself and also in establishing the company's position with lenders and investors whose funds would be required to finance our own laboratory work (and, especially in the early years, in solidifying our position with Battelle). The fact that RCA and IBM and GE wanted to be involved with xerography meant more than the money. As a native Rochesterian, Joe had been in awe of Eastman Kodak all his life, and he was especially eager to get Kodak working on some aspect of xerography, under license from us. One of the high points of the decade was the day we went up to the seventeenth floor of the Kodak tower to meet with senior Kodak executives and demonstrate (successfully) the superiority of one element of our process to the comparable element of their Verifax. One of the low points came when the Kodak people pointed out that what we proposed doing would cost many times what their process cost. The meeting provoked a long, almost anguished memo from Joe to the labs, about the need to concentrate on finding less expensive procedures.

Each of these relationships with a giant of American industry was a two-edged sword. We always had to be alert to the danger that one of these much larger licensees would come up with a product that would wipe out our prospects — and to the more subtle danger that one of them might become sufficiently enamored of xerography to want to gobble up Haloid and its patents, something easy and not very expensive to do because we were a publicly held company. A commanding position in Haloid stock could have been acquired without much strain by any of a number of the licensees.

There was, in addition, a danger to Haloid's reputation each time we lost the support of one of our larger collaborators. In 1956 Joe's father queried him nervously for an explanation of a recent decline in the price of Haloid stock. Joe blamed stories in the market about "delay and serious problems in connection with IBM, that the GE X-ray relationship was not in good shape. . . . Since we have used relationships like IBM and GE as assets in building our reputation and that of xerography," Joe concluded, "they can become enormous liabilities if anything happens to the relationship."

The first necessity was to maintain and strengthen our patent position. The original Carlson patents would run out between 1959 and 1961. To gain the advantages of the research we and Battelle were doing to make the process commercially viable, we needed patents on the improvements: selenium coating, "corona charging" of the selenium, "cascade development" of the toner, and a raft of others. At all times, we had to be careful about what we gave away. Government contracts were vital to us. When I assumed responsibility for government relations, I engaged the services of General C. T. Lanham — known to everyone as Buck — a shrewd observer and a splendid storyteller who was a good friend of Ernest Hemingway (which much commended him to Joe). Lanham became our vice-president and our eyes and ears in Washington, but government-sponsored research could be a trap, because the normal government contract could put its results in the public domain. We had to make sure that nothing in our arrangements with the government endangered our patent position.

In the patent area, of course, Carlson was the prod. As early as 1949 he had pushed Joe to convene a committee to examine what Haloid and Battelle were doing to keep control, and when the committee met he listed no fewer than sixty-two potentially patentable devices one of the two labs was trying to make — without patent applications. As a result, in 1950 Haloid hired its first inside patent attorney, Frank Steinhilper, who came on Chet's recommendation. But one man, Carlson kept saying, was nowhere near enough: Haloid and Battelle were being penny-wise and pound-foolish, saving money on the patent department and risking the loss of protection that might be vital to the future of a small company in what he was sure would be a big business.

In June 1953 Chet wrote Joe a letter proclaiming that "in our patentable inventions, Haloid-Battelle-Carlson hold the keys to possible dominance of a tremendous new industry. What Bell is to the telephone — or, more aptly, what Eastman is to photography — Haloid could be to xerography." From a legal point of view, this was an unfortunate letter, much stressed by counsel in the antitrust case against Xerox twenty-five years later (we won the case anyway), but it got Joe's attention, and it certainly expressed the drive and ambition that Chet was often able to instill in others working for his invention. In the summer of 1953, what Joe called a "royal commission" on patent problems was established, involving people from Battelle as well as Haloid, with me as chairman.

This was not an uncontentious group, because the question of who should pay for what was never far below the surface. According to the record, I pointed out that the problem troubling Carlson really affected him and Battelle more than it affected us: "By the time the basic patents expire," I said, "Haloid will have a lot of business, sales and engineering momentum, so that even without a strong patent position, or for that matter without any patent position, Haloid still would have substantial strength in xerography." Carlson then launched the discussion with a list of now up to one hundred "invention disclosures, of which, by very conservative estimate, at least fifty are now waiting for patent application." And I had to agree that "right now the patent program is substantially behind the research program."

The meeting did not greatly change anyone's behavior. Haloid still had only a two-man patent department. Liaison between the Battelle and Haloid labs was sporadic, and each organization handled its own patent applications. It was still not entirely clear who would own what in the patent area; and our contract with Battelle still barred us from suing against infringement of the patents they licensed to us — only Battelle itself could sue. Wilson wanted action, especially with regard to the protection on the machines we hoped to build in the next ten or fifteen years.

"We need now," Joe wrote me in November 1953, "a very realistic appraisal of the strength of our patent position over the next decade or two, an appraisal of what our patent position might be if a well conceived program of research and an appropriate patent program accompanying it were undertaken. We must know as a group (Battelle-Carlson-Haloid) what our maximum task is in this direction and then we have to match it up against the financial resources the three of us can muster and determine what part of that program we'll bite off, what part we may try to prevail upon others to bite off and what part we must forego.

"I do not have to tell you that responsibility for this work is great indeed," Joe added in a peroration that shows how nonindustrial and graceful his style could be. "It must be thoughtful, penetrating, imaginative, systematic, and fundamental policies of Haloid-Battelle and Chet himself will be based upon the outcome."

This produced a final meeting of my commission, and a recommendation that we add four patent attorneys to the Haloid staff (we added two) and hire specialized outside counsel (we employed the New York patent firm of Kenyon and Kenyon). The report was well received and circulated to the board of directors.

For me, personally, the patent commission produced an important result: it led to my becoming an officer of Haloid. Joe had long been after me to join the company so that I could speak with greater authority than an outside lawyer possessed in our negotiations with our licensees, and could ride herd on the patent work on a regular basis. Now he was pressing me to accept an appointment as vice-president in charge of licensing and patent development. I demurred, offering my customary reasons: I was a lawyer, not a businessman; I enjoyed practicing law, and I wished to continue serving my other clients as well as Haloid. He had found the answer to that: the work would not be that much more than I was already doing, he argued, and I could continue to handle most of it from my office at the law firm.

Joe, I think, had no notion of how unusual that sort of an arrangement was. Six years later, when I became chairman of the newly formed executive committee, with greatly expanded responsibilities including the areas of government relations, acquisitions, and international ventures, he wrote in the Xerox house organ that "Sol will, of course, continue in active practice as a partner in his law firm." Nobody else would have thought the words "of course" appropriate in that sentence.

My most important reason for taking the job, finally, was Joe's strong feeling that he and the company needed me. He was my closest friend, and he'd had a heart attack two years before. He felt that the company was at a critical point and that he would have that much less to worry about if I took prime responsibility for all its licensing activities and supervised the company's patent department. We talked about it on Sunday walks, during a family vacation in Bermuda, and at last I accepted.

What interested me most, both before and after I became vice-president, was the development of Haloid's licensing program. This had two purposes in my view: (1) to gain us access to minds that we couldn't hire and research facilities we couldn't afford to build; and (2) to protect us from predators. To achieve the first purpose, we required that our licensees grant a license back to us — *which we in turn would grant to all our other licensees* — on any patents useful in areas other than their own "field" that grew out of their work in xerography. Some of the licensees took umbrage at this requirement. One, the Keuffel and Esser subsidiary of the German film company Agfa, submitted our proposed license agreement to the Justice Department for an advisory ruling without telling us about it. In the absence of case law on a unique agreement, the Department's lawyers might have found it an interesting challenge and we could scarcely sustain the uncertainty (let alone the expense) of a suit against our practices. I wandered down to Washington for what I described as "a friendly sort of bull session" at the antitrust division, to see if we were in any peril. This was 1952, in the declining days of the Truman administration, and there was a new head of the division. I wrote Joe that the new man had "shaken up not only

personnel but confidence, and it is almost impossible to obtain any
assurance as to the position which the Department is likely to take
when confronted with a set of facts."

I was of the opinion that what we were doing was not only proper
but legal, and fortunately that proved to be right. When at last we
were sued — twenty-five years after that visit to Washington — we
won.

Our aggressive promotion of licenses also served my second purpose, because it involved us with the major competitors of the great
corporations that might otherwise have looked at this little company
with the interesting patents as a tempting acquisition. Because we
were also tied in through licenses with GE and Western Electric and
Stromberg-Carlson, an RCA or an IBM could not possibly buy us
up without creating an antitrust issue that the Federal Trade Commission and the Justice Department could not ignore. I described
this patent and licensing program as the creation of a "protective
picket fence" around Haloid and later Xerox; and inside that fence
we were indeed able to cultivate our own garden.

Although we had renegotiated our Battelle contract in 1951 to
acquire an exclusive license under the patents, carrying out this
strategy in tandem with someone else was awkward. We were,
moreover, beginning to look abroad for partners to market and perhaps produce xerographic products in other countries. In 1955 we
decided we would have to plunge, and buy up Battelle's rights in the
Carlson patents. What looked like the most important of them
would expire as early as 1959, and the other basic patents would
lapse in 1961, which made these rights a rapidly wasting asset —
but by the same token the tax laws would permit fast depreciation.
Again the two of us went to Columbus, where we offered Battelle
twenty-five thousand shares of Haloid, plus five hundred thousand
dollars a year for three years and thereafter a continuing royalty of 3
percent on xerographic sales until 1965. (The five hundred thousand dollars a year was not that much of an offer; our 8 percent royalty to Battelle on our sales of xerographic products ran that high in
1955.) To our amazement and delight, Clyde Williams of Battelle
suggested that the foundation might prefer ten thousand additional
shares of Haloid each year rather than the cash payment, and toward the end of the year the deal was closed. In hindsight, we paid a
spectacular price, for within a decade each of those blocks of ten
thousand shares would be worth about $5 million. But to Haloid in

the mid-1950s, finally facing the costs of developing the office copier that had been in our minds from the start, the Battelle deal offered more than control of the patents. Between the tax break and the substitution of stock for royalty payments, it also increased the cash available for our activities by more than a million dollars a year.

For Haloid, which we would rename Haloid Xerox in 1958 and the Xerox Corporation in 1961, it was the moment of truth. We would still license, and hope for royalties on uses of xerography other than copying, and sponsor work in the physics of this still partly magical process. But we were now far enough along, and big enough — and brave enough — to recognize that no one but ourselves could make our dreams become reality. In a speech I made to our employees not long before I left the company in 1966, I recalled this history and said we had buoyed ourselves through the long years with Toynbee's "admonition . . . that every problem is truly an opportunity." We now were ready to grasp our apparently insuperable opportunity.

5

Breakthroughs

IT WAS A MEASURE of our optimism that Joe and I began worrying as early as 1953 about the expansion of xerography to lands beyond our borders. We had turned over the international marketing
of the Xerox Standard A to Addressograph-Multigraph, for the useful product the system made was a master for the A-M lithography
printer. But A-M, for all its early professions of eagerness, had done
little to sell the process abroad. And now we were moving into production on the Copyflo, a machine competitive with the A-M
printer for many applications, where we could scarcely count on
A-M's help. We were busily registering patents in Europe and
Japan and Australasia. If we were going to have patents in all these
places, we should have products there, too.

We had commissioned a study from a consultant who was supposed to be expert on the markets for U.S. technology abroad, who
presently delivered to us a handsomely designed and printed tome
that contained disappointingly little we did not already know. We
had already begun to receive tentative inquiries from European
companies. John Dessauer's family had long controlled a German
paper company in Aschaffenburg, which his brother was now running. We had gone through long and not very happy negotiations
with the American branch of Agfa, and another German company,
Kalle, had expressed an interest. We had a letter from Gestetner in
London, and we had been visited in Rochester by the president of

the Mason Company of Manchester. There also had been another visitor to Rochester, a tall, witty, amiable man named Tom Law, who was almost deaf and almost blind, but remained very alert and brightly attentive to everything around him. We liked him immediately. He was managing director of Rank Precision Industries, a division of the Rank Organisation in England, best known as a movie producer and distributor but also involved in the manufacturing of cameras and film products.

Law came to us through a mutual Bell and Howell connection. Bell and Howell cameras were then being made in the United Kingdom by Law's factory, and we were in the process of arranging a license to Bell and Howell for photographic uses of xerography. Charles Percy, then chairman of Bell and Howell, suggested that on his way to or from Chicago, Law should look in on Haloid, and the upshot was an invitation to us to demonstrate our process in London in the spring of 1955, for the top executives of Rank. Among the recommendations from our highly paid consultant had been that senior executives of Haloid go to Europe and meet with potential licensees, to show and discuss what we had to offer. Neither Joe nor I, nor our wives, had ever been abroad except for our brief vacation together in Bermuda. The more we thought about Law's invitation, the more enthusiastic we became. Our consultant, we decided, had been insufficiently ambitious. What we wanted in Europe was not licensees but partners, who would become foreign manufacturers of xerographic products. We would give ourselves some time; we planned a thirty-day trip.

Demonstration was, necessarily, the basic Xerox sales technique, and Joe had become an adept ringmaster for our presentations. This was not easy for him. He was a shy man, subject to great nervousness before important meetings and public appearances. (Like others with that problem, however, Joe became quite resourceful once on stage. For years a favorite story at Xerox was about the time Joe was demonstrating the Copyflo, and someone had forgotten to attach the paper to the end roller. The Haloid sales staff in attendance covered their eyes in horror as the paper piled up on the floor. Without changing expression, Joe instructed one of the attendant engineers to carry the paper flood out to the audience, so everyone could see the quality of the reproductions the machine made. This greatly enhanced the effectiveness of the demonstration, and was written into the script for future presentations.) Although the trip to Europe would involve an unprecedented run of presentations, Joe immersed himself eagerly in the planning of it. He gave loving attention to all the details, from the transformers the machines would need to operate at European voltages and frequencies to the tourist attractions we should visit and even the shows we should see in London. (From the beginning, it was one of the pleasures of doing business with Rank that we went to the theatre in London — anything we wished to see — often as Rank's guests.)

We sailed on the *United States.* This was, of course, before the arrival of the transatlantic jet; but even after flying across the ocean had become routine, Joe and I would try to budget our time so we could go one way by ship. We stayed at Claridge's, but set up our demonstrations in the Piccadilly Hotel, a noble but then somewhat seedy structure from which one could see Buckingham Palace. We both found it extremely exciting to be in London. Joe was an omnivorous reader of British literature and social thought, larding his speeches with quotations from English authors; he felt himself at the source. There was an election in progress and we went out to watch Anthony Eden, then Prime Minister, give a street-corner speech in his district and handle Labour and Communist hecklers. I visited the law courts and the Inns of Court. Meanwhile, an English engineer who had recently come to work for Haloid set up our clumsy three-box copying machine in the conference room at the Piccadilly. He put it through a rehearsal before the arrival of our guests from Rank, and it caught fire. Fortunately, we had brought the right spare parts, and there was just enough time to get the smell of smoke out of the room before the Rank delegation arrived.

The group was headed by John Davis, managing director of the Rank group of companies, and "headed" was the word. Muscular, heavy, domineering, and bald, Davis cleft the air as the prow of the *United States* had cleft the waters — with magisterial confidence. We would see a great deal of John in the years ahead, in London, other parts of Europe, Japan, and Rochester (for he became a member of the board of Xerox), and I rarely knew him to be burdened by humility. He clearly considered us barefoot kids from the country and thought we would be dazzled — as in truth we were — by him and Lord Rank, their company, and their life-style. Our audience (several of them wearing bowlers) gathered around our machine as we put it through its clumsy paces and showed the rather fuzzy copy it made. Davis exchanged glances with Lord Rank and

Tom Law and then with Ronald Leach, a Rank director who was also the managing partner in the London office of Peat, Marwick and Mitchell and later would become a close friend and valued intermediary in the dealings between Rank and Xerox. "Quite," Lord Rank said, and moved toward the door. Davis made a clucking sound, " 'Kyou, 'kyou." We all shook hands, and the delegation departed, but I think Davis had decided at that moment that he wanted xerography for Rank. A few days later he entertained us at an elaborate lunch in the Dorchester Hotel, at which he laid out a rather grandiose plan for a Rank-Haloid joint venture that would operate worldwide.

We continued our busy visit. We made a further demonstration at the Piccadilly for Bernard Mason of the Mason Company, toured the Gestetner factory, and went to Edinburgh, to the offices of Ferranti, which was interested in the uses of xerography for X rays. We then continued on to France and Germany, for meetings with Agfa and Kalle, and with John Dessauer's brother Guido, and then to Italy. At each of our meetings, Joe and I had to be erudite about the technology of xerography. My wife, Toni, who was the only member of our party with scientific training (and who had installed an early Xerox copier in our home to experiment with patterns in electrostatic charging as an art form), would sit us down in the hotel room and we would go over the nature of the xerographic process yet again, to make sure we were ready for questions. At one of these meetings, Joe caught my eye while making an apparently knowledgeable response to an engineer's searching technical question, and we both almost broke up.

My recommendation on our return was that we seek to form partnerships with two European firms, one on the continent, in Holland or Germany, and one (or more) in Britain. Joe pondered for six weeks and then concurred. We agreed to try to set up joint ventures with Agfa in Europe and Rank in London; Haloid and its partner would each have a 45 percent interest in the resulting company, and Battelle (which had not yet been bought out) would have 10 percent. But Bernard Mason came to Rochester to plead the case for his company, and was so persuasive that we reached a tentative agreement to set up a Haloid Xerox, Ltd., in England, with Mason supplying half the capital. Then it turned out that Mason didn't have the resources — and John Davis, who did, was in New York and wanted to see us. Rank was not interested in a deal for Britain alone.

Davis wanted a joint company that would have the exclusive right to make xerographic products everywhere outside the United States and Canada. And he was willing to put up *all* the capital. In principle, provided Rank was willing to sublicense Gestetner, Ferranti, and Agfa for specialized fields, we were willing to take the plunge.

Davis, Leach, and Law came to Rochester (I arranged to have the local news show on WHAM-TV cover their arrival at the railroad station, to show that we had some theatrical influence ourselves), and we began serious negotiations. This was 1956, when our only xerographic products were the giant Lith-Master and the almost equally enormous Copyflo; and what really interested Davis was a desktop copier. He kept saying he wanted to see the Haloid factory, and he wished our schedule of meetings and entertainments at home, at the Genesee Valley Club, and at the Rochester Club could be relaxed to permit a visit of inspection. Finally, he said with wide eyes, "You know, I don't believe you *have* a factory" — which was quite true, for almost all the parts that went into those early products were made elsewhere, and merely assembled in unfinished loft space we rented for the purpose.

The outlines of the deal we could make with Rank became visible during this visit, although the details were almost another year in negotiation. Both Mason and Agfa, which sent a team of German engineers to Rochester, kept trying to convince us that they should be included. On the trip to London during which we finally came to terms with Rank, Harold Webb of Mason, who was a Member of Parliament, gave us one of the great experiences of our early travels by taking us to dinner at the House of Commons and a night session of Parliament.

Our agreement with Rank was that there would be a joint venture to be called Rank Xerox, and Rank would manage it; Joe and I would be on the board. Rank Xerox would manufacture and sell all xerographic products to be made abroad under our patents (which by now meant all the patents; we had concluded our deal with Battelle), and would have full rights to issue sublicenses under the patents, everywhere in the world outside the United States and Canada. We would contribute our overseas patents and our know-how, and they would put up all the money. Their initial investment would be the sterling equivalent of $2.5 million. Each partner would own 50 percent.

Although this was by far the best offer we had from any of our potential partners, it was still a hard bargain if you believed — as Joe and I did — that Xerox products were going to be not only very useful in the world, but also very profitable. At a late stage in the negotiations, when we were in Davis's impressive and book-lined office in London, Joe and I suggested that a fairer way to approach the division of profits would be to set a ceiling on the fifty-fifty split. Above that level, the Haloid contribution of patents obviously would be a greater factor than the merely financial contribution by Rank, and we should begin to receive royalties that would give us two-thirds of all additional earnings. Davis accepted our proposal, suggesting a ceiling set at six hundred thousand pounds. Joe and I were delighted with the offer: Davis may have thought this was an impossibly large projection for the company's annual profits, but our sights were set considerably higher. We did not, however, wish to accept this proposition too quickly. So we objected, and asked that our share of profits go to two-thirds at a level of five hundred thousand pounds. After some considerable discussion back and forth, I suggested that we follow an old American practice and flip a coin. Davis and Leach were intrigued — and then delighted when they won. We were happy, too.

Rank Xerox came into being on May 1, 1957, and the occasion was marked two days later by a lunch for three hundred people at the Grosvenor House. From the start, Rank Xerox manufactured machines, plates, and powders, and prepared its own sales and marketing literature. We were taken to a storefront in Holborn where a Copyflo was running for the edification of the public (which, however, was not to be edified; the crowds walked by, and nobody took any interest). Later in that 1957 trip we went to the multilingual Hannover Fair in Germany to observe Rank's introduction of xerography on the continent. Here we were not ignored. Joe and I watched with pride and fascination as people crowded around the exhibit. Joe wrote his father that "it was exciting for Sol and me to read the story of xerography told in German, French and Italian."

What had held up the introduction of the one-stop automatic single-sheet office copying machine was, simply, the fact that we did not know how to make it. Chastened by our overoptimism on the original Standard A, Joe was determined not to offer the market a product until it was high quality, operable by a secretary without engineering training, and reasonably economical. Sometimes Carlson was sharply impatient. He went to New York to the National Business Show in 1953 and wrote Joe bitterly that "small copiers were the hit of the show. I was chagrined, however, to find that Haloid and Xerox were not represented." Joe replied that we had not tried to rival Thermofax and Verifax at the show because he didn't feel that Haloid had a competitive product.

"Against considerable pressure, including yours," Joe wrote to Chet that November, "I have stood out for the past couple of years against the development of a small office copying device along any lines suggested up to date, on the grounds that such developments were not sufficiently promising against competitive ones on the horizon to warrant the tremendous cost of developing, tooling, producing, and, most of all, marketing. . . . When you say we missed the boat completely, I, of course, believe the opposite. I believe that if we had taken the wrong boat two years ago we would be infinitely worse off now. Now we know what the real copying competition is. Let's assume it's Thermofax and Verifax. They have shot their wad. . . . Now we know what we have to do. Either we can beat these processes inherently or we cannot. If we can we'll develop processes to much tighter specifications than we would have two years ago and thus save ourselves hundreds of thousands of dollars. If we cannot we also will have saved hundreds of thousands of dollars and we will devote ourselves to profitable lines of application rather than to dead ducks. . . . The reason I have been begging for hectograph and mimeograph and multiple copy techniques, etc., is to present a process that will do things that no other process will do."

What we had in the Standard A and the Copyflo was at bottom a traditional photography system, with a camera in one section, a developer in the next, and a printer in the third. Both used a flatbed press, which required that the selenium plate be moved back and forth to precisely the same locations for each new document. What was needed was a process that employed a rotary action, so that only the paper would move through the machine. This became possible in the mid-1950s, when Clyde Mayo and Harold Clark created the selenium-coated drum. Like the piston in the cylinder of the automobile engine, the drum would be subject to different forces as it moved. In one revolution, it would be charged; in the next, it would register the patterns of light and dark; in the next, it would be coated with toner; in the next, it would print the paper; and then it would be brushed clean in preparation for the succeeding cycle. All this had to be done, of course, with great speed and precision, and much more had to be designed: an optical system that would rapidly scan a page with light to be reflected on the selenium drum, a selenium coating that could be discharged instantly and completely to avoid double exposure effects, a very precise paper feed to get the page onto the drum at the right instant — and, most difficult, a means of taking the paper, which was attached to the drum by an electrostatic force, off the selenium and over to a tray where the "ink"would be fused on by a quick pulse from an electric heater.

The costs of solving these problems were staggering. Every year John Dessauer would bring in the budget for xerography research and Haloid controller Harold Kuhns would mournfully shake his head and say "Gee! Gee!" over and over again. In 1958 our total cash flow was less than $5 million, and we budgeted almost $2 million for research. But slowly, with many wrong turns and failures, the laboratories and shops brought in the answers. Ways were found to get the necessary even coating of selenium on the drum. An ingenious pattern of mirrors and prisms took the reflected light from the paper to be copied to the drum. An engineer in Mayo's group designed a blower that produced a tiny puff of air to waft the xeroprinted paper from the drum to the adjacent heating frame. Under Dessauer's supervision, a team was formed. Clark and his group of Ph.D.'s explored physical principles, helped by consultants from various universities. One of them, John Bardeen, a Nobel Prize winner for his work on the earliest transistors, became a member of the Xerox board. Mayo ran a machine shop in which trial solutions for the problems were hand-tooled. Horace Becker, in one industrial slum or another (for we rented the cheapest space we could find), turned Mayo's designs into prototypes that could be sent out to various manufacturers with detailed specifications. Merritt Chandler, a veteran production engineer Joe had recruited from the automobile industry, organized an assembly line.

Fortunately, these were fascinating problems for the engineers; they worked nights and weekends on their own motion. "Everybody was keyed up," Becker told John Brooks of *The New Yorker* some eight years later. "You couldn't tell an engineer from an assembler in that place. No one could stay away — you'd sneak in on a Sunday, when the assembly line was shut down, and there would be somebody adjusting something or just puttering around and admiring our work." The original Xerox 914 (named for the maximum dimension of the paper it could handle) had no fewer than 1,260 separate components to be assembled; the salesmen liked to say it was more complicated than a car.

For all the talent and money and time, it came slowly. Parts that worked adequately in their independent testing would be recalcitrant when linked. The timing of the steps was so delicate and crucial that what had produced handsome copies last night often yielded nothing but streaks and smudges this morning. Humidity conditions affected the quality of copies. Time after time there were heartbreaking results. You might find a better way to do one of the steps (develop a better toner, for example, that lay more evenly on the plate) only to find that it created problems with the other steps (the toner would smudge on the paper). It took fourteen years from the first license on the patents to the introduction of the 914, and repeatedly we found that what we had learned last year was not necessarily useful this year.

It was in this context that we discussed asking Bell and Howell or IBM to manufacture the Xerox machine, and in this context, too, that our people pleaded to be given the chance to do it themselves. I never heard Joe question the soundness of the decision to stop seeking a partner for domestic manufacture, but there were days when we wondered about the dimensions of our ambition. Over and over again, the 914 copying machines we were assembling failed to work when we tested them, and when we tried to substitute parts they didn't fit. Suppliers with whom Haloid had enjoyed long and cheerful relationships, whose work was perfectly satisfactory for Rectigraph cameras and the Copyflo, could not understand how close the tolerances had to be if their parts were to be truly interchangeable in this instrument. Becker and Dessauer toured suppliers' factories to carry the word of quality control. In one frantic two-week period in 1959, Joe held a meeting at the assembly plant at eight o'clock every morning, to check out what people had done the day before to cure production failures and eliminate production bottlenecks.

The worst time of all was the month after we began shipping machines to users. John Brooks describes what happened: "Just at the moment the public spotlight was full on it, the 914 turned out to be a veritable Edsel. Intricate relays declined to work, springs broke, power supplies failed, inexperienced users dropped staples and paper clips into it and fouled the works (necessitating the installa-

tion in every machine of a staple-catcher), and the expected difficulties in humid climates developed, along with unanticipated ones
at high altitudes. 'All in all,' Becker said, 'at that time the machines
had a bad habit, when you pressed the button, of doing nothing.' "
And Brooks's list of troubles leaves out the worst single horror —
the fact that the first two hundred 914s we shipped caught fire. If
the air puff that separated the paper from the drum malfunctioned
even very slightly, with too much push on the paper or too little, the
paper came in contact with the heating element. As responsible corporate citizens — to the dismay of our sales department — we
added a small fire extinguisher to the external trappings of the copier. Describing this problem and trying to lighten a very dark moment, I told the Board of Directors that we had inadvertently
managed to produce an ideal machine for the CIA: it burned everything before copying.

What saved us during those desperate months was the enormous
usefulness of the product (when it worked) to those who first acquired it. Contrary to the predictions in the study Arthur D. Little
had done for IBM, the first users of the 914 found their employees
not only willing but eager to make a trip to the copying room, because the Xerox machine was faster and better than its predecessors
and rivals. We also benefited greatly from the resourcefulness of the
sales staff that had been carefully assembled by C. Peter Mc-
Colough, then our bold and farsighted vice-president for marketing
(later chairman of the board and chief executive officer of Xerox),
and from our own very unusual business arrangements, which assured that our customers suffered inconvenience but not loss when
our equipment failed. In the sales strategy we developed, it was our
revenues that suffered if our product was unsatisfactory.

We did not sell the 914; we leased it. The terms of the lease, essentially, were payment by use: the number of copies made was
metered, and the user was billed accordingly. This added something
else that could go wrong; and the meters on the early 914s had a tendency to jam, register too few copies, or count each ten as one hundred. When one of the copiers failed to work, the blow was not just
to our reputation and future sales but to our income, and we had a
direct stake in getting the unit repaired, fast. We had staffed up with
repairmen working out of every sales office, and we gave them a lot
to do. (The average age of our staff in the field, as Joe reported to an
annual meeting, was twenty-six.) Gradually, as we took over the

manufacture of more of our own components and schooled our suppliers to the details of our needs, the number of calls for repairmen diminished, and we were able to concentrate on a more attractive problem: the fact that demand for 914s was dramatically above projections and we had no way to produce as many as we could place. A few years before, we had acquired a hundred acres of land in suburban Webster and had built a research facility for xerography. Now we moved the production of the 914 out of the four-story building we had rented near downtown Rochester and out to a new factory hastily built to our designs on our land in Webster.

The decision to lease the 914 had come only after protracted discussion. Haloid had leased xerographic products from the beginning, because the machines were so expensive that few potential purchasers would have been willing (or able) to risk the money. The first commercial placement of the Standard A, for example, had been with the motor vehicles bureau of the State of Michigan in 1949. The bureau had to make huge numbers of copies of forms for distribution to county offices, and was willing to pay eighteen hundred dollars a year to rent what were then the seven separate components of a copier. But it never would have paid the eight to ten thousand dollars we would have required to make a sale profitable. That was one machine; even little Haloid could easily finance that. With the 914, however, we were dealing in thousands of machines, to go into businesses of different natures and sizes.

Several members of our board thought the risks of financing this volume of placement were beyond anything Haloid Xerox could carry. That was the sort of thing IBM did. They could afford to push their receipts forward in time. Others were concerned that the rental that might be charged to a corporate headquarters, or to a big law office or accounting firm that might run a copier eighty hours a week, would be prohibitive for a small company that might need no more than a thousand copies a month. Nobody thought of a middle route between the IBM model of monthly rentals and the conventional direct sales strategy until John Glavin, the younger brother of our investment banker and board member Charles Glavin, who was working on the new products planning staff, noted the stamp machine in the mail room and rushed to Joe with the idea of metering the copies. Joe and I had a talk about the Pitney-Bowes model that Sunday while walking around the reservoir. Pitney was a small company, too. The executive committee was intrigued. After I had looked into the legal implications and found no impediments, the policy was set.

The development team, meanwhile, was working on ways to reduce the machinery of the 914 to a size that could stand on a desk. Every piece of market research we did indicated that the sales potential for such a machine was far greater than that of the still elephantine (if no longer gargantuan) 914. Dessauer reported back that the 914 processes simply could not be concentrated into that small a space: they would have to design new components. Some $20 million was spent from 1960 to 1963 on engineering and tooling up for our new 813 model (which was to handle paper up to the 8 × 13 legal pad — but when we went to production we boosted it to 9 × 14 to increase its utility).

The 914 had been an unimaginable success, largely responsible for boosting the company's total operating revenues from $33 million in 1958 to $176 million in 1963. With the 813 and a new large, high-speed 2400 model (which made forty copies a minute), three years later Xerox had lifted its revenues beyond the half-billion-dollar mark.

Income before taxes, which had been $3.7 million in 1958, crossed the $100 million mark in 1966, still rising. And there was much more on the come, for the leasing method of sales postponed income into future years. Xerox was listed on the New York Stock Exchange in 1961, and investors quickly accorded it one of the highest price-earnings ratios in the market. At the listing ceremony on Broad Street — very exciting for us, although clearly old hat to the participants from the exchange, who did it several times a month — Wilson recalled to Keith Funston, president of the exchange, that they had been in the same class at the Harvard Business School. Surprised, Funston responded that he had no recollection of that. Joe didn't mind: a corporate giant named Xerox had just been born, and this he was sure Funston would remember.

At business schools, the rise of the Xerox Corporation has long been a favorite case study. It illustrates perfectly the theory of the "cash cow" that pays for the emergence of new products. Photographic papers and Rectigraph machines were the cash cow; year after year they generated the revenues that enabled Haloid to make the investments in xerographic research that later paid off so spectacularly. (In due course the 914 performed the same service for the

813 and its successors.) It isn't so easy to manage these things as it is to describe and analyze them after they have occurred. The Haloid people who were pulling the load were conscious of the fact that their company's earnings were being used up, and thus their own rewards were being limited, in an expensive search for what many of them considered pie in the sky. And in this context it did not help that Joe, John Dessauer, and I kept speaking of xerography in such idealistic terms.

It isn't easy to call up again the heights to which our ambitions for xerography soared, thirty, twenty-five, twenty years ago. "We envisage," Dessauer told a stockholders' meeting, "that communications in general, and especially graphic communications, are on the threshold of changing our national and international life to a degree not yet comprehended by most people. It is becoming abundantly evident that we are in a new stage, one substantially different from earlier stages such as oral culture, alphabetic civilization, or book-oriented society. The combination of the electronics revolution and revolutionary imaging methods, along with satellite telecommunications, will permit contemporary man finally to be able to master time and space in an unprecedented way." We saw xerography at the center of these developments, as the output system for the computers, the path to improved X rays and air traffic control, the "camera" that would make the pictures from the satellites more useful, the generator of long-distance facsimiles that would improve communications among peoples, not only nationally but globally. Chester Carlson was sure that xerography would become the means by which integrated circuits would be etched onto transistors. Joe and I were impressed, even though we didn't really know what that meant.

More than that, we were developing our own theories of the role of business in American society. "To realize its full promise in the world of tomorrow," I said in a speech to the Conference Board in my last year with Xerox, "American business and industry . . . will have to make social goals as central to its decisions as economic goals." Even before the giant success of the early 1960s, we sought to make Haloid Xerox a force for the improvement of the city of Rochester, to help the schools and the university, educational television, and the cultural life of the city. When the urban riots came — and Rochester, astonishingly (for we had thought of ourselves as the residents of a lucky and happy city), had the very first of them —

we helped organize the response of the corporate community to the misery revealed so suddenly on our streets.

For many of the employees of the old Haloid Company, all this was remote. What they could see in the late 1950s was that top management was risking their company on a project in which they had no part, to some degree at their expense. One of Joe's greatest accomplishments was that he managed to keep all these people productive, mostly cheerful, through the long years of discouragement. In the end, they would be richly rewarded. John Dessauer estimated that no fewer than forty of Haloid's executives became millionaires from the stock option plan adopted in 1954 as a supplement to the company's long-standing profit-sharing program. There were long years and miles to travel before that happened, however, years when key people in Haloid remained with the company simply because they saw the stars in Joe Wilson's eyes.

Haloid's special need for good human relations extended far below the executive suites. It was a unionized company. Following a nasty strike in the 1930s, and over the violent objections of Gilbert Mosher, the company's absentee boss, Joseph R. Wilson had signed a contract recognizing the Amalgamated Clothing Workers as bargaining agent for Haloid employees. Joe believed in unions, and had good relations with Abraham Chatman, the local leader of the Amalgamated (then a strong union in Rochester, which was the home base of some of the leading makers of men's clothing). Joe contributed to and served on the board of the hospital built as a memorial to the union's longtime leader, Sidney Hillman. And he was more than willing to "post" the new jobs that would be opened up by the growth of the xerographic end of the business — to make them available first of all to existing employees, as part of a union contract. But the skills required to make Xerox copiers were different from those employed in the manufacture of photographic papers or even cameras. Arrangements were made at the Rochester Institute of Technology for special courses in xerography to be offered to Haloid employees at company expense. Inevitably, there was a haze of suspicion of management intentions on the shop floor, and Joe personally not only handled the key negotiations with Chatman but made the presentations to the workers.

Moving the executives around was more difficult, and in some cases an impossible task. In 1958, after two years of correspondence between the two men, Joe retained the services of a Cleveland in-

dustrial psychologist named Dr. Paul Brouwer. Brouwer became a
regular visitor to Rochester, where he would chat with the Haloid
Xerox senior executives and the ambitious middle managers who
reported to them; and then he would talk things over with Joe. He
was a man of charm and considerable common sense, who knew that
his job was essentially to sustain and occasionally direct Joe's own
instincts. As I look back, I find it interesting that on almost every
visit he would stop at my law office, where he would discuss the
company and its people at length. He looked upon me, he said, as a
non-threatening figure in my relations with the others at Haloid
Xerox, because I was maintaining my independent status as a practicing attorney.

Because Haloid had been a family company, its corporate organization was rather unusual. Joe as president was, in effect, chief executive officer, and his father as chairman of the board had an
essentially honorary status and advisory function. When Joseph R.
cut back his involvement, he was succeeded by Homer Piper, the
chemist who had in the 1930s created Haloid Record, the paper that
carried the company through the Depression and was still, into the
1950s, the foundation of its earnings. This opened the door for John
Dessauer to assume the role and title of director of research and
development. When Piper retired, the chair passed to John B. Hartnett, who had organized the Haloid marketing operation (permitting the promotion of Peter McColough), and then to Harold
Kuhns, the company's controller (permitting a better title for Kent
Damon, who as treasurer was arranging the rather intricate pattern
of borrowings and stock sales by which the development of the 914
was financed). All these were Haloid people; only Dessauer and Joe
himself spanned the two parts of the business. I was entirely on the
xerography side; and for many in Rochester and elsewhere the symbol of change in the company in 1961 was as much my election as
chairman of the board as the adoption of the name Xerox Corporation.

Through much of the 1950s, the company had a five-member,
informal executive committee that met a few times a month at
the Rochester Club (there being no office at Haloid sufficiently private for such meetings). It consisted of Joe himself in the chair,
Dessauer, Kuhns, Hartnett, and me. In 1959, as the company began its rapid growth, we agreed that something more formal was
required. Joe proposed and the board approved the creation of

such a committee, with me as chairman. Later, the membership fell to four, when Kuhns and Hartnett dropped out and McColough was added.

I continued to chair it until I left for Washington. After 1961 I held three titles: chairman of the board, chairman of the executive committee, and general counsel. This confused the management consultants dreadfully, and sometimes bewildered the outside world, too. In 1965 I made a speech before the New York Society of Security Analysts, and in describing my role told them the fable of the man who created a new kind of creature by crossbreeding a tiger and a parrot. When asked what the animal was good for, he replied, "I don't know, but I'll tell you this: when he talks, we listen." By then, the structure of Xerox had been pruned and simplified considerably. Joe, of course, was its center. There was no "chief operating officer." Instead, three of us had designated areas of responsibility: I was responsible for international activities, patents, licensing, legal activities, acquisitions, and government relations; Peter McColough, for domestic production and sales; John Dessauer, for research and development.

At no time did I abandon the private practice of law. Haloid soon became my largest client, but I had a number of other corporate clients. As the work grew, so did the office, and I was fortunate enough to pick up several extraordinarily able new associates, most notably Richard Buxbaum, who later became a law professor at the University of California at Berkeley. But the tasks began outrunning the available manpower, and in 1958 we merged Sutherland, Linowitz and Williams into the much larger firm of Harris, Beach, which became Harris, Beach, Keating, Wilcox, Dale and Linowitz, with approximately fifty lawyers. A member of the firm, Albert H. Swett — who later succeeded me as Xerox general counsel — became my chief legal associate on Xerox matters. Between the legal work and my responsibilities as a corporate officer, Xerox took about three-fifths of my time, but I fought successfully to save the rest for others. I worked mostly out of my law office. When I was a vice-president of Haloid, I never had an office in the old headquarters on Haloid Street. When the company moved its offices to Midtown Towers, there was an elegant suite for the chairman, but I was in my law offices far more often than I was there.

By 1966 we had outgrown everything. Offices were scattered all over Rochester as we awaited the completion of Xerox Square, our ornament to the city's skyline and contribution to its amenities (we had included a skating rink, like Rockefeller Center's, just for the fun of it). Incredibly, our little company had become one of the twelve largest in the United States in terms of the market value of its stock. (The figure was $4.5 *billion*, twice as great, Joe told the 1966 stockholders' meeting with considerable awe, as the market value of Chrysler or U.S. Steel, and roughly equal to that of Gulf Oil or Standard Oil of California. "These companies," he added, "are five or ten times larger than we are" — but Xerox stock had a higher price-earnings ratio than any other of the nation's hundred largest corporations.)

That spring, Joe moved up to chairman of the board (holding the function of chief executive officer), and Peter McColough was made president and chief operating officer. I continued as chairman of the executive committee and general counsel — and became chairman of a newly formed Xerox International, with direct line responsibility for what had recently become the fastest-growing part of the company.

The metamorphosis of little Haloid into giant Xerox made surprisingly little difference to Joe and me in our daily lives. I had already purchased the lovely house we left behind when we went to Washington; we wished for nothing better. Joe and I still went for walks on Sundays, wrote memos to each other, and met frequently at the company and on social occasions, when Joe usually wanted to talk, at least for a few minutes, about something related to work. We had already been presidents of the City Club and the Chamber of Commerce, and we were both on the board of the University of Rochester — Joe had become a trustee at the age of forty, the youngest ever to be so honored. When he called me with the news on a Saturday afternoon, he announced with delight that the appointment had come "five years ahead of my schedule." (He always had a schedule of accomplishments; he could never understand that I didn't.) In 1959, as the first 914s were coming off the line, he became chairman of the board of the university.

Of course we moved now, both as businessmen and as citizens, onto a larger stage. There was a growing sense of wonder about Xerox as people in Rochester began to feel that their city had been blessed with "another Kodak." Where once the company had been involved with public-affairs shows on local television and the proposal to take the third VHF channel allocated to the city and use it for an educational station, now we sponsored "CBS Reports," the coverage of the national conventions on ABC, and the four-part series on the United Nations that roused the storm of protest from the right wing. Where once we had known the mayor of the city and our local Congressman, Kenneth Keating (who was, in fact, a law partner of mine after I merged with Harris, Beach), now we were invited to meet and dine with the President at the White House and to chair nationwide civic organizations. We could make a contribution to the aesthetics of our society, commissioning the design firm of Lippincott and Marguilies to make the Xerox copiers ornaments of the office, and the architects Welton Beckett and Associates to make our new factories and Xerox Square structures in which our employees and our city could take pride. Where previously we had worried that some large corporation might acquire little Haloid, we now had the delightful opportunity to scout around for acquisitions that might complement the activities of Xerox. I was given the responsibility for finding the right businesses to buy.

The most obvious area for us was publishing; and in publishing the most obvious target was something that involved a microfilm process, for we were the proprietors of a system that inexpensively turned microfilms back to printed pages. In 1962, after arduous negotiations, we acquired University Microfilm of Ann Arbor, Michigan, the outstanding preserver of scholarly documentation. A few years later we acquired from Wesleyan University, which had found itself in a somewhat awkward position vis-à-vis the Internal Revenue Service as the proprietor of a profit-making enterprise, all the operations of American Educational Publishing, the nation's largest producer of elementary school materials, including the magazine *My Weekly Reader*. The price we paid made Wesleyan one of the best-endowed small universities in America. We moved on in education by purchasing Basic Systems, Inc., a group of bright New Yorkers (mostly former teachers, which we found attractive) who were pioneering in the new field of programmed instruction, which turned out not to have the promise they or we had thought.

By the mid-1960s the federal government had made what we all thought would be a major commitment to the improvement of American education: Lyndon Johnson's Great Society could scarcely be anything but a slogan without a better-educated population, and the President himself, of course, was a former school-

teacher. Both personally and for business reasons, Joe and I were enthusiastic about the prospects.[1] Early in 1966 I told a meeting of the
Cleveland Security Analysts that "the twenty-five centuries since
Plato have seen less growth in our ability to transfer knowledge between men than in any other area of human endeavor." I noted that
other large corporations — I mentioned IBM, Time Inc., General
Electric, and RCA (we were now playing in the big leagues ourselves) — had also made commitments to education. "Perhaps
among us," I said, "we can find the means to revolutionize educational technology and bring great rewards to ourselves while at the
same time serving an essential human cause."

We were also interested in acquiring technologically innovative
companies with products that could contribute to xerography, and
especially to the extension of its uses. The one such acquisition in
my time was Electrical Optical Systems, the property of an ingenious, aggressive, charismatic physicist named Abe Zarem, a Silicon
Valley–style entrepreneur before there was much silicon or a valley.
His inventions, we thought, would contribute to the perfection of
xerographic cameras not only in copying machines but also in exotic
uses like space probes. When it appeared that EOS was going to be a
drain on Xerox resources rather than a contribution to them, Joe and
I contented ourselves with listening to Zarem's ideas — which we
always enjoyed doing — and trying to control Zarem's budget.

The company's giant acquisition, a $1 billion purchase of Scien-
tific Data Systems, occurred after I had left Xerox. Once Haloid had
lived in fear that IBM would create its own office copier and grind
down its small competitor; now Xerox was going to compete with
IBM at the very center of the giant's lair. Joe called me in Washing-

---

[1] This idealism, incidentally, turned out to be a petard on which we could occasionally be
hoisted, and by the most articulate people in the country, too. Marshall McLuhan wrote in
American Scholar that "xerography is bringing a reign of terror into American publishing,"
and we learned one day with horror that a mention of Xerox at a meeting of the Authors
Guild had created a wave of booing from writers who felt, with considerable reason, that il-
licit copying was vitiating their copyrights and diminishing their already meager incomes.
Even more serious was the devastation wrought upon scholarly publishing by the loss of
multiple subscriptions from academic departments and libraries at universities, which had
once purchased a number of copies to keep faculty and students current with the leading edge
of research, and could now take a single journal and make whatever duplicates were wanted.
We supported a new copyright bill pending in Congress to help authors and publishers col-
lect from the making of Xerox copies, we cultivated the leadership of the Authors Guild at
lunches, we contributed twenty thousand dollars to the creation of a new copyright clearinghouse. This was a problem that would not go away, however, and the new copyright legislation that eventually passed (more than a dozen years after this first cut at a solution) has not
yielded a remedy.

ton to tell me about it, and when I reacted with some hesitation, he was not disturbed. He noted gaily that I had always been a worrier — and I reminded him that lawyers are paid to worry.

What changed most of all between 1955 and 1965 was that we found the world outside the United States. This happened partly, I am sure, because we wanted it to happen: long before we had ever been abroad, we had become committed internationalists deeply aware of global interdependence. Among the pleasures of Haloid's growth was the business reason it gave us to learn firsthand how they order things in other countries, but we became world travelers out of necessity as well as pleasure. Our ventures abroad required constant attention, and frequently an admixture of discipline, from Rochester. Because we were no better than equal partners in Rank Xerox, and our British partners were sometimes unwilling to consider us real equals, the management of the overseas involvements required time for negotiation and renegotiation by someone in a position of authority. One of the reasons Joe felt I should be chairman of the executive committee, and then chairman of the board, was to magnify my voice when I spoke to outside companies — including Rank. Almost from the beginning, I was responsible for our international activities, and my appointment as chairman of a new Xerox International in the last months of my association with the company merely made formal a responsibility I had been carrying for years.

The marriage with Rank had not been made in heaven, and it did not always run smoothly. Some of the difficulties were merely embarrassing and expensive, like the moment when Rank Xerox began marketing our 914 copier, so triumphant in the United States. They discovered only after the first dozens of units had been shipped that the doorways to British offices were smaller than the doorways to U.S. offices and the machine would have to be downsized — not enough to force redesign of the interior, but enough to be very costly. Underlying all our discomforts with Rank was something much more significant — the fact that for some years office copying did not catch on in the United Kingdom to anything like the extent it did in the United States. In America, "to Xerox" soon became a verb in such common use that we had to wage a full-scale campaign and push on all the print media, demanding the invariable use of the capital "X," respecting a trademark that otherwise we might lose. In Britain, both attention and revenues came much more slowly.

The Copyflo, which was all Rank had to sell for a while, never really caught on because the British made much less use of microfilm than we did. While the 914 far exceeded Rank's expectations of it — Davis had been interested originally only in a desktop copier, and pressed us incessantly to get that work done before Kalle in Germany made a version of the RCA Electrofax that would drive Xerox from the European market — it never, in a sense, entered the culture. On visits to America, Davis would marvel at all the publicity Xerox received and wonder how Rank Xerox could rouse the same kind of public curiosity. As late as 1966 he wrote plaintively (and only half jokingly) to Joe that he and I should make sure we had time on a trip to London for a dinner Davis and the investment house of Kleinwort Benson were planning for one hundred "leading investment people," because "the City still cannot believe that the business of Xerox and Rank Xerox exists."

One problem we encountered was that Rank Xerox sought to make money from sublicensing in ways that collided with our domestic strategy. An executive named Peter Faulkner served as deputy to Tom Law, the managing director of Rank Xerox and our basic (always pleasurable) contact in England. Law also had responsibility for the Rank Precision Industries factory, and delegated various of his Rank Xerox duties to his deputy. Faulkner became involved in disputes with Stromberg and RCA at a time when Haloid Xerox was closely associated with both, and then became upset (as did Davis) when we pointed out that these American companies already held valid sublicenses from Rochester for the work they were doing abroad. Frightened by Kalle's claim to be able to produce multiple plain paper copies from a zinc-oxide-coated paper plate, Rank Xerox refused to grant the German manufacturer our standard Electrofax license. Meanwhile, Faulkner sold what it purported to be exclusive sublicenses for Electrofax to Senox in Germany and Savin in Japan. It fell to me to work through and straighten out the relationships among the various companies and to settle with Rank Xerox the proper division of licensing labors internationally.

After the 914 took off and other American makers of copiers were scrambling frantically to find ways of competing with Xerox, we began to focus attention on Japan, which was obviously going to become a major market for copiers. Because the Japanese language didn't permit the use of typewriters, and calligraphic pens didn't make carbon copies, Japan was an immense market for photocopying machinery, most of it inconvenient, slow, messy wet stuff. Fuji Film Company, one of that country's largest producers of photographic equipment, had not only pronounced a strong interest in dry copying but had experimented in its laboratories with the creation of xerographic products, using our published patents and descriptions of our procedures.

As early as 1957 Fuji Film executives had corralled Harold Clark, who was visiting Japan as a tourist, and enticed him to a tour of their factory and discussions of the possibility of a license from Haloid. On Clark's return to Rochester, he discussed his Japanese experiences with Wilson and Dessauer, and we put Fuji in touch with Rank Xerox, which had just acquired the international rights. We all agreed that we didn't want a license-and-royalty arrangement in Japan; we wanted a full-scale joint venture. Rank Xerox hired the firm of Charles Rayden, who was supposed to know about possibilities in Japan, to scout the field for the best partner. He came up with Nippon Electric and Toshiba. Law then decided to go look for himself, and did so in the autumn of 1959. On the spot, he agreed with our tentative assessment that a deal with Fuji offered the greatest opportunity, and he worked out the general terms of an agreement under which Fuji would produce and sell xerographic machines and supplies for the Asian market. And then — nothing happened.

The difficulties lay for the most part with MITI, the department of the Japanese government responsible for conserving foreign exchange — and for preventing foreigners from owning a significant share of a Japanese manufacturer. Tom Law came to Rochester to discuss the problem, and proposed that I go to Japan with him to help resolve the dispute. Over Thanksgiving weekend in 1960 I made my own first trip to Japan to help the negotiations along. I found the Fuji people understandably confused. They knew what an immense success the early 914s had been in the United States, but they also had an Electrofax license from RCA for a machine they could produce by themselves. Thanks in large part to the personal relationship we developed with Setsutaro Kobayashi, the chairman of Fuji Photo Film — and later with Tony, his son, who would follow his father as president of Fuji-Xerox — difficulties were worked out. Rank Xerox remained the main channel of communications with Japan, but I continued to be involved in the negotiations. Joe and I went on the board of Fuji-Xerox, and we frequently attended the board meetings in Tokyo.

The Japanese were marvelously inventive in selling the 914. To prove that it made seven copies a minute, they would make Xerox copies of the customer's watch, showing the second hand advancing. We had our share of problems: our worldwide claim that Xerox copies could be made on *any* paper was defeated by Japanese rice paper; and the idea of leasing was quite foreign to Japanese practice. A bank wrote angrily to Fuji-Xerox that it had been slandered by the implied suggestion that it could not afford to buy a copying machine. The Japanese were not in those days ten feet tall in technology. A recent official history of Fuji-Xerox discreetly reports "the difficulty of maintaining product quality equal to that of imported machines, since certain parts and materials could not be obtained in Japan." Teams of engineers came from Rank Xerox in Britain to help out, and presently the quality of Xerox products from the Fuji factories was equal to that in the United States or Europe. I made special trips in 1962 and again in 1964 to participate in the introduction of the first Japanese-made 914s and 813s. By 1965 Fuji-Xerox was profitable after only thirty-six months, and looking for markets in the rest of Asia — first the Philippines, then Okinawa, Korea, Thailand, Hong Kong, and Taiwan. In each of these places, their first market was the U.S. military, and then the use of xerography spread rapidly to local industry.

Another source of tension between Xerox and Rank was the British company's failure to develop a Latin American market. I raised the subject at many Rank Xerox board meetings, and in private conversations with Tom Law, who kept saying, "You can't rush these things, Sol. Let's do them at the right time." The fact was that Latin America was not a priority for Rank, and it was for us. We could see our competitors gearing up to get a head start there. Moreover, as our interest in education grew, and Kennedy's Alliance for Progress gathered its brief head of steam, we saw an opportunity to do work that would be important as well as profitable — provided we had our franchise in Latin America.

In 1962 Joe and I decided that the only way out of our dilemma was to try to buy up the Rank Xerox rights in the Western Hemisphere. Davis did not welcome our approach; when we first raised the subject he indicated that this would be "very expensive" for Xerox. (Davis was now on the board of Xerox; he knew what we could afford.) On the other hand, he was anxious to acquire stock in Xerox for Rank — he had been after us to sound out Battelle on the chances of buying some of their stock — and we knew it. Eventually, we paid ten thousand shares of stock (then worth more than $2 million) plus a royalty on our Latin American sales to get back the Latin American rights in which Rank had only a halfhearted interest.

Staffing for Latin America would obviously be the key to our prospects there. We had been warned in dire terms about the horrors that would lie ahead if we got involved with the wrong people. I hired as my deputy for this area a trilingual Brazilian named José Bejerano, who had worked for Petrobras, the Brazilian state oil enterprise, and he put us in touch with potential partners in the more important markets: Mexico, Venezuela, Brazil, and Argentina. We wanted joint ventures rather than agencies, and we were prepared to train both sales and service personnel at our expense, some of them on site and some in Rochester. We were also willing to promise some opportunity to manufacture xerographic supplies locally, although the manufacture of machines would have to be some time off. We needed people with the right abilities, the right imagination, the right attitudes, and the right relationships — all four. Bejerano lined up groups of both business and government people for us to meet, and Joe and I went off together early in 1965 on a fast trip to Caracas, Rio, São Paulo, and Buenos Aires.

I found it an eye-opener. I was fascinated by the vitality and enterprise I found in South America, by the depth of their problems and of their commitment to make a better life, by their need for the communications services and educational technology we hoped to bring. We met Presidents, central bankers, lawyers, businessmen, and the U.S. ambassadors. I spent an evening with Lincoln Gordon, our ambassador to Brazil, who, in the course of a long conversation, indicated he would be interested in Tom Mann's job as Assistant Secretary for American Republic Affairs in the State Department — which is where I found him when I became ambassador to the Organization of American States eighteen months later. This brief trip south turned out to be important to Xerox, which was to find a major outlet for its products in Latin America, but far more important to me, for my first flashing contact with this fascinating world was surely among my strongest reasons for accepting the OAS post when President Johnson offered it to me in the summer of 1966.

Lyndon Johnson, who was an omnivorous consumer of documents and kept up with the business scene, took an interest in Xerox from the beginning of its skyrocket rise. He cultivated the Republican Wilson as well as the Democratic Linowitz. Joe, too, was invited to dinners and other social functions at the White House, where the President danced with Peggy and charmed the Wilsons as he did everyone he set out to charm. Joe became a fund-raiser for Johnson in the 1964 election and a supporter of the President inside the business community.

Joe was pleased with my increasing involvement in government advisory committees on international and educational affairs. We often discussed the possibility that I would take one of the appointments the White House was suggesting to me, which would require my departure from Xerox, at least temporarily. Both of us recognized that my position at Xerox was inseparable from our personal relationship. The question was, who would succeed me as general counsel, not who would undertake the other responsibilities. When the day came for my departure to government service, Joe issued a characteristically generous statement that the company had been honored by my appointment. He said he himself would become chairman of Xerox International, and left the post of chairman of the executive committee open as a kind of candle in the window. But he fully understood when, three years later, I decided to remain in Washington.

Paul Hoffman, who had left Studebaker for government service and then returned to it as a member of the board of directors, gave me a piece of advice: cut the cord. Your presence on the board, he said, would remind people that you were once chairman, and would tempt you to comment on how things used to be done. They don't need that, and neither do you. It was good advice.

Toni and I saw Joe and Peggy socially, shared pleasures and heartaches with them. I remained on call for Xerox if needed — as I still do. Peter McColough and I have long been friends, and I have an avuncular feeling for the current chairman, David Kearns, who while still in high school dated the baby-sitter for our daughters. More than that, I am still a believer: when Kearns tells me about the exciting things that are being done in the Xerox laboratories, I hear the fire bell ring again. I still know in my heart that xerography is not just a branch of the office-machinery business, but an invention with manifold applications, some still hidden in the womb of time, that will increasingly make a difference in people's lives.

I remained in Washington as a lawyer, not as part of government, working in the private sector as a senior partner in the law firm of Coudert Brothers. Since leaving the OAS in 1969, in fact, I have never been on a public payroll. But I had become, and I remain, a public man. Thinking back, it was a natural result of the dreams and ideals Joe and I had shared through the almost twenty-five years of our friendship.

PART III

The Washington Years

6

Private Organizations

RETURNING FROM THE OAS to private life was more wrenching than I had expected. This was in no way a reflection on Coudert Brothers, where my work as a senior partner engaged primarily in international law practice was stimulating and absorbing. I was especially happy with my personal relations in the firm, the chance to work with my old acquaintance and colleague Struve Hensel; with Alexis Coudert, whom I had come to know and admire when we had both served on the International Law Committee of the New York State Bar Association some years before; and with Charles Torem, head of Coudert Frères in Paris, whom I had retained on behalf of Xerox several years earlier. Still, it was hard and a little unsettling to return to the relatively narrow concerns of even the largest corporate clients — however intellectually stimulating the issues might be — after almost three years of dealing with matters that involved the vitality, perhaps even the fate, of nations.

Throughout my years in Rochester, I had been active in civic and national causes, and my understanding with the Coudert executive committee was that as a senior partner in the law firm I would continue such participation. As the rest of this book will demonstrate, a large part of my time since 1969 has been allocated to government service and to policy-oriented private organizations, but most of it has gone to the practice of law and to service on corporate and educational boards. I was brought up in a tradition of the bar that held that it was unseemly self-promotion for lawyers to discuss publicly the magnitude of the interests they represented, or even to list the

names of their clients. The Supreme Court has since ruled that the
canons of ethics that forbid advertising violate the First Amendment, and I have no quarrel with the Court's decision. That an activity is permissible does not make it desirable, however, and I feel I
would impinge upon the necessary trust between attorney and client if I were to describe in the context of personal memoirs the work
I have done as a lawyer for particular clients.

Similarly, I feel that a board member serves in a context of confi-
dentiality. Since my return to private practice I have served on four
corporate boards — Marine Midland Bank, Mutual Life Insurance
of New York, Pan American World Airways, and Time, Inc. All
four had to make policy decisions of great import to the enterprise
during my time as board member, and I worked hard on my boards.
I am or have been on the executive committee of all four boards, and
I have chaired the audit committee and the nominating committee
on several of them. I believe you should not accept appointment to a
board unless you are ready to make a commitment to be conscien-
tious in attendance and participation, to read all the necessary material and remain alert to developments that may affect the company. I
think most board members these days agree with me: we have gone
far beyond the point where a man went on a board of directors because he was a friend of the chairman and found the meetings a
pleasant way to spend an hour before going to lunch and discussing
one's golf score. The chairmen agree, too, sometimes a touch reluctantly. I asked one of them recently whether he regarded the board
as a burden he had to bear. "Not really," he replied. "But I do have
to spend so much time preparing for board meetings that it's a
chore." I said, "That's the best thing we do for you."

Among the cherished souvenirs on the walls of my office is a
scroll presented to me by the board of Time, Inc., on the occasion of
my recent retirement from that board. "Frequently," it reads, "you
have asked 'have you thought about?', almost always on matters that
needed more thought." I am proud of my contributions to the deliberations of these boards, but I feel that both the deliberations and
the contributions are matters to be kept under seal.

During these years I have also been a trustee of my alma mater,
Hamilton College (from which I hold an honorary degree that gave
me special satisfaction, for it was, I am told, the first time Hamilton
had ever made such an award to an active trustee), and of two great
universities, Cornell and Johns Hopkins. (Earlier I had also served
on the board of the University of Rochester.) Here, too, difficult

decisions had to be taken during my watch, on the board level. I did not join these boards for reasons of prestige or to help rubber-stamp the actions of an academic administration. As a trustee, I meet with students and faculty as well as with administrators. I serve on working committees, and at board meetings I try to ask the right — if difficult — questions.

Moreover, I have a point of view that has not always been popular. I believe that universities have to take responsibility for the education of their students, whether or not the students or even the faculty think so. The science courses I took because Hamilton forced me to do so have stood me in good stead, and I think the scientists of my generation have been better at their work because their colleges made them study languages. Once, in the 1960s, a member of the faculty at one of the universities where I serve on the board explained to me with patient condescension that he and his colleagues could no longer tell their students what they should study, because the world had changed so much that the students' opinions about the proper curriculum for higher education were as valid as those of the professors. I suggested to him that he and those who agreed with him should immediately resign their professorships because they had declared themselves incompetent. Still, it seems to me that the issues the universities have had to resolve and the options they considered should be brought to public attention only — if at all — by the people who were on the firing line every day, the presidents and deans who have had to live with the decisions as no board member did. I am especially reluctant to parade my contributions to these debates, because I had opportunities to take a place on the firing line — three universities flattered me with invitations to become their president — and I declined.

I was chairman of the Jewish Theological Seminary of America for several of those years, honored by the chance to work with the erudite and saintly (but also amusing) Rabbi Louis Finkelstein and then with his gifted successor, Dr. Gerson Cohen. For a few years I was chairman of the executive board of the American Jewish Committee. When the campuses erupted after Nixon sent U.S. troops to Cambodia, the American Council on Education, the association of the nation's colleges and universities, asked me to chair a National Commission on Campus Tensions, including students, psychologists, and politicians as well as university faculty and administration. This was a distinguished group. Among our members were Whitney Young and Bill Moyers and the presidents or chancellors of several great universities: Kingman Brewster of Yale, Robben Fleming of Michigan, Vivian Henderson of Clark College, Charles E. Young of UCLA, and Alexander Heard of Vanderbilt. Our report was accepted across a wide spectrum of political opinion, although it clearly tagged the Vietnam War as the root cause of disturbance, and blamed many of the most serious student riots on provocation by the government. (We did not contend that the war was the *only* cause: the colleges had been unresponsive to their students in many ways, and too many of their students were not ready to accept the disciplines of higher education. The riots on campus were also symptomatic of greater problems outside. Clark Kerr, former president of the statewide University of California system, noted that the colleges were like the canaries coal miners had kept on their helmets as a test for leaking methane: if the canaries keeled over, the place was dangerous.)

Among those who took an interest in our report was President Nixon, who invited me to the White House to discuss it with him. I found him ill-at-ease and remarkably insecure. He had obviously been briefed on me, and went out of his way to make comments like "You know, I went to Whittier College, not as good as Hamilton, but a good school" and "I know you went to Cornell Law School with Bill Rogers." I remember thinking to myself that this was an incredible experience: the President of the United States was working to impress *me*.

I also served on the board of the American Red Cross, and I continued my involvement with the International Executive Service Corps, a privately sponsored Peace Corps with a business slant, of which I had been cofounder (with David Rockefeller) in 1964. I was also a member of Nelson Rockefeller's Commission on Critical Choices for Americans, and I still believe this distinguished bipartisan group of leaders from various walks of life might have provided useful as well as wise guidance if its work had not been aborted by Rockefeller's elevation to the vice-presidency by Gerald Ford — who, incidentally, also had been a member of the commission and a contributor to its deliberations. I spent some time trying to convince congressional leaders that the commission should be made an official body to enable it to complete its work, but on both sides of the aisle Senators and Congressmen saw it as something Rockefeller might use as a launching pad to the presidency, and neither the Democrats nor the prevailing school of Republicans wished to encourage that.

* * *

Three of my activities during the eight years of the Nixon and Ford presidencies were especially time consuming, emotionally satisfying, and, I believe, important: the National Urban Coalition, the Federal City Council (where I continued as president until 1978), and the Commission on United States–Latin American relations.

Since 1964, I had been deeply conscious of the depth and intractability — and of the racial aspects — of America's urban problems. That was the year Rochester exploded in the first of the great riots that were to wrack our cities for the next half-dozen years. The episode began when the police brought dogs into a black neighborhood to search for a young criminal, and ended some days later with Joseph Avenue a wreck of looted and burned shops, and the National Guard stationed all over the city. Joe Wilson and I were astonished, for we had seen a contented (others said "smug") Rochester, a cheerful city of well-paid, skilled workers who did interesting jobs for well-meaning employers like Eastman Kodak and ourselves. We thought the people of Rochester were lucky, and knew it, and felt grateful to be living there. We had not paid attention to the fact that Rochester was also home to a growing black underclass who did not participate in the city's prosperity or in the amenities it offered. The riot was a terrible shock to the entire white leadership of Rochester.

Toni and I had been friendly with Mayor Peter Barry since 1958, when as head of the Chamber of Commerce I had been chairman of a small group that went to France for ceremonies through which Rochester was officially "twinned" with the city of Rennes. We had then proceeded to Israel together in a group that also included the president of the University of Rochester, Cornelis W. de Kiewiet, and Paul Miller, the chairman of the Gannett newspaper chain, which was then based in Rochester. When the riots came, Barry asked me to join a committee he formed to study the reasons and remedies for the city's racial tensions. Xerox as an employer could help a little. We were expanding our work force, and the union could agree without discomfort to a special training program to prepare the residents of what we learned to call "the ghetto" for the skilled jobs in our factories. I learned in the committee, however, that the problem was far deeper than any solutions the city's employers could find, and that the ills of the ghetto could not be cured without the participation of the victims.

Having made that rather courageous analysis, our committee summoned the "agitator" Saul Alinsky to organize the poor black

people of Rochester. I had recently been President of the Chamber
of Commerce, and I arranged a lunch for him with the city's leading
businessmen. He denounced Eastman Kodak; he was profane and
obscene; he was brilliant, irascible, and infuriating; he praised the
Black Muslims for instilling self-discipline; he said all the things we
didn't want to hear. But we could also see — most of us could
see — that he had a wise sensitivity to the lives of the people in our
slums, and we funded him to come make us uncomfortable.

This sort of thing takes time, and before Alinsky and his disciples
could mount their challenge to the city's white leadership I was off
in Washington dealing with the international side of underdevelop-
ment. While I worked on programs to relieve Latin American poverty, I was always conscious of eerie similarities between what I saw
in the horrible shantytowns of the Latin countries and what had
been revealed to me in the slums of Rochester. Among those who
knew of my continuing concern about our cities was John W.
Gardner, former head of the Carnegie Corporation who had been
Secretary of Health, Education, and Welfare in the Johnson cabinet
and had left to form an Urban Coalition Action Council, which became the National Urban Coalition.[1]

The name was to some extent misleading, for the essence of the
urban coalition movement was local rather than national. Its philos-
ophy was an insistence that we are all, really and truly, in the same
boat — rich and poor, black and white, young and old — and that
the agony of our cities cannot be ended without the best efforts of
all. Hunger and wretched housing, unemployment and dead-end
jobs, bad education, inadequate public transportation, discrimination in the provision of police, fire, and sanitation services — these
were not problems someone could solve with the passage of a few
resolutions or even the adoption of some good ideas. The chairman
of the board, the shop steward, the black pastor, the consumer advocate, the police sergeant, the city council member, the school
principal, the unelected leader of the people who live in the housing
project — all have a contribution to make, and programs developed
without their contribution are likely to fail, however well inten-
tioned or well funded.

---

[1] I had known Gardner for some years, and had been at the meeting at which Johnson first
suggested to Gardner that he join the administration. Gardner had said no. I told him, "You'd
better prepare to go to Washington, because it sounds to me as though the President really
wants you."

The force that drove the coalitions at the start was, of course, the riots themselves, the warnings of "a long hot summer" ahead. Businessmen were forced to understand that plans for their companies were flawed at the foundation if the cities where they operated were to go up in flames at irregular intervals for reasons the leaders of those cities did not understand or even recognize. By the same token, the responsible and even the irresponsible leaders of the black community knew full well that whatever the visceral satisfactions of revolt, the losers in each of these episodes were the people who lived in the shattered neighborhoods,who paid a fearful price for the temporary palliatives of a little attention, a little funding, a little improvement of the conditions that had sparked the riot. When the cities were under threat, it was not hard to persuade their leaders that the potential antagonists should, as Lyndon Johnson liked to say, reason together. As the threat faded in the 1970s, the drive to cooperation diminished. I think it was Whitney Young of the Urban League who said to me that what the cities needed was some way to "institutionalize the riots."

What kept the coalitions going beyond the immediate stimulus, however, was something both more trivial and more profound: the fascination of all the participants with the experience of meeting and relating to people so entirely different from their past acquaintance. One of the most active of the urban coalitions was the one in Detroit — called "New Detroit" — where Henry Ford II and Walter Reuther of the UAW, who had got used to each other, found themselves equally appalled and impressed by the firebrands from the black ghetto, their articulate fury, their despair . . . and their dreams. The quality of raw experience of the urban coalition meetings was later caricatured as "radical chic," but not much was radical or chic about the businessmen who squirmed in their chairs listening to these strangers who insisted they were "telling it like it is." Some became immensely defensive, some were moved by their contact with sufferings they had known previously (if at all) only as statistics or as stories in charity appeals, some busied themselves usefully with bits of remedies that were in their power to devise — but few were unmoved. They did not send their assistants or their vice-presidents to the meetings; they came and subjected themselves to tirades from people who were "unfair," whose arguments were "simplistic," whose demands were "impossible" —but who knew whereof they spoke. It was theatre, but much of it was also truth.

The local coalitions needed a national clearinghouse so they could keep in touch with each other and share both successes and failures. And they needed national representation, for much of the money coming into the cities for purposes central to the coalitions' work came from Washington, and a great range of national policies ostensibly without an urban focus — tax codes to highways, energy, environment, health — might have a disproportionate and sometimes deleterious effect on the cities. The National Urban Coalition was of necessity a coalition of coalitions, rather than an organization that controlled its subsidiaries; but it had some local functions, especially in cities like Chicago and Atlanta, where strong mayors who were hostile to "participatory" decision-making prevented the creation of any meaningful coalition. And it performed the necessary function of holding congressional feet to the fire and forcing national attention to urban problems.

Andrew Heiskell, chairman of Time Inc., had been involved with both the New York and the national coalition, and I think it was he who first suggested to Gardner that I might make a suitable replacement when Gardner left in 1970 to start Common Cause. Both came to me, separately and persuasively, and I accepted, but only with conditions. Gardner had been a full-time chairman, and I could not do that; I would need a full-time president to run the organization on a day-to-day basis. They agreed, and chose Jack Vaughan, who had been ambassador to Colombia and director of the Peace Corps. Then they carried the good news to a board meeting — and all hell broke loose. Who was Linowitz? I hadn't been involved in the work of an urban coalition, I was being imposed on the group in a way that violated the ethos of the movement . . . and I wasn't black. Neither was Vaughan. It was blacks who were being victimized in the urban crisis. The national coalition had a black vice-president who was being passed over for the top job — the able Carl Holman, an academic from Atlanta University, a poet, and later a cherished friend. Dr. Kenneth Clark wrote an angry letter to the *Washington Post* denouncing the appointments as a gesture that reinforced the stereotype that blacks weren't capable enough to run national organizations.

I received an invitation — it was, in effect, a summons — to meet with the black leadership at the New York offices of the United Negro College Fund. The group included Whitney Young, Vernon Jordan, Roy Wilkins, and other black leaders, and they were upset. I had never had that sense of bitterness and anger directed at me, and from people most of whom I'd never known. They felt a proprietary interest in this organization. I was an outsider; I had not paid my dues. They proceeded to tell me, often in very strong language, how questionable a choice I was to be chairman of the National Urban Coalition.

I listened dutifully for an hour, and then I got a little angry. I told the group that I had not sought this position. I knew from Gardner and Heiskell that the organization was running down — the senior businessmen had either stopped coming to the meetings or had made the local coalitions a toothless division of the Chamber of Commerce. I felt strongly about improving the relationship among people in this country, and about the need to do something about urban problems. If they felt I didn't know anything about the National Urban Coalition or black problems, I *knew* they didn't know anything about me. I suggested that they give me six months, and we would talk about it again: if they didn't like what I had done, I would be happy to leave. Not long after those six months were up, Vaughan went off to run Senator Fred Harris's campaign for the Democratic nomination for the Presidency, and I promoted Holman to president, which staunched that wound. Eventually, the black leaders and I became good friends.

I remember wondering at the time whether Gardner, although white, had been acceptable because he was not Jewish, and I was unacceptable because I was Jewish. Having been the only Jew in my class at college and very often the first Jew on a corporate or university board, or in a social club, I am sensitive about the subject — but I also know that it does not over time govern what happens. Many blacks find Jews in a controlling posture in their lives — as the storekeepers, teachers, lawyers, and doctors in the ghetto, and, indeed, as leaders in civil rights movements — more often than they find other whites. They resent what they consider a facile identification many Jews feel with "victims of discrimination," because they regard the discrimination against blacks as qualitatively and quantitatively more debilitating than anything the Jews experience. For Jews, who cannot forget history and the Holocaust, this insistence that blacks are always worse off can be disconcerting or worse.

These conflicts were controlled and even hidden in the 1960s and early 1970s, but they emerged, sometimes ferociously, when less-qualified blacks began to displace Jews in higher education and even in some jobs. I have always been on both sides of these issues. The word "quota" troubles me: it's in the genes. And I know that it is unfair to say to black kids, "You don't have to make it; we'll put you through." At the same time, I sympathize with the argument of the black leaders that it is fiction to say that we all start from the same place, and an injustice to ask their young people to compete in what is supposed to be a fair race when their starting line is far behind that provided for others. What I know is needed on both sides is a sympathetic perception of each other's concerns and a gentle care not to give offense. Recently, however, leaders have arisen on both sides who lack this necessary sensitivity. The worst of this was still in the future in 1970, of course, and I had no difficulty looking at the work of the National Urban Coalition in an entirely national perspective. Jew or Gentile, Hispanic or Anglo, black or white, we all had our work to do.

There were three central tasks: revitalizing the local groups, spreading the word of what was working from city to city, and refocusing national attention on our cities, which were increasingly, as I said in a speech, becoming "black, brown, and broke."

To stimulate the local coalitions, I invited a number of their full-time executive directors to join the national board, and I toured the country, seeking especially to bring business participation back up to the levels of a few years before. But in the Nixon days, when, as Carl Holman put it, "we had a President who had declared that the urban crisis was over," the most important work was in Washington itself. I agreed that we could not hope to solve urban problems by "throwing money at them," but in 1971 there was little danger that such an approach would be tried. It was vital to keep before the cabinet and especially the Congress the fact that our decaying cities could not be rescued without intelligent help from the federal government. Exhortation, I knew, would not get us far; other claimants for federal support had more political influence than the National Urban Coalition could muster. But if we gave the Congress a fully developed blueprint, we would at least win their attention, and if we could generate a program that commanded the support of our diversified board, they would have to take us seriously.

With this in mind, we staffed up to create the "CounterBudget," a category-by-category if not line-by-line review of federal spending to show where money could be saved from less-vital programs, and money could be gained from tax reform, to pay for the rescue of our cities. We were not shooting from the hip: every change we suggested was buttressed by expert testimony. I don't know how many generals and admirals our defense panel consulted before submitting its recommendations. It was a first-class piece of work, endorsed in full by a board that included men of diverse views: from David Rockefeller and James Roche, chairman of General Motors, and Hy Romnes, chairman of AT&T, to George Meany, Whitney Young, John Lindsay, and Father Hesburgh of Notre Dame. (We dedicated it to the memory of Walter Reuther, who had been among the strongest supporters of the project on our board and had died while the CounterBudget was in preparation.) The result received not only attention but acclaim over a wide political spectrum. Senator William Proxmire called it "the most important piece of work ever done by a nongovernmental body in dealing with the United States budget." Nervously, the Nixon cabinet members received us and went over our proposals with us, and there were extended hearings in both the House and the Senate. It is probably fair to say that we got more publicity than action, but the CounterBudget was certainly on the minds of the Congressmen who later created the Congressional Budget Office as a countervailing force to the executive branch.

There could be no doubt that the question of race was critical in any effort to deal with our urban problems. In an attempt to revive the concern for race relations that followed upon the riots, we established a new commission headed by Senator Fred Harris of Oklahoma and former New York City Mayor John Lindsay (who had been cochairman with Illinois Governor Otto Koerner of Lyndon Johnson's National Commission on Civil Disorders) to retrace the steps of five years before and report on progress or the lack of it.[2] The report dismayingly demonstrated that little had been achieved in dealing with the root causes of the problem. Again, we garnered a harvest of publicity, but not much action. Still, it was important to the businessmen who were investing their time and effort in the urban coalitions to have this sort of attention. Here and there around the country there were beacons of light, job programs and educational ventures that worked, community relations initiatives that were building bridges of trust nobody on the outside knew about — although they would have learned a great deal quickly

[2] Koerner could not contribute to the new commission because he was in jail, convicted of abusing his office. Carl Holman says that it was an insistence by an Illinois group to which he was speaking that he not make reference to the "Koerner Commission" that led John Gardner to decide that the corruption of American politics was an even more basic national problem than the condition of the cities. He turned over the chair at the National Urban Coalition (but remained on the board) because he felt that the crusade he called Common Cause was a condition precedent to saving the cities.

about the consequences of distrust if such bridges had not been in place. One of my favorites was a radio program started in the Detroit area called "Buzz the Fuzz." It was a call-in show giving people a chance to vent their anger or dissatisfaction directly to the chief of police, and to make suggestions for change in police procedures. Through the cross-fertilization efforts of the national office, we were able to stimulate similar programs in a number of cities.

We were never simply a pressure group with our hands out for public funds. We thought it would be helpful to create a million public-service jobs, partly for training purposes, partly to meet public-sector needs, but we both recognized and acclaimed the genius of private enterprise as the central creator of jobs for Americans. The first role of government, we argued, was to create a climate for growth in the private sector. Prosperity might not lift all the boats, but it was everybody's best chance. Reading and meeting with academics and with coalition participants all over the country, I developed or adopted some pet ideas. A few of these now look rather inappropriate: a year before New York teetered on the edge of bankruptcy, for example, I was arguing that most of our cities, and especially New York, had the power to expand their borrowings and should do so for public-works projects that would create both wealth and jobs. Others have proven out, like urban homesteading — giving poor people decayed and unoccupied houses, instruction in how to fix them up, and credit for parts and skilled labor, with agreement that their "sweat equity" would make them homeowners.

Particularly in the first year, when we were organizing for the CounterBudget and the Lindsay-Harris commission, I was also a fund-raiser for the National Urban Coalition, knocking on the doors of corporations and foundations. McGeorge Bundy at the Ford Foundation was especially generous, and the coalitions owe a great deal to his informed support. When I arrived, the cupboard was bare; when I moved over to a much more inactive role as cochairman in the autumn of 1973, we were quite soundly funded. But most of our cities are still, alas, increasingly black, brown, and broke, and we have not yet mustered the national will to stop the decay.

Not long after I stepped down from the chair of the National Urban Coalition, I took on the presidency of a very different but not unrelated Washington institution, the Federal City Council. Founded in 1954 by Philip Graham, this unique organization has a membership of 175 "trustees," 150 of them leaders of the private sector in this most federally impacted of all cities, the other 25 a selection of key people in the national government — cabinet members; the directors of the Office of Management and Budget, the General Services Administration, the Post Office, the Environmental Protection Agency, and so forth, and the chairmen of the House and Senate committees charged with District of Columbia affairs. (These "federal trustees" were not part of Graham's original group; they came on board when Kennedy took office.) The private-sector trustees are businessmen, professionals, and educators. They all serve as volunteers — indeed, they pay dues to help support the council's work.

A brilliant lawyer who had married into the family that owned the *Washington Post*, Graham saw a capital city run by remote control, with all significant decisions in the hands of a national President and Congress who had other things on their minds. The interests of the residents were often secondary to those of an array of little kings in the federal government. Despite the great growth of the government during the war and postwar years, the city was running down, being drained by suburbs that held out far more in the way of amenities. This was bad for business, and it was business that provided 70 percent of the jobs and much of the vitality of Washington. Graham conceived the Federal City Council as an all but invisible catalyst that would bring the District's businesses and residents into fruitful interaction with the federal authorities. The choice before Washington, he said, was between progress and decay; the Federal City Council would mobilize the forces on the side of progress.

Graham's group cut its first teeth on the urban renewal project in southwest Washington, and over the years extended its scope to education, transportation, housing, water supply, and economic development. In the 1970s a new element entered the equation, when the city achieved partial self-government, with an elected mayor and a city council. But it continued to be true that the most important plans for Washington could be made only with the consent of Congress and the cooperation of the executive departments. And the makeup of the new city government — overwhelmingly black because the residents were overwhelmingly black — meant that sophisticated intermediation between the local authorities and their federal controllers (and between both and the business community) became more essential than ever. On the most rudimentary level, the fact that the federal government had the power to declare prop-

erty exempt from local taxes — and did exempt for one reason or
another roughly half of the city's land — meant that the provision of
amenities by the municipality was a function of congressional appropriation.

From the beginning, the influence of the council radiated from
three focal points: a president whose work was primarily national in
scope and who had significant government experience, a chairman
chosen from the local business community, and a full-time executive
vice-president who pulled the threads together for the part-time officers and the committees that concentrate on specific problems. I
became president in 1974, and served until 1978. My predecessor as
president had been George McGhee, an oil man who had been
Under Secretary of State and ambassador to Germany and Turkey;
my successor was James T. Lynn, a lawyer who had been director
of the Office of Management and Budget and Secretary of Housing
and Urban Development. It was our task to be knowledgeable about
the ways of government, the life cycles of urban neighborhoods, and
the arguments that move businessmen to action. To the extent that
we were effective, of course, much of the credit goes to Kenneth
Sparks, the executive vice-president, who was always there.

A great deal happened on my watch at the Federal City Council.
Most notable was the arrival of limited "home rule" and a true city
government dedicated — not unreasonably — to improving the lot
of the residents who had elected it, sometimes at the expense of the
business interests, and thus the business prospects, of the city. Doc-
trinaire local politicians, heady in the sweet air of freedom, proposed
rent control and consumer protection ordinances, among others,
that could have greatly impeded the economic progress the District
badly needed. And many who had bitterly resented the intervention
of physically present but politically remote federal authorities now
found that with the devolution of power in the city, to councilmanic
districts and even neighborhoods as well as to the new municipal
government, they simply couldn't find out what was going on. Our
small staff at the Federal City Council had to become a source of
detailed information as well as long-range plans. The task was made
more difficult when the White House disbanded its long-established
capital city liaison office, and turned over functions relating to the
city to the national Domestic Policy Council. Fortunately, many
people who had been elected to Washington's new municipal government as firebrands soon realized that there was work to be done
as well as speeches to be made. And as trust and confidence grew,

we were able to draw the teeth from some of the more dangerous legislation being considered by the new city council.

We also had to face the death of certain comfortable assumptions. The Federal City Council had been among the prime movers of Metro, the Washington subway system. In the planning for it, we had assumed an area population of about six million, and a cost of about $3 billion. By the mid-1970s it was clear that the population would be about one-third lower than our estimate, and the costs would double. (To complete the system today will cost over $10 billion.) In the mid-1970s it also became apparent that the supposed steady growth of federal employment would not happen, and that Washington would have to face the business cycle in ways never before contemplated. As inflation eroded the values of rental property, especially that under the threat or reality of rent control, we had to look at support for the private sector in housing the middle class in Washington, in addition to our ongoing programs to help house the poor.

For some years we had recognized the need to work cooperatively with the suburbs in Maryland and Virginia. As we looked at the economic development of the region in the mid-1970s, we realized that we had common interests with Baltimore, and that much of the hope for commercial and industrial progress lay in the corridor between the two cities. I organized a committee that worked with the Greater Baltimore Committee, eventually with success, on the organization of a "common market" group to promote private investment in the region. And we ventured onto the road, which is still being traveled, to exploitation of the city's status as an international as well as a national center, with more than a tenth of its "domestic product" directly traceable to international activities.

We also participated in the horror story of Union Station, where the expenditure of tens of millions of dollars had destroyed the railroad station and created a useless National Visitors Center. The concept may have been viable, but the execution had been execrable. Our study groups helped to save Metro, and made a contribution to the rationalization of the water-supply projects in the Potomac River basin. With help from Rosalynn Carter, who came to some meetings of the Council, we helped persuade the White House to reestablish its District liaison office. And the Federal City Council can surely take some of the credit for the planning that led to the construction of the Convention Center, although it was not until after my time that Congress could be persuaded to get out of the way of that project and let the city proceed on what was in truth its own business.

Among the improvements during my term was a reorganization of the private-sector efforts to help the District. Following the presentation of a report commissioned from Thomas Fletcher, former deputy mayor of the city, who had moved on to the Stanford Research Institute, two research organizations were merged into one more capacious institution; a Community Foundation was created to receive charitable gifts for the benefit of the city; and the tasks of directly promoting the city's commercial and industrial growth were allocated to the Board of Trade, permitting the Federal City Council to specialize in dealing with the various levels of government. I was able to report to the Council with great confidence that the leadership of the Board of Trade was happy to accept the added responsibilities, because my brother R. Robert Linowes, head of his own law firm in Washington and Silver Spring, was then its president. To the extent that there was a power structure in the civic betterment organizations of the national capital, one local wag commented, it played tennis together on the weekends.

Throughout the years between the Johnson and Carter administrations, I maintained my interest and involvement in Latin American affairs. In the first year after my departure from the OAS, I made a number of speeches critical of the Nixon administration's neglect of our neighbors, urging that the government pick up the threads of opportunity — commercial, cultural, and political — that lay all about us. Even after I became absorbed in urban problems, I attended meetings at the Center for Inter-American Relations in New York and maintained my close relations with the Latin ambassadors, who would frequently call to discuss hemispheric developments. Early in 1974, after I had cut back on my involvement with the National Urban Coalition, David Rockefeller came to me with the suggestion that I chair a Commission on United States–Latin American Relations, to be set up under the aegis of the Center in New York.

For once, the reason to seek added attention to this region of the world was not failure but success. At the end of the 1960s and in the early 1970s, Latin America as a whole had actually exceeded the growth targets set in the Alliance for Progress. Although there was no general Common Market, there was an Andean economic community including Bolivia, Chile, Colombia, Ecuador, Peru, and

Venezuela. Brazil in particular was becoming a significant exporter of manufactured products. Literacy had expanded everywhere on the continent, university enrollments had multiplied, and the technocratic-professional cadre was greatly enlarged. The achievement was not universal, but it was widespread. The nations to our south had become in every way less dependent on the United States. The time had come to recognize their growth and strength, and to adjust American policy to a new reality. Indeed, some glimmerings of that need had penetrated the gloom and discouragement of the Watergate-driven administration. At three meetings of Western Hemisphere Foreign Ministers — in Mexico City, Washington, and Atlanta — Secretary of State Henry Kissinger had been unusually forthcoming, at least verbally, and his colleagues had been significantly accommodating.

The twenty-three-member commission I formed and chaired was strongly staffed and included a wide range of opinions. The membership was most distinguished, including four men who had been or would be cabinet members (Michael Blumenthal, Nicholas Katzenbach, Peter Peterson, and Elliot Richardson), six significant academics (Chancellor Alexander Heard of Vanderbilt; Presidents Clifton Wharton of Michigan State, Theodore Hesburgh of Notre Dame, and Arturo Morales-Carrión of the University of Puerto Rico; and Professors Samuel Huntington of Harvard and Harrison Brown of Cal Tech), investment and commercial bankers, businessmen, publishers, and lawyers. The Rockefeller, Ford, and Clark foundations supported the project. We worked for five months and came up with a report that made strong recommendations, yet commanded universal assent from a group that did not start off with much agreement.

Its central statement was that the United States no longer had a "special relationship" with the nations in this hemisphere, and could no longer assert an exclusive and unquestioned right of leadership. Latin America was emerging on the global scene, and the United States should learn to work with the Latins not as clients but as part of the developing world. While maintaining our concern for the observance of human rights, we should establish a policy of nonintervention in the internal affairs of our neighbors, refrain from economic as well as military threats, loosen the quarantine of Cuba, negotiate a new treaty to govern the operations of a Panama Canal that was, after all, part of Panama, and help stabilize commodity prices and open our markets to Latin American products. We should work more closely with the region's multinational organizations — the OAS in political matters and the Inter-American Development Bank in economic affairs. Our private investments in the Latin countries should promote the transfer of modern technology to their industries. "The United States and the nations of Latin America," I wrote in my introduction to the report, "complement each other and need each other."

Some of this was too optimistic. Although the report was well received, and became the basis for a continuing resolution that passed Congress in 1975, it did not produce major changes in U.S.-Latin American relations. Soon the economies to our south began to develop the pathologies that came to such public prominence in 1982. Their growth had become too dependent on borrowed money, especially bank loans. The Andean Common Market lost thrust. Far from becoming an entering wedge for poor-country cartels that would push up the prices of the raw materials needed by the industrial nations, OPEC had become an exploiter of the Third World. Inflation spread through the continent like a disease.

Politically, too, there was much to be troubled about as 1975 wore on into 1976. The Latin involvement in global politics stepped into the sterile swamp of the "New International Economic Order," a series of rhetorical demands on the industrial countries that were obviously satisfying to make but also obviously fruitless. As part of their identification with the formal Third World, many of the Latin governments lined up at the United Nations behind initiatives abhorrent to us — notably the resolution that declared Zionism a form of racism. Military governments were strengthening their grip on the continent, a development not unwelcome to our national security establishment. Our relations with tyrants had grown too cozy at a time when the continent was, as we would later write, "suffering a plague of repression."

In 1976, then, the Commission was reconstituted, and issued a second report that reiterated a number of the 1974 proposals but also broke new ground. It placed greater emphasis on arms limitations and nuclear nonproliferation, the securing of human rights throughout the hemisphere, the role of the World Bank in Latin American economic development, and the need for an American initiative to help stabilize commodity prices. And it stressed the great urgency of negotiating a new Panama Canal treaty.

7

The Panama Canal Treaties

EVEN AT THE VERY beginning, any objective observer would
have had to recognize that Theodore Roosevelt's 1903 treaty with
Panama gave too much to the United States and too little to Panama.
The Americans who lived in the Panama Canal Zone, however,
liked the status and privileges that came with residence in an area
governed by the U.S. military and essentially barred to all
Panamanians except those working for the United States. They had
friends and relatives back home who were happy to help them protect their perquisites. And they had further help from millions of or-
dinary Americans whose history courses had proudly presented the
construction of the Panama Canal as a great American accomplishment, in which Panama had merely provided the place where the
ditch could be dug. By the 1970s the persistence of this unfair treaty
had become a source of festering unrest and disturbance not only
between the United States and Panama but also in American relations with all of Latin America — and in American domestic politics.

For the Panamanians, the arrangements established by and under
the treaty were a source of shame. By the terms of the treaty, the
United States had taken control "as if it were sovereign" over the
canal and a ten-mile-wide zone that cut Panama in two. This foreign
presence in the midst of Panama — U.S. governance of the nation's
only deep-water ports; the PX culture of the zone; the U.S. courts;
the second-class citizenship and reduced wages of the Panamanians

who worked in the Zone — had been a bone in the throat of Panamanians, rich or poor, educated or illiterate, across the political
spectrum. In compensation, the United States paid Panama an annual subsidy of $2.3 million, taken from the toll receipts of the canal.
And by the terms of the treaty, our presence was to last forever: "in
perpetuity."

Negotiations to replace this anachronism had been in progress
since 1964, mostly as the result of the vicious riots around and even
in the Panama Canal Zone in January of that year — the first for-
eign-affairs crisis of the new Johnson administration. These negotiations had in fact produced a viable draft treaty in 1967 — one of
the more cheerful moments of my time as ambassador to the
OAS — but that deal had been aborted by premature and hostile
publicity in both the United States and Panama, and the treaty was
never even signed by the two Presidents who announced the agreement, let alone submitted to their legislatures.

In the early 1970s Panama had moved its dispute with the United
States out of the bilateral focus and onto the world stage. General
Omar Torrijos, chief of the National Guard, the rough, shrewd,
strong man of Panama, in whose hands rested all major domestic
and foreign policy decisions, had successfully maneuvered to get a
meeting of the UN Security Council in Panama City. At that meeting, by prearrangement, a resolution was introduced calling for
unrestricted Panamanian sovereignty throughout the isthmus. It
was gleefully supported by the Communist bloc and vetoed by the
United States, standing alone. (Torrijos sent a menacing message to
UN Ambassador John Scali that if he planned to cast a veto he
would be well advised to do so from the airport, a joke that was not
soon forgotten at the State Department.) By inserting the canal dispute into an East-West context, however, Torrijos had won Henry
Kissinger's attention. The head of the team Lyndon Johnson had
appointed to negotiate with the Panamanians was Robert B. Anderson, a Texas lawyer who had been not only President Eisenhower's
Secretary of the Treasury but his reputed choice to replace Richard
Nixon as his Vice-President in his second term. Nixon knew this,
and, not surprisingly, Anderson had neither access nor influence in
the White House. Nixon accepted Anderson's resignation and in his
place installed Ellsworth Bunker, who had just returned from a six-
year tour of duty as U.S. ambassador to South Vietnam.

William Jorden, a former *New York Times* foreign correspondent who was then on the staff of the National Security Council and later became ambassador to Panama, states in his book *Panama Odyssey* that Bunker was an inspired choice. He was indeed. Already nearing eighty, this tall, erect, canny, courteous Vermonter was a negotiator of vast and successful experience. He had presided over the resolution of the war in Yemen and the withdrawal of Egyptian forces from that country, and had managed the transfer of the western half of New Guinea from Dutch to Indonesian sovereignty. He had also been the U.S. representative handling the immensely difficult negotiations in the Dominican Republic in 1965. And he was a master at handling egocentrics, having started his diplomatic career as Dean Acheson's ambassador to Perón's Argentina. As a result of his tour in Saigon, moreover, Bunker was probably held in higher esteem at the Pentagon than any other American diplomat.

The first fruit of Bunker's labors in Panama was a Statement of Principles to govern the creation of a new canal treaty, signed in early 1974 by Kissinger and Panama's Foreign Minister Juan Antonio Tack. Central to these eight sensible principles were a term of years for the new treaty, to replace the "perpetuity" proclaimed in 1903; Panama's prompt assumption of administrative powers over civilian life in the zone and gradual acquisition of control over the operation of the canal; increased benefits for Panama from the canal tolls ("a just and equitable share"); and the maintenance of American military bases on Panamanian soil to help assure the "protection and defense" of the canal. At Bunker's suggestion, the signing was staged in Panama for the massed television cameras of the Western Hemisphere.

In the 1974 report of our U.S.–Latin America commission, we had hailed this Kissinger-Tack agreement and called for a prompt follow-through to a new treaty. But as often happens with agreements in principle, the words so ceremoniously attested in Panama proved an ambiguous guide when it came to writing a binding document. While Bunker and the Panamanians bickered, Congress took a hand in the negotiations. A Kentucky Republican Congressman named Gene Snyder attached a rider to an appropriations bill for fiscal 1976, prohibiting the expenditure of funds "to negotiate the surrender or relinquishment of United States rights in the Panama Canal Zone." The Senate refused to go along — mostly, William Jorden reports, because Bunker had called some chits and mobilized effective opposition. The House thereupon rejected the conference report because it lacked Snyder's amendment. The best the State Department could get was a softening of the form of the resolution from direct prohibition to a statement of the "sense of Congress." This was better than nothing, but scarcely a portent of success when the time came to submit a treaty.

The idea of a new treaty was not entirely without friends in the House. Congressmen Lee Hamilton of Indiana and David Obey of Wisconsin went to Panama for a long weekend in November 1975 and came back with a statement that "the only sure course to preserve rights in the Canal Zone is to work with the Panamanians to negotiate a new system of relationships." They also warned that "members of Congress should be aware that their comments on the Canal are closely followed and widely reported in the Panamanian press.... To seek to prevent a draft treaty from even being submitted to Congress serves no useful purpose...." In presenting their report, Chairman Thomas E. Morgan of the International Relations Committee was careful to note that their findings "do not necessarily reflect the views of the membership of the full Committee."

Many politicians found that the sanctity of the 1903 treaty could be an emotional cause for large numbers of voters, mostly but by no means exclusively on the right wing. The House that demanded the Snyder restriction, after all, was the very Democratic body elected in the aftermath of Richard Nixon's resignation. In 1976 the Panama Canal "issue" became one of the most important supports for Ronald Reagan's challenge to Gerald Ford for the Republican nomination. Reagan once told me that he had not made the Panama Canal a major issue in his campaign until after he received uproarious approval when he answered a question on the subject by denouncing the Ford administration for its willingness to "surrender" U.S. sovereignty over the Panama Canal Zone. "When it comes to the canal," he said to wild applause — over and over again: it was part of his stump speech in the primary campaign — "we bought it, we paid for it, it's ours, and we should tell Torrijos and company that we are going to keep it." With the tide running against him in Texas, Ford backed away from the established American negotiating position. "The United States," he said, "will never give up its defense rights to the Panama Canal and will never give up its operational rights as far as Panama is concerned."

It was in part because of the damage being done to the negotiations about the future of the canal that I decided to reconvene the Commission on United States–Latin American Relations in 1976. (The other major reasons were the dangers we saw in the Latins' escalating bank debt, and the great abuses of human rights through much of the hemisphere.) In our second report, which was designed to influence the winner of the election, we wrote that "the most urgent issue the new Administration will face in the Western Hemisphere in 1977 is unquestionably the smoldering dispute with Panama." Although the document was not published until December, its contents were known to the actors in the Panama drama some time before. I was not surprised, therefore, when Panama's Foreign Minister, Aquilino Eduardo Boyd, who was in the United States for the meetings of the UN General Assembly, took me aside at a reception the day after the televised Carter-Ford debate on foreign policy.

In response to a question by a reporter, Carter had said that he "would not relinquish practical control of the Panama Canal Zone any time in the foreseeable future." Boyd wanted to know, not unreasonably, what Carter meant by that. I said I was sure it was not as bad as Boyd feared, but I would find someone more authoritative to tell him so. Cyrus Vance was serving the Carter campaign as an adviser on foreign affairs. He was an old friend, and someone who knew about Panama firsthand, having gone down to the zone as Lyndon Johnson's Deputy Secretary of Defense to report on the status of the military after the 1964 riots. I called him to relay Boyd's query. He said he would speak with Stuart Eizenstat, the candidate's sensible and thoughtful guru on various issues. Vance called back to say that Eizenstat wanted me to tell Boyd that statements spoken in the heat of debate in response to a reporter's question should not be taken as determining the policies Carter would follow as President; the Democratic platform plank on Panama had accepted "the principles already agreed upon," and Carter had no intention of repudiating them.

Vance's nomination as Secretary of State was among the earliest of Carter's announcements after his election, and presently I had a call from Cy asking me to come over to the first-floor office at the State Department traditionally occupied by the incoming Secretary. We talked together for several hours about people he thought he might ask to serve with him and about the problems the administration would have to face, and he asked me whether I would be interested in joining the team. I told him my obligations were such that I could not accept a full-time appointment, but I would be interested in a troubleshooting assignment where he thought I might be useful, provided it was understood that I could not abandon my legal practice or my directorships on several corporate boards. Then he said that what he had in mind — and he had already discussed it with the President-elect — was the Panama situation.

During the election campaign, two months before the publication of the second report by our Commission on United States–Latin American Relations, Vance had written a long memorandum to Carter that stressed the need for action on the canal treaties: "The new Administration," he concluded, "must face up to completing the negotiations and carrying the battle to the Congress." In the late November conversation between Carter and Vance that led to Vance's appointment, Carter had, with no great enthusiasm, accepted this approach. It was decided that, as earnest of his intentions, the President would invite Foreign Minister Boyd of Panama to be the first official of a foreign country to meet with him in Washington. Next, the thought was, I would replace Ellsworth Bunker as the head of our delegation to the negotiations.

That I said I could not do. Ellsworth Bunker was a good friend. He had been my predecessor at the Organization of American States, and his guidance had been invaluable to me there. Moreover, he had organized my introduction to a number of Washington institutions and personalities whose acceptance makes it possible for people to function effectively in that unique environment. To take an example not quite so trivial as it sounds, he had arranged my membership in the 1925 F Street Club, a place where a number of the people who run Washington — and some of the people who run the rest of the world — can meet in privacy to sort out what they are doing. (I took Supreme Court Justice Abe Fortas to the F Street Club for lunch soon after I joined, and he asked me how I had gained entry: to the best of his knowledge, Jews had not been members of the F Street Club before. Now there are a number of Jewish members.) I was not willing to be the instrument by which Bunker's thirty years of service to his country would come to an end. In addition, I did not think I could be more effective than he was as our negotiator. If Bunker himself thought I could be helpful, however — if he asked me to join him as co-negotiator of the new treaty — I said I would be willing to accept. A few days before the inauguration, Vance called and said the President had approved naming me as co-negotiator, and I reminded him that it was Bunker's invitation I required.

Three or four days later, I was in a conference at Seven Springs Center outside New York City when I was called out of the meeting for a telephone call from Ellsworth, who asked me to join him. It didn't seem to him in any way unreasonable, he said, that the new President would want his own man in such negotiations, especially if the administration planned to make a strong push for a new treaty. In addition to picking up much of the load, I would symbolize for the Panamanians the President's seriousness in seeking a balm for this long-standing hemispheric irritation. Bunker said he wanted me to become co-negotiator, and he meant it.

This was not quite the end of it, for I had to be sure that Vance and Carter understood — and the White House Office of Ethics approved — my continuing to practice law and serve on corporate boards while representing the President in the canal negotiations. Vance assured me that there was no problem, and reminded me that he himself had served on just those terms as Averell Harriman's deputy in the negotiations with the North Vietnamese in the 1968 Paris talks. Among the useful oddities of American governance is a provision whereby citizens can serve in special ambassadorial assignments under presidential appointment but without Senate confirmation. Since 1968, however, a new law, designed to keep the President from using this provision to get around the Senate's confirmation powers, had restricted such appointments to no more than 180 days a year. This time limit would later play a significant role in the concluding phase of the treaty negotiations. My appointment took effect on February 12, 1977, which meant that August 10 was the last day in that year on which I could officially speak as the President's ambassador.

I had met Jimmy Carter once before, during the course of his campaign for the nomination. Clayton Fritchey, the Washington columnist, had given a sizable dinner party for the candidate at his home. Although Carter was the guest of honor, few people at that time took his candidacy very seriously. During the cocktail hour I found him standing alone, looking around at the Washington establishment whose support he needed so he could run against them. We had an interesting talk. He had, typically, done his homework, and he knew who I was; we talked about the urban situation and

about Latin America, on which I found him surprisingly well informed. He spoke Spanish, he said — and he did, too, with an un-
mistakable Georgia accent — and kept working at the language by
reading a chapter from a Spanish-language Bible every night with
his wife. I found this a charming example of taking a practical benefit from one's spiritual exercises. Later in the evening, when Carter
was table-hopping among the dinner guests and stopped off at my
table, Katharine Graham, publisher of the *Washington Post,* asked
him several penetrating questions about Europe, and he dealt with
them frontally and vigorously. He was articulate, and he had, I
thought, a sophisticated knowledge of world affairs.

Now I saw him in the Oval Office to receive instructions and was
given a considerable mandate. This was Vance's approach, too.
Commenting on Johnson's instructions to him when he was told to
prevent a Turkish invasion of Cyprus in 1967 ("Do what you have
to to stop the war. If you need anything, let me know"), Vance
notes in his memoirs that "nothing can be more helpful than such
instructions and the confidence that they inspire." President Carter
wanted a treaty fast, to get it through the Senate before the 1978
elections were on the Senators' minds. The deal should be, as he
later put it in a personal letter to General Torrijos, "generous, fair
and appropriate." It would have to be acceptable to all the Departments of the U.S. government — Defense, Treasury, and Commerce as well as State — but I could be assured of his help in
bringing the others in line. My mission was to get the job done, and
how Bunker and I did it was our problem.

Even before my appointment was announced, I began work at an
office in the State Department. I brought one assistant with me —
Ambler Moss, who had been my aide ten years earlier in the OAS
post and then had acquired a law degree (at my urging) and joined
me at Coudert Brothers. There he had spent several years, first in
Washington and then in our Brussels office, putting his great lin-
guistic skills and scholarly accomplishments at the service of the
firm's clients in the common market. He would continue at the State
Department after the treaty was negotiated. Later he would serve as
ambassador to Panama (for President Reagan, by reappointment, as
well as for President Carter) before becoming the dean of the Graduate School of International Studies at Miami University in Florida.
Ambler pulled together for me a documentary history of the previous fourteen years of negotiation. Fortunately, the early history of

the canal itself was immediately accessible in David McCullough's splendid book *The Path Between the Seas*. I began a round of meetings with Bunker's negotiating team.

Quite early in the process I worked through in my own mind both the strategy and the tactics I thought we should employ to make these six months different from the preceding thirteen years. The cornerstone of the strategy would be to divide one treaty into two. The first of the two treaties — and we would insist on agreement on this treaty before we would proceed to the second — would deal solely with security questions, the authority of the United States to protect the canal from armed challenge of any kind, in partnership with Panama or, if necessary, unilaterally. We called it the "Neutrality" Treaty, because in form it was proclaimed as a way of protecting universal access to the canal. The second treaty would deal with Panamanian sovereignty in the Canal Zone, money matters, control of the company that operated the canal, the rights and privileges of American citizens working for the canal company (an immensely complicated question, and very emotional for the individuals concerned), and the logistic details of the presence of American forces on Panamanian soil. The two documents had to be separate because the key elements of the first would be permanent, while the second would provide a fixed cutoff date, after which the canal operation would belong to Panama.

Our tactics had to be tripartite. First, we had to get the Defense Department totally committed to the negotiation of a new treaty in a manner that would let us say to the President and Congress that we had fully taken care of the security interests of the United States. Second, we had to win the trust of the Panamanian negotiators and of their leader, who were deeply skeptical of all American claims to be ready to renounce voluntarily a treaty so immensely advantageous to the United States. And in the end, we had to have a document we could sell to sixty-seven U.S. Senators, in the face of public-opinion poll data that showed the overwhelming majority of voters opposed to "giving away" the Panama Canal. To negotiate a treaty and have it fail in the Senate would be the worst of all worlds. It would provoke an uncontrollable explosion of wrath in Panama and poison our discourse with all our neighbors to the south.

Some of the State Department people on Bunker's team had been dealing with Panama matters for a decade or more. Suggested proposals to the Panamanians on security matters had been transmitted

back and forth between the State and Defense departments over
and over again. Generally, they were returned from Defense, after
long delays while the Pentagon bureaucracy spun its wheels,
with amendments and reservations much longer and more detailed
than the proposals themselves — and, of course, much less acceptable to Panama. The way to deal with the Panamanians, it seemed
to me, was to isolate the things that were vitally important to them
but not to us — control of Ancón Hill, for example, the highest
spot on the isthmus — and yield there, while requesting their cooperation in some areas that we cared about much more than they
did. In that way, fundamental trust might be constructed, piece
by piece.

As I worked through the material, I would wake up in the middle
of the night obsessed with an idea. Then I would go to the next
day's meeting full of enthusiasm, and a bored voice from some member of the team would say, "Nineteen seventy-one, we tried that";
or "We brought that up in nineteen sixty-nine"; or "That was tried
six years ago, it's old hat." There was frustration and weariness in
their voices. They clearly felt that the Panamanians did not really
want a deal and that the canal issue was too useful to the local politi-
cos to be sacrificed at the altar of national interest. Moreover, the
old-timers patiently explained, you couldn't win: any concession
you made to the Panamanian negotiators they simply "banked," accepting it as their due, and then the negotiations would have to start
from there. The Defense Department was not seeking a deal, either.
They liked the 1903 treaty, and their representative on the negotiating team, Lieutenant General Welborn ("Tom") Dolvin, although
charming, capable, and full of goodwill, was bound by rigid instructions to hold his ground.

Both Ellsworth and I knew this negative approach was no longer
realistic. There had been one crucial change in the chemistry: we
now had a President who was truly insistent on getting a treaty, and
was prepared to pay a political price for it. We went together to the
Defense Department to see Secretary Harold Brown (a renowned
physicist and former president of Cal Tech) and General George
Brown, the bomber pilot who had become chairman of the Joint
Chiefs of Staff. In George Brown we almost had an ally; while still
chief of the Air Force, he had visited Panama and met Torrijos, and
the two men had hit it off, soldier to soldier.

Bunker and I had armed ourselves with half a dozen possible formulations of a treaty clause that would guarantee American rights to defend the canal, drawn to our order by the Office of the Legal Adviser at the State Department. I put them all on the table for the Secretary and the Chairman of the Joint Chiefs of Staff. They could take any of them — or, indeed, write their own: "I would welcome your language," I said — and we would see to it that precisely those words appeared in the Neutrality Treaty. The two Browns chose one of the formulations and rewrote it from two sentences to one. As it appeared in the final document, this "Brown-Brown" sentence read, "The United States of America and the Republic of Panama agree to maintain the regime of neutrality established in this Treaty, which shall be maintained in order that the Canal shall remain permanently neutral, notwithstanding the termination of any other treaties entered into by the two Contracting Parties." If we could sell this sentence to the Panamanians — and it would be a hard sell, for it put us back in the world of "perpetuities," which Panama considered one of the most poisonous aspects of the original document — the Defense Department was committed to support a new treaty.

There remained the question to which no answer could possibly be found in Washington: did Torrijos really *want* a new treaty, or did he want a crusade? That was the first thing Carter had to know: was Panama ready to negotiate a treaty he could present to the Senate and the American public? Bunker and I and ten associates flew to Panama City on February 13 to find out.

Rarely have I had such a discouraging experience as those first ten days in Panama. We were given a reception at the airport, where our host was Nicolás González-Revilla, the new foreign minister. Boyd had been removed from office upon his return from Washington. This was a signal of uncertain portent. Boyd had been a fiery spokesman for anti-American resolutions at the United Nations before his appointment, whereas González-Revilla, who was quite young, had been ambassador to the United States and a sympathetic figure. On the other hand, Carter had just made an investment of time and attention in Boyd, and their meeting had gone well. From the reception we were flown directly to Contadora, a lovely island in the Pacific that was being developed as a resort community, and lodged on the top floors of a new hotel built on land owned by Gabriel Lewis Galindo, who would soon become Panama's ambassador to the United States. There was a casino on the ground floor, and there were tennis courts, beautiful beaches, and sailboats — all one might wish for a tropical vacation. There was a conference room, too, but we didn't make much use of it. And I had not come to Panama for a vacation.

The first day after our arrival was declared by our hosts a day of relaxation and recreation. The second day there was a brief formal meeting with the senior member of the Panamanian negotiating team, Rómulo Escobar Bethancourt, a sharp, fifty-year-old lawyer and former rector of the University of Panama, and a man long associated with left-wing causes (he had been a member of the Communist party in his youth); and with Edwin Fábrega, an architect who had also been rector of the university and was known to be a close friend of General Torrijos. Escobar spoke no English; Bunker and I spoke little Spanish. Much of the meeting dealt with arrangements for translation and interpretation. That afternoon we met with the larger Panamanian team, and Bunker made a presentation of the American position on what we considered the three crucial questions: the neutrality of the canal, the duration of the new treaty, and the defense of the canal during the new treaty and after its expiration. He also handed over a written statement of U.S. views on a large number of other issues.

We had not come, of course, to negotiate with ourselves, and Bunker's statement was in large part a restatement of positions taken in previous meetings. There had to be some proof of new intentions, however, and that was provided by a concession on the duration of the treaty. The Ford administration had talked in terms of at least forty years, and we offered an expiration date in the year 2000. Otherwise, it was what the Panamanians had heard before, and for some reason they had expected much more; they didn't like it. Moreover, a personal letter from Carter to Torrijos, which they had been told to expect, had not yet arrived, for reasons nobody ever discovered. The Panamanians took notes on Bunker's statement and pocketed the written document, said coldly that they would consider it, and agreed to another meeting at four o'clock the next afternoon.

That meeting did not start until six, because the Panama delegation was late. And when it arrived, we found it had come to fight, not to bargain. A furious Torrijos had sent a very capable young Panamanian lawyer, a graduate of Yale Law School, to play bravo and deliver — in English — a denunciation of the United States, its exploitation of the Third World (especially Panama), its perfidious bargaining tactics, and its bad manners. Bunker was a man of great patience, stiff posture, and few words, who intervened rarely in the sessions and only when he had something important to say. On this occasion, he let his irritation show, feigning deafness to give him an excuse to interrupt the bravo's tirade. At the end, he said that he would not listen to such an "attack on my country," and led our team out onto the terrace. Some of the group felt we should simply walk out and go home, but Bunker and I thought that was not what the President expected of us. Now that the Panamanians had got this diatribe off their chests, it might be possible to start serious negotiations in small groups and private meetings if not in formal sessions.

When we returned to the conference room, Bunker suggested that the Panamanians look again at the document he had offered the day before, and at some new material he now supplied, and make their counterproposals. I urged them to remember that we did not have, and the President did not have, plenipotentiary powers. What we could offer was constrained by our judgment of what the Senate would accept. They should study our proposals seriously, as ideas put forward by people who wanted to find a solution. We would try to find a way to meet their needs, but they had to consider ours. Escobar's native courtesy now responded. Having put on his show, the aggressive lawyer had returned to Panama City while we caucused on the terrace — and we agreed on another meeting. Then that meeting was postponed, by the Panamanians, with the solicitous thought that both sides needed time to ponder what had just happened. Obviously, we were on the island to hold still there, and they would come when it suited their convenience, with whoever felt like coming. I felt it was patronizing. Then, two days later, we were told there would be a meeting, informal, just Escobar and Fábrega, Bunker and me, and the translators. Nothing was accomplished, but Escobar admitted that the United States was indeed serious in its desire to reach an agreement. That could have been seen, although I did not see it at the time, as reason for the beginning of hope.

It was now the weekend, and the rhythm of these negotiations had always been such that no work was done on weekends. Bunker went sailing in a boat the Panamanians put at his disposal when he came to Contadora. Ambler Moss and I went walking on the beaches, permitting me to manage my irritation in the company of a friend. Escobar, it later developed, went off with Torrijos to Colombia for the carnival celebrations, and when the time came for the Monday session he was still there. For me, this was the low point of the negotiations, for it argued that the Panamanians were not serious about arriving at a new treaty — certainly not in the time frame of my six-month tour of duty.

To the next meeting, at which they presented their counterproposals, they sent Fernando Eléta, a very charming man at the center of Panama's society. He bred racehorses and owned the nation's most successful television channel, and was also an old friend of mine from the days when I was OAS ambassador and he was Panama's foreign minister. He joined Escobar in listing what was to us an incredible series of demands for the new treaty. I listened and said I was "shocked," and could see no point in prolonging our meetings; we would go back to Washington and report to the President. The word "shocked" amused the Panamanians and kept recurring in later months: I would start a response to a bargaining point they had made by saying, "Frankly, I must admit that I am . . ." and Escobar would lean forward and supply the word "shocked," and we would all laugh. As this meeting ended, Escobar called me aside and asked me to join him and an interpreter for breakfast the next morning before we left Contadora for the airport. This was not an occasion for substantive discussion, but Escobar ended the meeting by saying, with a confidential air, "You must not be so disappointed; you must have patience." And this word of wisdom enabled us to say to Carter that while the sessions in Contadora had gone badly there was at least a chance that Panama was simply testing the new men in and from Washington, and we should try again.

Next time, we met privately — no announcements, no communiqués, no press. We set it up for a mid-March Saturday in New York, but that turned out to be the day of a snowstorm that closed the New York airports, and the meeting was held in Washington at the residence of the Panamanian ambassador. The building had been vacant for a month (Lewis had not yet been appointed), and it was bitterly cold. Bunker and I kept our overcoats on for the morning session, and the atmosphere of the negotiations was not much warmer. The young lawyer who had uttered Torrijo's diatribe was there, although he didn't say much, and the one addition to their team, Aristide Royo, the bright young minister of education, was an unknown quantity even to the Panama experts on our team.

Yet it could be argued that in this March meeting both sides made their important points. Thereafter, the Panamanian negotiators, I think, understood that the United States would require agreement on a security treaty before anything else could be negotiated. They retreated occasionally from that understanding, because Torrijos had vowed he would not go that route. We were asking them to trust us to a remarkable degree, because the slightest hint in the free press of Panama that the government had given way on this issue before the others were resolved could have provoked an all but unmanageable uproar. Meanwhile, Ellsworth and I had to put our trust in a number of Senators, not all of them known for reticence. We were committed to consulting with the leaders and some of the more interested followers as the negotiations proceeded, and a leak from the Senate would have been devastating. Let the cynics note that despite the passions raised by the canal issue, the dozens of Senators who knew our strategy played the game by our rules until the very last days.

By the end of the March meetings, Bunker and I understood that we were not offering Panama enough. We were led to that understanding partly by Bill Jorden, our informed and capable ambassador to Panama, who sat in on these March negotiations and on occasion acted — it is one of the roles of an ambassador in such circumstances — as an advocate for his hosts. Escobar, although emotional and florid, was an effective spokesman. Bunker and I were constantly impressed with his ability to deliver an organized and logical oration for as long as an hour without consulting notes or documents. His colleague Royo, young, handsome, and sharp, a good lawyer with ambitions that were in fact to be realized (for Torrijos later made him President of Panama), proved to be a man well informed on what his principal really needed, and he had a sense of humor, too. (His formal status was as co-negotiator: if we had co-negotiators, Panama would have co-negotiators, too.) We were, Escobar and Royo pointed out, offering an end to the juridically separate canal zone — but what our military demanded in terms of the control of "Lands and Waters" for the American military presence and operation of the canal boiled down to a continuing zone not that much smaller than what we had. If the civilian employees of the Panama Canal Company got the same extraterritorial rights that American military personnel had in the standard Status of Forces Agreement we require wherever Americans are stationed, Panamanian authority would be of little account. If Panama was to take seriously our need for security, we had to take seriously their need for sovereignty.

Still, the immediate reaction to the March meeting, on both sides, was that it had been a failure, and that a great deal of further preparatory work would have to be done before the negotiators tried again. During the month of April, both sides restated positions through normal and informal diplomatic channels. Torrijos returned to his campaign to bring international pressure on the United States, and unwisely chose Libya's Muammar Qaddafi as his instrument, visiting Tripoli and posturing with the foreign leader whom American professional and popular opinion considered one of the least trustworthy in the world. The love feast with Qaddafi roused the Jewish community in the United States against Torrijos. This would lead later to charges of anti-Semitism, which were especially upsetting to Torrijos because his wife was Jewish and the small but influential Jewish community of Panama had been among his earliest and strongest supporters. Nevertheless, the feeling on both sides was that we had to try again. Torrijos filled his vacant ambassador's slot in Washington as a gesture of goodwill, and added his friends Fábrega and Rory González, one of his close companions, to the negotiating team. González was a bluff, blunt man of no great diplomatic grace, but he spoke good English and had a son in an American boarding school; Torrijos must have felt we could relate more easily to this representative than to some of his professionals.

The new sessions began on May 9 and ran for more than two months, with only occasional interruptions. By the traditions of the negotiations, their location should have alternated between Panama and the United States, but I was not going to risk Contadora again — and I had a good reason to insist on remaining in Washington: I had eye troubles that threatened to lead to a detached retina, and my doctor wanted me to stay near him and his hospital, just in case. So we started in the Panamanian embassy, which was, as Escobar stressed in his opening statement, Panamanian soil. When it became clear that these meetings might make significant progress, however, we moved to the businesslike conference room of the Deputy Secretary of State, where there were simultaneous translation facilities. With Ellsworth's agreement, I presided over every session, day after day.

Some repetition goes with the territory in these things. Positions are stated and restated and restated with increasing amounts of irritation, anger, and disappointment when the other side refuses to accept — seems to refuse even to consider — your arguments. Sometimes the anger is real, sometimes it is posturing, and I had to learn the signs that distinguished the two. Bunker sat at the table immobile, and I tried to do the same. Escobar was jiggling all the time, revealing his impatience, and I wouldn't give him the satisfaction of revealing mine. But it was important to keep a good humor, to know when to make the wisecrack that would get everyone to laugh.

Ellsworth and I shared a suite at the State Department, down the hall from the conference room, and we met every day before the session with the Panamanians. We talked over what had come in overnight, reports from our embassy in Panama City, answers from the staff to questions we had assigned the night before, usually investigations of the factual basis for arguments the Panamanians had advanced at the previous meeting. We would get to the conference room ten or fifteen minutes ahead of the Panamanians, make sure the interpreters were in the booths, and drink the first cup of coffee. The spirit in which we approached a day's sessions would, inevitably, be a function of what had happened the day before. Some meetings were tense, difficult, even hostile, leaving us wrung out at their conclusion and still anxious the next day. Escobar often felt compelled to make a speech at the end. He was a powerful and eloquent fellow, and we knew he had been speaking to Torrijos. The conclusion of such a speech was usually a statement that the Panamanian side saw no point in coming back to the negotiations, to which we would reply that we thought both sides should think over what had happened, and see whether we could do better tomorrow.

We were being tested, of course — we knew that. And we were testing them. As in any negotiation, you try this out, you try that out, and after a while you become more sensitive. You begin to listen for what the people on the other side don't say as well as what they do say; you get a sense of the significance of their gestures, especially, perhaps, their signs and gestures to each other. As time went on, we went into the conference room with an increased sense of anticipation that something of value could come out of it.

A few of the problems could be finessed with language. We got away from the hated word "perpetuity," for example, by substituting the word "permanent." This happened at the negotiating table during the wrangles over the first treaty. I had said finally and flatly that there was no hope of pushing a treaty through the Senate unless it gave the United States an enduring right to protect the canal and its neutrality, and they had said that their first and unchangeable mission was to rid Panama of the incubus of "perpetuity." All I could do was reiterate our need for "something lasting." I added the word "permanent." Suddenly, Escobar and Royo looked at each other, and Escobar nodded: *"Permanente"* — that, for some reason, was a word they could live with.

For a long time they questioned whether we were really leveling with them: it was a surprise to them that the President of the United States could not simply get something through the Senate, and they needed some time to accept the fact that we meant it. When Lewis came as ambassador, he was a big help. He was in and out of the White House frequently. The President liked him, and found it easier to relate to someone who was a businessman rather than a diplomat. Lewis could convince Torrijos that Carter was serious. Torrijos had developed a theory that because he and Carter were both farmers, they understood the world the same way. And it was Torrijos himself, of course, who made the decision that the security treaty could be dealt with and agreed upon at the top of the agenda.

That decision was expressed to us in the most careful, basis-for-discussion way, because the Panamanians wanted to have a grip on what we would really give on the sovereignty issues before they took the step. I called Clifford Alexander, Secretary of the Army, a lawyer who had been a friend before he went into government service, and told him that unless the Pentagon softened its stance on several specific questions relating to "Land and Waters," the negotiations were likely to abort. Alexander knew the issues well; the Secretary of the Army was *ex officio* the president of the Panama Canal Company and a member of the commission that ran the zone. We made an appointment to meet the next morning.

Bunker and I went to the Pentagon with a list of the things we thought the Panamanians needed and ought to have, because we had been assured that the United States could carry out its security responsibilities without them. The most important was control of the two deep-water ports and the railroad connecting them; the most symbolic was authority over Ancón Hill, the highest point in Panama, with nothing more than a lease to the United States of the administrative offices, the hospital, and the schools we had built on its slopes. (Ellsworth and I broke the tension in one meeting devoted to Ancón Hill by solemnly telling the Panamanians that they could have it if they would rename it Bunker Hill.) The President wanted a treaty; these were the things that were holding it up. The Brown-Brown formula for meeting America's security needs would work without them. Would the Army, which basically controlled the zone, approve our offering them to Panama in return for the security guarantee that was all the Secretary of Defense and the Chairman of the Joint Chiefs of Staff said we needed? Alexander said he would get back to us; I said we had to have word that same day. The next meeting with the Panamanians was scheduled for three o'clock. We waited for Alexander's call while the others assembled in the conference room, and just before three the call came. The Army would go along.

Even after that meeting, it took a week's work in the conference room, but on May 26, with no publicity whatsoever, the two delegations agreed on the principles that would inform the "Neutrality" Treaty. I called Carter, and for the first time told him that I thought there might be a deal. For the remaining weeks of the negotiations — and there were six of them — the President involved himself personally. I saw him several times a week, occasionally with Bunker but more often just the two of us, a few times with members of the White House staff. We talked about organizing the campaign that would be necessary in the country and in the Senate to win approval of the treaties, we talked about the policy problems related to eliminating the special privileges of the Americans living in what had been the zone, we talked about the economic issues the Panamanians raised once the security question was off the table, and we discussed the details of the two treaties.

One had to be careful in working with President Carter not to let the conversation be dominated by details, for he seemed to feel that he had to know them in order to be truly in command. He *clutched* for information. I remember one meeting when he asked, almost out of the blue, what tonnage of U.S. shipping had transited the canal the year before. There was only one correct answer to such a question, and that was, "Mr. President, I don't know." I gave that answer, though, as it happened, I did know. But to give the President the number would have been the first step down an endless path. The next question would have been about the value of the tonnage, then its division among the various commodities and manufactured goods that were shipped through the isthmus, and the use of the canal by other nations, and so forth.

The President knew he had this tendency, if only because the press was always criticizing him for taking too much time with details. As he later said to a meeting at the Woodrow Wilson Center, some years after leaving the presidency: "That was my life, my training. I am an engineer by training." He did not mind when someone he trusted led him away from the details to the larger question that had to be decided. At these meetings on Panama, Carter and I became — and remain — friends. He gave me authority, and I used it. Only twice, at the very end, did Ellsworth and I feel it necessary to come to him for a decision.

Having taken care of military security on the one side and pride on the other, the negotiations now proceeded to economic questions, and quickly ran aground. In the first few days, the Panamanians made it clear that they would expect a large compensation from the United States for all the years they had received virtually no share in the benefits the United States derived from the use of "their" canal — and then a large annual subvention for the duration of the treaty, as ground rent for the facilities the U.S. would continue to control. They had been building this case for a long time, and they presented it with passion.

They pointed out that tolls for transit of the canal had always been set low, at a level just sufficient to pay running expenses plus the interest on the bonds sold to build it. This represented an enormous subsidy to U.S. and other shipping, which Panama in effect had been forced to pay; it should now be returned, they argued, with interest. Imports to and exports from the zone had been free of Panamanian tariffs and export duties, at immense cost to the Panamanian government. Residents of the zone paid neither sales tax nor income tax to Panama. Panamanians had been forbidden to open shops and hotels inside the zone, greatly limiting the economic benefit the nation could have received from the presence of the canal. All this injustice would now have to be remedied, with cash. And in the years to come, Panama should receive its "just" share of the money shippers saved because they did not have to circle the continent or use land routes to move merchandise from one ocean to the other.

In reply, I told the Panamanians that it was wholly unrealistic to think that Congress would appropriate American taxpayers' money for the purpose of persuading the Panamanians to take away "our" canal. We brushed their arguments aside, and they ignored ours. During this preliminary bout, no figures were put on the table.

Memorial Day weekend arrived. The Panamanians went off to visit a U.S. boarding school for the graduation of the son of one of the delegates, and I looked forward to some time with my family. On Sunday, however, I had a call from Ambassador Lewis. Escobar was insisting that he and I have lunch together — alone, no staff, no interpreters — on the following day. We met at the Mayflower Hotel and went into the restaurant. This was the first time Escobar had ever tried to speak English with me, and he was clearly nervous about it. He had a martini, and then another martini, and then another.

Then, in a stumbling, not wholly comprehensible way, he laid on the table the dollars and cents of what the Panamanians expected to get. Their economists and statisticians, he said, had worked out that what the United States *really* owed Panama for this three-quarters of a century of occupation was more than $6 billion. But they recognized that this figure was unrealistic and because of their desire to conclude the treaty quickly and not make too much trouble for President Carter, they would settle for one billion, twenty million. Plus, he added as an afterthought, an annual payment of three hundred million. Dollars. It was a bad lunch. I told him — he seemed to have even more trouble understanding me than I had understanding him — that the *only* money Panama could hope for would be a return from increased tolls, which our economic forecasters would help us set at a level that assured Panama a fair and appropriate income. But it was absolutely impossible to ask Congress in these circumstances to appropriate money to be given to Panama.

The next weeks became a tangle of bad vibrations. The Panamanians went home to report to Torrijos and the Council of State, and came back with a raft of changes to be made in the neutrality agreement we had reached on May 26. "The U.S. negotiators," Ambassador Jorden writes in his book, "had not reckoned with the Panamanians' proclivity to change their minds, and the equal tendency to become ensnarled in words and footnotes." We certainly hadn't: nobody would willingly devote weeks of his time to negotiations if he had to reckon with the other parties' proclivity to change their minds after an agreement was reached. The agreement was still secret, and the Panamanians could go back on it, but Bunker and I, having told Vance and Carter that we thought we had a deal, were now forced to return and say, "Maybe not."

Jack Anderson now weighed in with a column saying that Torrijos had made an alliance with Qaddafi and Panama would become an outpost of Arab influence and anti-Semitism in the Western Hemisphere. The political attaché in the U.S. embassy in Panama met with opposition political leaders, as was his job, and a report went back to Torrijos that he had said the only thing holding up a treaty was Torrijos's reluctance to sign off and deprive himself of the political issue. The report was false, but that scarcely mattered. In Panama City, a private in the U.S. Army — not an American citizen, but a mentally unstable Dominican who was accelerating his citizenship application by serving in the Army — got drunk and shot a Panamanian policeman, and in the police station boasted that he had taken his gun with him because he was going to kill Torrijos.

The next meetings were supposed to be in Panama, which I was still against after my experience in Contadora; I thought the atmosphere in Washington was infinitely more businesslike. And because of my eye problem, my doctor strongly urged that I remain near home. So on June 13 in Washington we started all over again, with hostile negotiations that led up to a passionate repeat — this time by Escobar — of the denunciations of the United States we had heard at the first meeting in Contadora. But as the emotions simmered down, it became clear that some of what had upset Torrijos could be handled by changes of language or form rather than of substance.

Moreover, the economic argument moved to a new ground, where it seemed to us that Panama had a strong case. The United States had agreements for bases in many countries — Spain, Portugal, Greece, Turkey, the Philippines — where we paid the host country for the use of facilities. It was unreasonable of us to ask that in Panama alone we should get our bases for nothing. The man who made the argument, and had done the economic analysis of what our pattern of payments elsewhere would mean in Panama, was Nicolás Barletta, Minister of Planning (at this writing, President of Panama). Completely fluent in English, he was a brilliant economist with a Ph.D. from the University of Chicago, where one of his teachers was George Shultz (at this writing, Secretary of State), who remembers him well and affectionately. He convinced us that we could not simply dig in our heels. If no payments to Panama could be written into the treaties, we had to find a mechanism outside the treaties that gave Panama some economic assistance. Ten years earlier, I had participated in the CIAP meetings that recommended allocation of funds from different U.S. aid programs — and from the international agencies — to development programs in various Latin American countries. Here, again, it should be possible to pull together, for the benefit of Panama, a number of U.S. assistance agencies.

With the approval of the President, I arranged for Barletta to meet with Richard Cooper, Under Secretary of State for Economic Affairs, and Anthony Solomon, Under Secretary of the Treasury for Monetary Affairs. Between them, with help from AID, the Export-Import Bank, and the Overseas Private Investment Corporation — and the Defense Department in the area of military assistance — they organized a package of loan concessions and loan guarantees worth about $350 million over five years.

Meanwhile, we squeezed a little more money for Panama out of an econometric model of the total revenues that could be expected from different levels of canal tolls. With assurance to Panama of a toll rate of thirty cents per ton, and the transfer of certain revenues from the debt service of the Canal Company to the Government of Panama, we could predict that the canal would yield Panama $40–$50 million a year, in contrast to the $2.3 million under the old treaty. The numbers had been developed for us by the Stanford Research Institute. Barletta, a trained economist before he was an advocate, agreed with them. The total was far less than Panama had demanded, but probably as much as Panama could absorb. At a meeting in the White House, Panama Ambassador Gabriel Lewis recommended to the President that he write Torrijos a personal letter certifying that there simply was no possibility of any money beyond what was now on the table. Between Carter's letter and Barletta's recommendation, Torrijos reluctantly acceded.

We were now well into July, with the draft of the second treaty already submitted, and we were still not out of the woods. In June, Torrijos had sent down a new military negotiator to work with our General Dolvin, and they did not get on. Aspects of the "Lands and Waters" agreement that we had thought long settled suddenly opened up again, and Dolvin reacted by demanding a more specific provision that U.S. forces could intervene anywhere in Panama if necessary to safeguard the canal. This had been put in writing two years earlier in a Status of Forces Agreement, which was quietly incorporated by reference in our "Neutrality" Treaty, and the Panamanians found its repetition not only demeaning but politically dangerous.

On July 14 I ran into a press problem that almost disrupted the negotiations. I had accepted an invitation from Godfrey Sperling of the *Christian Science Monitor* to discuss the status of the negotiations with a group of thirty correspondents and columnists at an off-the-record breakfast. My meetings with Carter had included discussion of how to organize the campaign that would be needed to sell the treaties to the Senate and the public, and this breakfast seemed a natural step in the sequence. Representatives of the wire services had not been invited, and thus were not bound by the participants' pledge not to divulge what I said. They got a garbled version of my presentation from someone, and put on the wires a set of specific figures that they attributed to me, plus a statement to the effect that the United States had retained the right to "intervene" militarily on Panamanian soil after the year 2000. There was an uproar in the Panamanian press, and opponents of the treaty in the U.S. Senate took advantage of the situation to leak to reporters some of what Bunker and I had said in confidential briefings on the Hill. Bunker and I met with the Panamanian negotiators in special session, and I gave them a copy of what I had actually said at the breakfast, which they found innocuous enough. The storm passed.

Another issue long settled then surfaced when the President responded to a question in a "town meeting" format in Yazoo City, Mississippi, and made much of the fact that the treaty gave the United States an exclusive right to build a separate sea-level canal in Panama. Such a canal had been much in the minds of American negotiators in the Lyndon Johnson days, when the Navy wanted a waterway large enough to pass its nuclear-powered supercarriers and the engineers believed it would be possible to dig canals with nuclear explosions. Now, however, the only pressure behind it was the Alaska delegation in the Congress, which wanted to be able to ship Alaskan oil directly to the Gulf and Atlantic ports in supertankers. Senator Mike Gravel of Alaska had piqued the President's interest in this proposition a few days earlier. Long before my arrival as co-negotiator, Panama had agreed to give the United States the right to build a sea-level canal, and our draft of the principles had locked it up in iron, as lawyers do when an issue is really moot and there has been no dispute about it. Now, with the President's prestige engaged, Panama demanded an equal voice in determining where, how, and by whom such a canal might be built.

Finally, at the very last minute in the Washington talks, Barletta grew concerned about the figure of thirty cents per ton on the canal tolls. He was an economist; he saw inflation heating up in the United States. Within a few years, the thirty-cent figure might be inadequate. As a matter of prudence, Panama required an escalation clause that would allow the toll to rise as the purchasing power of thirty cents shrank. Bunker and I agreed that Barletta's position made sense, but we knew that the Treasury Department was opposed, and in any event we did not have time to put the question through the bureaucracies. Ambler Moss drafted a memo for me, recommending that the canal tolls be tied to an index of prices for industrial products in the United States, and we had it hand-carried to the White House. I called National Security Adviser Zbigniew Brzezinski, who added that memo to the list of things he would take up with the President just before he went to Plains, Georgia, for his vacation.

It had been arranged that the U.S. negotiating team would go to Panama Sunday evening, August 7, to leave three days for wrap-up negotiations and drafting before my commission expired. The Air Force plane that flew us to Panama would wait to fly us back on August 10, the last day of my ambassadorial appointment. As part of the final preparations, Torrijos was meeting on August 5 in Bogotá, Colombia, with the leaders of that country, Venezuela, Costa Rica, Jamaica, and Mexico, to gain their public support for the deal he was about to make. To their amazement, and to ours in Washington, he told the group that the negotiations were going badly and he didn't think there would be a deal. Friday night, as I was preparing to go out to dinner, I got a hurry-up call from Ambassador Lewis to come to the Panamanian embassy, which was maintaining an open line to Bogotá, to receive a message from General Torrijos.

In retrospect, this was obviously part of a strategy of pressure Torrijos employed through this final week, to see what else he could get. (In his book on the treaties, Bill Jorden speculates that it was also a ploy to ensure that the other leaders with whom he was meeting, several of whom were much more radical than he was, would commit themselves behind a treaty that granted Panama so much less than Latin rhetoric had been demanding for the previous decade.) We couldn't be certain Torrijos was merely operating, however, and in the back of our minds there was still our old worry that he did not really want an end to this old and politically useful dispute. As the evening proceeded, Lewis drew from Torrijos what he felt he needed on the issues that were still open, from specifics as narrow as the ownership of the Coco Solo Heights Housing Project and the toll escalation clause to generalities as wide as the provisions governing the implausible prospects of a sea-level canal.

Although Bunker and I had not thought we would be negotiating that Friday evening, in fact we had some authority to move. The President had already approved the toll escalation clause, and we knew from our conversations with Alexander that the Army had some give remaining on the "Lands and Waters" issues. The sticking point that night, oddly enough, was the sea-level canal question, for this was Carter's initiative, and in the end only the President could yield. We put in a call to the White House, and on Saturday evening we got our response. In a conference call from Plains to Bunker and myself, the President agreed to accept the Panamanian terms for American involvement in any new canal. The clause the Panamanians proposed, after all, while denying the United States an exclusive right to build, did give the United States a veto power over the construction of a canal by anyone else for the remainder of this century, and in effect it added up to the same thing.

When Bunker and I boarded the presidential jet for our trip to Panama Sunday night, we had cautious hopes that we might return with agreement on the substance of two new treaties, but we were keenly aware of the uncertainties. We were to dine that night with the Jordens at the embassy, and we asked Ambassador Lewis, who was traveling with us, whether there was any chance we could have a negotiating session that evening after dinner. He sent a message from the plane, and before we landed we knew that most of the Panamanian team would be waiting for us at the home of Rory González, to start work. We met for two and a half hours, discussing the basis for dealing with several unresolved issues, notably in the "Lands and Waters" area and in connection with the rights of non-Panamanian workers employed by the Canal Company. The spirit was cordial and cooperative, but I had no sense of denouement; they had said they wanted to complete the work before my appointment expired, but they did not seem to be in any hurry.

The Foreign Ministry had reserved a floor of the Holiday Inn in Panama City for negotiating sessions, and in the morning the negotiating teams broke into working groups to deal separately with the remaining disagreements. In the afternoon there was an open session with a large cohort of press in attendance, and we were stunned when Royo handed over to us, ceremoniously, a Spanish version of a complete redraft of the treaty we had submitted to them on July 10. We had assumed that we would be working from our draft, having heard nothing to the contrary; this public gesture was immediately disheartening, and boded ill. The Panamanians knew I could not participate in negotiations beyond Wednesday night, and it seemed impossible that their texts of so many contentious clauses could be reconciled with ours in forty-eight hours. Following the public presentation, Royo gave us an English translation of some portions of their document, which were in large part similar to our submissions, although there were some significant changes. We commissioned an immediate translation of the rest, to be delivered to me that evening at my room in the Ambassador's residence. At about the same time that the translation arrived, we received a message that the next morning's meeting had been canceled because members of the Panamanian delegation wouldn't be available until two o'clock in the afternoon.

I put the U.S. text and the translation of the Panamanian text side by side and compared them, paragraph by paragraph, until one in the morning. As I read, my heart sank and I became discouraged, then irritated, and finally angry. The Panamanians had once again exercised their proclivity to change their minds. When Ambassador Jorden looked in on me about midnight, I told him the situation was hopeless. In clause after clause, the Panamanians had made alterations that diminished the rights we had preserved through the months of negotiating.

The next morning, our negotiating team caucused at the embassy. We found ourselves in complete agreement that Panama had thrown a large monkey wrench into the works, and that the machinery for producing new treaties had ground to a halt. I authorized Jorden to communicate to the Panamanians, prior to the two o'clock meeting, how deeply we were disturbed. And I put in a call to Hamilton Jordan, Carter's assistant, to warn him that the negotiations might be about to collapse, and that the White House should be prepared to issue a statement detailing the terms we had offered, in hopes that the rest of Latin America would see the onus of the failure as resting on Panama.

On the plane going down to Panama, Lewis had told me that Torrijos had commented to him that in recent photographs he had seen I had looked sour, as though I had been "sucking on lemons." I shouldn't worry so much, Torrijos had told him — everything would work out all right when we got to Panama. When we entered the conference room that afternoon, Royo greeted me by saying in a jocular way that now I looked as though I had eaten a dozen lemons. I let him know that I was not amused. Escobar and Royo said that, given the impending expiration of my commission, they were prepared to continue this meeting as long as necessary to resolve the issues. I replied that we would, of course, be willing to work all night, but that there were so many new difficulties raised by their changes that I didn't see how we could possibly reach agreement. Royo then asked me to point out the changes that were troublesome to us, and I began a long litany.

Step by step, Escobar and Royo noted my objections and expressed their understanding of what was bothering me. A few of the passages that I found especially outrageous they treated as jokes. This was a new tone for the negotiations, and Bunker and I began to feel that perhaps there was some hope. We made it clear that we were relaxed about the possibility that we would go back to Washington Thursday without an agreement, which spurred their efforts to meet our objections. Early in the session, Escobar had said that one of their reasons for putting this meeting on its marathon basis was the hope that they could announce our agreement on principles Wednesday afternoon or evening.

Petty matters took up hours of time, however. There was, for example, the question of how much furniture a new U.S. employee of the Canal Company would be permitted to import to Panama, duty-free. They had inserted a figure of three thousand dollars; we thought that wildly inadequate. And the automobiles of Canal Company employees: they had inserted an insistence that although the cars themselves could enter duty-free, spare parts would be taxed. Once this tiny-work had been disposed of, as though it were something we could give them in return, the Panamanians suddenly demanded that we put in the treaty a guarantee that the total of American military personnel in Panama would never be greater than the total roster of the Panamanian National Guard. I said anything of that sort was out of the question, but this one they indicated was serious. They felt that they needed a limit on the extent of the American military establishment in their country after the treaties came into effect. They, too, had to get a treaty ratified, and according to the constitution Torrijos had promulgated some years before, the ratification would have to be by plebiscite. The issue of the U.S.

military presence was sure to be raised by opponents during the ratification campaign, and we had to protect our treaties and Torrijos. We said we would take the issue under advisement overnight, and the next day we found the words — a pledge that the U.S. forces in Panama would never be larger than they were now — that satisfied both sides.

The next morning, Escobar opened the meeting by saying jovially that he recognized this was my last day as an ambassador, and announced that "we will try to conclude agreement today as a present to Sol." It soon became clear that Torrijos had personally directed that ways be found to resolve the outstanding issues. In retrospect, although it was not apparent at the time, this cooperative attitude was inevitable. First at Bogotá, then with the redrafting of the treaties, Torrijos had taken his best shot at winning better terms for Panama. Now, as a responsible leader — and he was a responsible leader — he had to confront the realities. This was a negotiation between a superpower and a tiny principality on an isthmus. His only real weapon was the threat that by civil disturbance and sabotage he could block the operation of the canal. The canal was important to us, but not vital; it was Panama's lifeblood. The failure of the negotiations would have been tragic for us; it would have been catastrophic for him.

Our worst problem now was the scratchiness and tension between General Dolvin and the representative of the National Guard, who did not like or trust each other. But they were, in the end, subordinates of the co-negotiators. We pushed on Tom Dolvin, and they pushed on their colonel, and eventually the military working group signed off. We ticked off dispute after dispute, with the Panamanians accepting the substance of the previous agreements they had tried to evade in their draft, the Americans occasionally accepting changes of language that the Panamanians insisted were important to their internal politics.

At half past five in the afternoon, we were in agreement on principles, although a few minor details relating to the rights of Canal Company employees were still unresolved. I looked around the room and asked whether there was any substantive matter of any kind that we had not discussed and agreed upon, and received unanimous consent that all bases were covered. I pointed out that if later we found such disagreements, it would be terribly embarrassing to both countries and to us as negotiators. Escobar and Royo assured

me that what was left was trivia, easily taken care of in phrasing the
treaty language, and Ellsworth and I gave our consent to an announcement that we had reached an agreement on principles.

I had told Hamilton Jordan that the Panamanians would wish to
issue a statement, and we agreed that the United States should make
a parallel statement. Ambassador Jorden, as a former newspaper-
man, was assigned to prepare it. We kept the White House informed
almost on an hourly basis of the progress of the negotiations, and
Jordan worked with Jorden on exactly what the U.S. statement
should say. But there were no questions from the White House
about the substance we were settling with the Panamanians. It is a
measure of the trust the President placed in Bunker and me that he
permitted us to announce the triumphant conclusion of a negotiation that had run for thirteen years, under the aegis of four Presidents, simply on our assurance to him that we had reached
agreement on the terms of a treaty the United States could and
should accept.

At six o'clock, the four co-negotiators of the two sides announced
to the television cameras, microphones, and reporters assembled at
the Holiday Inn that the United States and Panama had reached
agreement on the outlines of two new Panama Canal treaties. Bunker and I then were taken to Torrijos's unofficial residence, to see
the man with whom, in effect, we had been negotiating for six
months. He was a fascinating person.

The son of a Colombian schoolteacher father and a Panamanian
peasant mother, he was in all the Latin senses a strong man. He was
an intuitive politician of great native intelligence, in his own way a
philosopher. He lived quite modestly — but at the same time em-
bodied for his people many of their dreams of what they would
want for their male children: power, respect, autonomy, an unchallenged machismo. Like his people, he saw the zone as a place where
the rich Americans lived while Panamanians remained mired in
poverty, and he was full of resentment. There was never any question that Torrijos was pulling the strings that moved his negotiators
in our sessions, and he unnerved us quite a while as to where he was
leading them. But the fact is that he wanted to be — and to be seen
as — a statesman; he wanted an achievement for the Panamanian
people, and indeed for the hemisphere.

For this celebratory occasion Torrijos was wearing a red shirt and
khaki trousers. He seemed younger, more fit, and much more at-

tractive than I had expected. He exuded vitality, and he greeted me by saying that he could tell from my smile that I was no longer sucking lemons. We sat together on a couch for forty-five minutes and spoke through an interpreter. He began by saying that he was very pleased the negotiations had been concluded successfully, and that he wished to apologize if at any time he had made our work more difficult by saying things that were offensive or inappropriate. Sometimes, he said, he got carried away. I conveyed President Carter's gratification and good wishes. We then talked about ways of ensuring that the treaty would be approved in both countries, and he used an interesting phrase: he and President Carter, he said, had different sets of customers to whom the treaty would have to be sold, and therefore would have to use different selling tactics.

He then raised the question of where the treaty might be signed, and said he would like to invite all the Presidents of the Latin American nations to come to Panama as witnesses to the signing. I said I believed that Ambassador Lewis had already conveyed this hope to President Carter, but no decision had been made. He seemed sensitive to the fact that it might be politically awkward for President Carter to come to Panama to sign the treaties. Interestingly, he suggested that when we held our background meeting with the American press we should sound them out on whether they thought it was a good idea to have the treaties signed at an elaborate ceremony in Panama. This led to a discussion of how to handle the press. We agreed that it would be a sensible idea to coordinate the more formal announcements of agreement that would be made within the next few days by the two Presidents themselves. It was a lighthearted and comfortable conversation, and Bunker and I returned to the ambassador's residence in high spirits.

Following dinner, I spoke on the telephone with President Carter. After congratulating us, and asking some questions about the treaties, he said he would like me to call former President Gerald Ford that evening (he knew I was friendly with Ford), outline for him the basis of the agreement, and tell him how much the President and I would value his support. Ford was at his home in Vail, Colorado. His reaction to my initial statement was, "I want to be forthcoming, and I will be forthcoming." I discussed the treaty terms, stressing that no appropriation would be required, and told him about the terms of the separate neutrality treaty. He said he liked what he heard — with some difficulty, by the way, because the telephone connection was poor — but that he would have to study the details before making a public comment. He promised to make no public statement until he had looked at the material we would send him, thanked me for the call, and said he would look forward to hearing from me again when I returned to Washington. We had started down the next road.

Two members of our negotiating team remained in Panama: Mike Kozak and Gerri Chester from the State Department's legal staff, who had found ingenious semantic solutions to negotiating problems through the six months. They and their opposite numbers in the Panamanian Foreign Ministry would now have to take the pieces of agreement their seniors had left on the table and stitch together the seamless garments of the treaties. Especially for Gerri, who had been five months pregnant when I came to the negotiating team and was now being separated from her two-month-old daughter by drafting chores, remaining in Panama when the rest of us went home seemed above and beyond the call of duty. She waved us off bravely. Her sacrifice can stand as a symbol of the competence, dedication, and endless work the professional staff gave to the treaties.

As the rest of us flew to Washington on the Air Force plane, we received a message that there would be a helicopter waiting at Andrews Air Force Base to take us quickly to the White House. We were impressed to find that it was the President's own helicopter. It whisked us to the White House lawn, where we found the President waiting for us, flanked by my wife, Toni, and Ellsworth's wife, Carol Laise, who was then director general — personnel chief — of the State Department. The entire White House staff was there, plus a hundred press photographers and newsmen covering the event. We walked across the lawn to the Cabinet Room, where we were greeted by Secretary of Defense Harold Brown, Warren Christopher, the Acting Secretary of State (Vance was traveling), the Joint Chiefs of Staff, and other officials. With the television cameras rolling, President Carter announced that he was firmly committed to the treaties. Ellsworth and I looked at each other, moved (and a little frightened) by the President's confidence in us. We knew the President had not yet seen the treaties, and was relying entirely on our judgment.

After the press departed, Bunker and I answered questions about the treaties for an hour and a half. The only question raised by the Joint Chiefs of Staff was whether military "cargo" could transit the canal without inspection by Panama, and I read them the relevant clause providing that assurance. The President on second thought had regretted our failure to gain an exclusive right to build a sea-level canal, and wondered whether Panama might be willing to grant such exclusivity if we promised in return — something we had not been willing to do before — that we would not negotiate for such a canal with any other Central American state. I discouraged the thought. The President also wished to be able to assure some opposing Senators, especially Jesse Helms, that there was nothing in the treaties that would require action by him prior to ratification, and I told him that was so, that he was in no way obliged to take any action that could be interpreted as an attempt to get around the Senate.

Then we turned our attention to what we could do to convince the Senate and the country that the treaties we had negotiated were in the best interest of the United States. We all recognized that we had done only the first half of the job. What we did not understand yet was that this first half had been less arduous, less complicated, and less emotional than the task that lay ahead.

8

Ratification

SEPTEMBER 7, 1977: the Panama Canal treaties were completed and ready for signature, prior to their presentation to the Senate for ratification. Toni and I were in a White House car driving down Constitution Avenue to the Pan American Union, the home of the Organization of American States, for the signing ceremonies. As we turned onto Seventeenth Street, I heard Toni gasp, "My God!" she said. "Look!" I followed her gaze and saw a crowd of people on the corner. Above them hung a large banner with my name on it, and beside it was a gallows from which a shouting, jeering mob was hanging an effigy labeled "Linowitz."

The fight over the ratification of the treaties was among the most emotional episodes in American politics in this generation — and because there were two treaties there were two fights: my strategy for getting from here to there returned to bedevil us. I saw a face of America I did not want to see, and it still haunts me. The hatemongering, the obscene letters we received, the threatening phone calls . . . I felt in danger in my own country. Indeed, I learned after several of the talks I made in support of the treaty — in Denver, for example, to a convention of the American Legion, and in Houston to the Chamber of Commerce — that in and around the hall security agents in abundant caution had established protective procedures of which I was unaware.

In time I came to understand the strong feelings of the many de-cent and well-intentioned people who were caught up in the emotions of this fight against the treaties. Their manners were bad because they were upset. In high school they had experienced a moment of exultation when the history books told them what Americans had done in Panama. The French couldn't build it but we could. American medicine defeated yellow fever. American engineering created a path between the seas. Now we were "giving it away" — not even getting back the money we had spent to build it — because Carter, Vance, and I were knuckling under to a "tin-horn dictator." The phrase was used repeatedly in the debates, which were broadcast live on Panamanian radio, through loudspeakers into the public squares, infuriating Torrijos, who listened every day, swallowing his rage, accepting the humiliation of the personal insults flung at him from the floor of the Senate. Someone said toward the end of this shameful display that a visitor from Mars observing this hemisphere in the first months of 1978, and asked which of these two countries had the developed economy and culture and the educated leadership, would never have concluded that the correct answer was the United States.

The Americans who lived and worked in the Panama Canal Zone enjoyed, as the Panamanians said, all the benefits of colonialism. They had their own police and courts that applied American rather than Panamanian law, their own schools and hospitals, their own post office, subsidized shopping at military PX's, subsidized housing that was not especially lavish but was kept neat and clean and pleasantly landscaped by low-wage labor from across "the frontier." They were paid better than Panamanian workers who performed similar jobs, and they had the job security of American military employees. Although we had built into the treaties assurances that they would retain their jobs, they stood to lose status as well as benefits when the 1903 treaty was abrogated. Like most people with special privileges, they insisted that they were indispensable, that the Panamanians could never run "our" canal. They had come from all over the United States, and the rumors and suspicions they spread in their letters home helped rouse a domestic constituency against the treaties.

Torrijos's past attempts to internationalize the dispute over the canal now hobbled his efforts — and ours. They gave his enemies an erroneous sense that there was a route to follow other than negotiations with the United States, and gave our opponents colorful and damaging ammunition. Torrijos had visited Cuba and Libya, and there were pictures of him with Castro and Qaddafi. (What would have been the most damaging picture, however, he had managed to kill. During his visit to Havana, Castro's brother Raúl, Cuba's Foreign Minister and a most mischievous man, had maneuvered him in front of a hammer-and-sickle banner. Torrijos's instinct had led him to look behind, and on seeing this background he had demanded that the film in the Cuban newsmen's cameras be destroyed, which it was.) Arnulfo Arias, the president of Panama whom Torrijos had ousted, was living in exile in Miami. All his political life, Arias had solicited the support of extreme left-wing elements in his country; now he encouraged Ronald Reagan and the American right wing to denounce Torrijos as a tool of the Communists.

This was the end of the 1970s, a time when many Americans felt we were in retreat, surrendering our rights and status all around the world. The morning of the day before the vote on the second treaty, Senator S. I. Hayakawa of California said he had awakened in the middle of the night with a feeling that our retreats had gone far enough; somewhere a line had to be drawn, and Panama was the place. He would vote against the treaty. But when the time came for the roll to be called the next afternoon, Hayakawa voted "Aye," and with one vote to spare, the Senate consented.

Those who voted for the treaties paid a price, as many of them knew they would. In a recent talk, former President Carter pointed out that of the twenty Senators up for reelection that fall who voted for the treaty, only seven were returned to Washington, and the mortality rate was almost as high among those who stood for re-election in 1980. In the 1984 Senate campaign in North Carolina, Jesse Helms attacked his opponent, Governor James Hunt, as a man whom I supported, who was thus by association an enthusiast for my surrender of the Panama Canal. The issue continues to be a fruitful source of outrage for right-wing groups. Not long ago, a nice little lady came up to me at a reception. She said she recognized me, and wanted to know if it was true that my most recent assignment had been in the Middle East. When I said it was, she nodded with satisfaction. "Thank God," she said, "they're keeping you away from our canals."

The need to win ratification had been at the forefront of our consciousness from the beginning. Ratification was the rationale for the two-treaty strategy, and concessions that might imperil ratification were always the point beyond which the Panamanians simply could not push us in the negotiations. After it was all over, and Ellsworth Bunker and I flew down with President Carter in June 1978 for the ceremony marking the actual exchange of the executed treaties, Escobar told me that sometimes he and Royo had thought I was using the threat of a Senate rejection as an argument to win concessions from them — an unfair argument, they felt, for it prevented compromise. Having observed the ratification debate, however, they now knew better. "You never lied to us," Escobar said. "You always told us the truth, and this we will never forget."

What I had said to the Panamanians about the perils on the path to ratification had been much more than just my opinion; it was the result of constant consultations with groups of Senators, starting in March 1977, as soon as I felt I had a grip on the issues and an understanding of the attitudes of the Panamanians. The first meeting was in the office of California Senator Alan Cranston, the majority whip. Among those in attendance were the majority leader, Senator Robert Byrd; ranking majority member of the Foreign Relations Committee, Senator Frank Church; chairman of the subcommittee on Inter-American Affairs, Senator Paul Sarbanes; and Senators Hubert Humphrey, Dick Clark, Milton Young and John Chafee. They were mostly Democrats, and mostly liberal Democrats — our friends on the Hill. I briefly described the state of the negotiations, and asked for their advice: what did they think we should require from the Panamanians, what was absolutely necessary if the Senate was to approve a treaty? Hubert Humphrey, by now ill and wasted, urged us on with characteristic passion, but what I got from a number of the other Senators was headshaking. They doubted that the President should be going into this fight at this time. They felt there was little or no support among their constituents for a new Panama Canal treaty, and some of them were unsure about it themselves.

On April 1, 1977, Bunker and I testified at a meeting of the Senate Foreign Relations Committee — the first meeting on Panama in five years. There was strong attendance: chairman John Sparkman, and Senators Frank Church, Claiborne Pell, Richard Stone, Mike Gravel, and John Glenn from the Democrats; Charles Percy, Jacob Javits, and Clifford Case from the minority Republican side. Four days later I had breakfast in the Senate dining room with Senator Chafee and eight Senators serving their first terms, including Haya-

kawa and Orrin Hatch from the Republican right and Donald Rie-
gle from the Democratic left. During the next few months, scarcely
a week passed without some informal meeting with a group of Sen-
ators. As the negotiations heated up in June, I spent an afternoon in
Senator Robert Byrd's office with representatives of the Defense
Department (Army Secretary Clifford Alexander and Chief of Staff
General Bernard Rogers) and a truly mixed bag of Senators —
Humphrey, James Eastland, Cranston, Sarbanes, Sparkman, Carl
Curtis, John Tower, Case, Barry Goldwater, Russell Long, and Paul
Laxalt. We had, my diary says, a "useful exchange." A week later
we were in Byrd's office again, with Cranston, Chafee, Sarbanes,
Richard Lugar, Edward Zorinsky, and Malcolm Wallop.

Meanwhile, I continued more casual, individual contacts. Senator
Goldwater was obviously a key. He had supported Ford's position
on Panama when Reagan was attacking it in 1976, and in his un-
diplomatic way had said that he thought Reagan would support it,
too, "if he knew more about the subject." I talked with Goldwater
several times, and once he told Bunker and me that we had brought
him "not all the way, but one hundred and sixty degrees around."
Long after others had despaired, I thought he might come down on
our side. I was wrong.

Other efforts were more successful. Bunker and I kept in touch
with Senator Howard Baker, the minority leader, and twice went to
his office to brief him on our progress. When I testified at the ratification hearings before the Senate Foreign Relations Committee that
Bunker and I had met with seventy Senators during our negotiations with the Panamanians "to assure that there would be understanding when we did come back with these treaties," Senator Baker
replied that "you did much more than anybody I have ever known
has done, and I congratulate both you and Ambassador Bunker."
Baker would work for as well as vote for the treaties, not because
there was anything in it for him (indeed, his stand on the Panama
Canal treaties was and remains a blight on his hopes for the Republican nomination for President), and not because we had cajoled
him into it, but because he had studied the subject. Once the treaties
had been signed and their terms were known, he had commissioned
position papers from a scholarly advocate and a scholarly opponent,
read both, and decided the advocate had made the stronger case.
And he went to Panama to meet Torrijos, to speak with both government and opposition politicians, and to see for himself. But it did

seem to mean a great deal to him that we had kept him well informed.

We also cultivated key members of the House of Representatives, which would eventually have to pass legislation to change the nature of the U.S. instrumentalities operating in the canal. We testified before the House Merchant Marine Committee, a painful experience because its chairman, John M. Murphy of New York (who later was convicted in the Abscam scandal), was a West Point classmate and friend of Nicaraguan dictator Anastasio Somoza (whom Torrijos detested), and gave hostile Congressmen freedom of his podium to hector us even though some of them were not members of his subcommittee. We lunched with House Speaker Thomas P. ("Tip") O'Neill to solicit his help; he was sympathetic, but said there wasn't much he could do.

The situation was asymmetrical, because the opponents of treaty change could spread their propaganda through the country, whereas we could not seek support for a new treaty that did not yet exist and might never become a reality. I did make one particular effort to blunt the thrust of those who were attacking the idea of a new treaty: I made contact with Ronald Reagan. He was then writing a newspaper column and making radio broadcasts, and the stump speech about the canal that he had used against President Ford was still part of his stock-in-trade. Senator Helms had made some personal attacks on me, related to the fact that my law firm had represented Chile in some technical matters, and that I as senior partner in Washington had been called on to register for the firm as an agent for Chile — which I did, for exactly one day, and then, by prearrangement (for we no longer represented Chile), I withdrew the registration. Helms also had made several speeches pointing out that I sat on the board of the Marine Midland Bank, which had a $2 million share of a syndicated $200 million loan to Panama. To avoid any appearance or question of impropriety, I had resigned from the Marine Midland board. Reagan had picked up a garbled version of these incidents and used them in a column. I wrote him a letter, saying: I know you're a fair man. Here are the facts of the matters you mentioned; I think you'll want to correct the record. And, by the way, some day when you're in Washington I would like to come in and talk with you and tell you what's really happening in the treaty negotiations.

About a week later I received a phone call that former California

Governor Reagan was going to be in Washington in connection with an appearance on "Meet the Press," and if I was free that Saturday morning he would be happy to meet with me at the Madison Hotel. We spent three or four hours together in his suite. He had before him a yellow pad on which were listed a series of questions. He would read a question, check it on his pad, and note down my answer. I had never met him before, and I found him very charming and likable. As he listened to my explanations, nodding pleasantly, I really thought I was persuading him. I suggested that he make a visit to Panama and see for himself what the situation was. He said that was an interesting idea and he might do it — but he never did.

Mrs. Reagan joined us for lunch, and we talked about movies and Hollywood and the Hays Office, which had censored the films of the 1930s and 1940s in rigidly strait-laced ways. Reagan talked about a movie in which he had played the great baseball pitcher Grover Cleveland Alexander, whose career had been blighted by double vision, and who woke one night and saw just one moon. His sight had been restored! He went out in the night to throw balls at a barn and see if he could regain his pitching arm. Alexander's wife in the movie, Reagan remembered, had been played by Doris Day. It was part of the story line that he had to sneak out of bed quietly so as not to disturb her, and the scene had been hard to film because the Hays Office would not tolerate a shot that showed the two of them in bed together. He shook his head in cheerful reminiscence and fell into the character of Grover Cleveland Alexander. There was the former Governor of California, getting up from the table in his hotel suite and enthusiastically showing his pitching form; the tableau is still in my mind.

Then Nancy Reagan left, and we returned to our discussion of the canal. At the end, he walked out to the elevator with me and said, "You've answered all my questions, and I want to tell you how much I appreciate it." I could scarcely wait to see "Meet the Press" the next day and hear the changes in his position that would be the fruits of my advocacy — but he went on television and said exactly what he had been saying before. I was disappointed, and decided I would have to try again.

Carter's first decision at our meeting on the afternoon of our triumphant return from Panama was that he would have to start immediately to gather support. He couldn't wait until the State Department legal staff and their opposite numbers in Panama completed the drafting of the details of the treaty. This was Thursday, August 11; the President wanted to make his statement to the press the next day, and he wanted Bunker and me to be with him to help answer questions. The press conference was called for two o'clock. As I was about to leave my office, I had a call from Press Secretary Jody Powell, who read me the proposed text of the President's statement. There were several points in it that would have aroused the Panamanians, and I dictated some revisions, all of which the President accepted. At the White House, he introduced us to the press corps, and we answered questions for forty-five minutes.

Two days later I had a call from William Buckley, Jr., who had been an opponent of treaty revision and a critic of the Torrijos government until late 1976, when he visited Panama, spoke with locals and zonians, and changed his mind. He said he wanted to let me know that his newspaper column the following Tuesday would endorse the treaties as Bunker and I had presented them, and that his magazine, *National Review*, would editorialize on our side.

On Sunday Bunker and I appeared on "Meet the Press."

On Monday, as I was completing a television interview for Globo TV in Brazil, I had a call from Hamilton Jordan: the President wanted me to go to Vail the next day with General George Brown and General Brent Scowcroft, who had been President Ford's national security adviser, to brief Ford on the details of the treaty in the hope that he might make a statement of support. We met with Ford for an hour and a half. One piece of our puzzle was still missing; Henry Kissinger, whose endorsement we and Ford had expected, had still not committed himself. But Ford saw nothing in the treaty different from what he had set out as the American objectives in the years when the negotiations had been carried out in his name, and Scowcroft concurred. "We don't have to wait for Henry," Ford said, and went out to give a handsome endorsement of the treaties, and the work Bunker and I had done, in a statement to the press.

On Wednesday there was another hearing before the House Merchant Marine Committee, a four-hour spectacle covered by the television networks. All but one or two of the members of the committee attacked the treaties; many of them attacked Torrijos and the government of Panama; several of them attacked me.

On Thursday I went to New York for a meeting of the board of Time Inc., and then on to Denver, where the next morning I was to address the Internal Affairs, Americanism, and National Security

Commissions of the American Legion at the annual Legion convention. I was received courteously by the several thousand in this
group, and I hoped I had changed some minds — but there was no
doubt the Legion would persist in its long-standing opposition to
"giving away" the canal.

The next week Toni and I tried to give ourselves what we regarded as a well-earned vacation in our summer home near Rochester, but the phone never stopped ringing. Often enough, it was a call
from Panama. Not surprisingly, some of the peripheral arrangements we had glued together during those last frantic days in Panama were coming unstuck in the drafting process, and the State
Department legal people wanted guidance. Or it was Hamilton Jordan or Landon Butler in the White House, or Bunker, or Ambassador Gabriel Lewis of Panama. In theory my term of service had
ended, and I had no authority to speak for anyone — but, whether I
liked it or not, these were considered "my" treaties. Both the
Americans and the Panamanians seemed to feel that when they had
a problem, I might be able to find the words that would express the
agreements I thought we had reached.

Early Wednesday morning, August 24, the President himself
called. His first words were, "How's the treaty coming along, Sol?"
I said it seemed to be progressing; there was work to be done, and
there were new and old disputes every day, but nothing surprising
had happened. He asked whether the work could be finished in two
weeks, and I said I thought it could — maybe sooner. Then he told
me that two weeks was an outside limit, because he and Torrijos
were about to schedule a signing ceremony for September 7. He had
accepted Torrijos's suggestion that the heads of government of all
the OAS member countries should be invited to witness the signing
and attest their satisfaction. For Carter to go to Panama would have
been politically dangerous, and might harm the ratification campaign, and Torrijos had agreed to come to Washington instead. The
OAS headquarters was in Washington, and it would be appropriate
for Torrijos to travel for a ceremony to be held under OAS auspices. While in the United States, moreover, Torrijos could meet
with Senators and others, and demonstrate that he had neither
horns nor a tail. After I had thought about this for a while, I called
Ambassador Jorden in Panama and suggested to him that he urge
Torrijos to wear a business suit rather than a uniform in Washington, a suggestion Torrijos — who *always* wore a uniform — rather
uncomfortably accepted.

The day after Carter's call, I tried again with Ronald Reagan, this time in New York, where he was staying at his friend Justin Dart's apartment at 870 United Nations Plaza. Ellsworth Bunker joined me. We gave Reagan a full exposition of the treaties, and made our arguments: they preserved the security of the United States and enhanced the long-term security of the canal itself; they imposed no economic cost on the United States; indeed, they might carry economic benefits, because they would improve our relations with the Latin countries, which were major markets for American products. Reagan listened carefully and thoughtfully, asked penetrating and pertinent questions — many of them, disconcertingly, the same questions he had asked me in the spring. I asked him point-blank whether he planned to lead a campaign against ratification, and he said he did not, but would continue to assert his own opinions as an individual. We had about an hour with him, and at the end he authorized us to make a statement to the press that we had answered his questions fully. "But," he added, "I'm going to end up on the other side." That evening he made a speech to a convention of Young Americans for Freedom, and its tone was muted. Significantly, he indicated that he recognized the need for a new treaty, but he said he could not accept the terms of the treaties we had negotiated.

On Friday we were back in Washington, and I spent the day in the State Department conference room with Bunker, the Panamanian negotiators, and some of the U.S. legal staff who had returned from the drafting meetings to brief us. The issues were post office facilities and PX privileges for employees of the reconstituted Canal Company. It took time, but the tone was not discouraging. Clearly, everyone (except, of course, the zonians) wanted a deal. By then it was known that the signing was to be September 7. We worked again, mostly on the same material, on Saturday, with much telephoning to and from Panama.

On Monday Bunker and I went to the White House to brief the cabinet on the treaties and to answer questions, most of them from Special Trade Representative Robert Strauss and Attorney General Griffin Bell. That afternoon we gave another briefing, for the assembled Latin American ambassadors to the White House and the OAS. The next morning I appeared on the "Today" show and discussed the treaties, and then lunched with Bunker, General George Brown, and two of his predecessors as Chairman of the Joint Chiefs, Generals Lyman Lemnitzer and Maxwell Taylor, whose support was considered essential. They made no commitments, but in the end they endorsed ratification. The opponents of the treaties were making a considerable tactical mistake, charging that the President had bullied the Joint Chiefs into supporting the treaties against their judgment of what was important to the security of the country. This infuriated General Brown and his colleagues, and offended their predecessors, who considered such attacks demeaning to the military.

From the lunch, Bunker and I returned to the White House for the first of what would be a series of meetings to win grass-roots support, state by state. For each of these meetings, the President solicited from the Senators of two states a list of their constituents who would be particularly interested in learning the details of the treaties. The White House then added some names on its own, and invitations went out to the Governors of the states, local political and business leaders, and others.

The first states were Georgia and Florida. The Governors of both states were present, as were the Senators, a number of the Representatives, and well over a hundred state officials, businessmen, labor leaders, educators, lawyers, and so forth. The White House dining room was converted to a lecture hall for the occasion. The briefing was by National Security Adviser Zbigniew Brzezinski, Deputy Secretary of Defense Charles Duncan, General Brown, and me. The President then spoke for twenty minutes, and took questions. I thought the event was a triumph: 90 percent of those who came were opposed when they arrived, and 90 percent seemed supportive when they left. Dean Rusk, who had become a law professor at the University of Georgia on leaving the State Department, told me he thought the presentation was very effective; so did Governor Reubin Askew of Florida. We did it again two days later, for citizens of West Virginia and Arkansas, also, I thought, with very good results. The President stayed at this meeting for an hour, and at the end remained to shake hands with all the participants.

I spent the next few days cultivating some conservatives whose help we needed — I lunched with columnists George Will and James J. Kilpatrick — and inviting business leaders to a breakfast at the White House to precede the September 7 signing ceremonies. Seventy-five or eighty people attended, including the chief executive officers of DuPont, AT&T, IBM, and General Electric; George Meany from the AFL-CIO; Vernon Jordan of the Urban League; and Father Theodore Hesburgh of Notre Dame University. Secretary of State Vance led the briefing, with participation by Bunker and me, Brzezinski, Secretary Brown and General Brown, Vice-President Walter Mondale, and Carter himself. After the breakfast we did our briefing again for four important Senators — John Stennis, Henry Jackson, Sam Nunn, and Robert Morgan. They asked hard questions, which we thought we answered; but only Morgan seemed fully committed to the treaties. From the briefings we went to lunch at the Council of the Americas, for the eighteen visiting heads of government and Vice-President Mondale.

That evening, before the television cameras of the world, the treaties were signed by Carter and Torrijos, who gave each other the traditional Latin *abrazo* and then shook hands with all their peers. The visiting Latin American leaders signed a Declaration of Washington that expressed their gratification. Of the twenty-six nations represented at the ceremony, only Mexico withheld its approval. Then we all went to the White House once again for a state dinner, a truly festive occasion, with Isaac Stern and André Previn playing violin-and-piano sonatas by César Franck and Aaron Copland. The guest list was a collection of celebrity and significance, including, for example, Muhammad Ali and Ted Turner. At the dinner I sat with President Pinochet of Chile, who told me that he would prefer to spend time with his grandchildren, and hoped he could save his country for democracy. Like General Stroessner in Paraguay, he had his own distressing definition of "democracy."

On September 8, the next day, the House International Relations Committee held hearings on the treaty from ten in the morning until four in the afternoon, broken only by a recess to permit some of us to attend a lunch for the heads of government given by the Senate Foreign Relations Committee in the caucus room of the Old Senate Office Building. This House Committee was much friendlier than Merchant Marine, and the atmosphere was not only civil but cordial. (But as we were testifying in the House, Ronald Reagan testified in opposition before a Senate committee.) In the evening, Torrijos was host to a dinner for Mondale at the Panamanian embassy. He was relaxed, and seemed confident despite his civilian clothes. He told me he was "relieved." So was I.

Then the bad news began to arrive. CBS News carried a report that Senator Goldwater was about to announce his opposition to the treaties. I called Frank Moore, chief of congressional liaison for the White House, and he said the story was true. He had talked to

Goldwater, who said he had read the documents and could not support them, but he did not say why. He did tell Moore that he had received eight thousand letters from various people in Arizona opposing the treaties, and that the deluge was continuing. Moore suggested that I talk to Goldwater. I tried but couldn't reach him. Moore and I spoke with the President, who said he would call Goldwater himself. The President couldn't reach him, either. On Saturday Moore located Goldwater, who was at a friend's house on the eastern shore of Maryland, and when I spoke with him the Senator said he could not see any point in talking with Carter on the subject: "It would be a waste of time for both of us."

These were the days when we began to get glimpses of the troubles that were to grow out of the speech the Panamanian negotiator Rómulo Escobar Bethancourt had made to the Panama Assembly on August 19, outlining the treaties and acclaiming his representation of his country in the negotiations. The enemies of the treaties in Panama, who were loud and not negligible in number, were the people Escobar had always considered his friends. Defending himself in the Assembly, and in a press conference on August 22, he denied that the United States would have any significant rights relating to the possible construction of a sea-level canal; he said that Panama had not accepted any obligation to keep the canal open permanently; and he insisted that "we are not giving the United States the right of intervention."

These statements were made while the final document was in process, but we knew that what would be in the ultimate text was quite different from what Escobar was saying. No one thought that Escobar had gone off the reservation on his own, which made his remarks especially disturbing. Torrijos had told me that he and Carter had different customers to sell on the treaties and would have to use different approaches. The Escobar speeches sounded suspiciously like a Torrijos approach to his selling problem. Americans who had not been involved in these matters — even supporters of the treaties — believed that Panama was enthusiastic about our agreement and that all the problems were in America. We knew that the treaties were a far cry from what Torrijos had promised his people. He had always said, for example, that he would never agree to give the Americans a right to "intervene." Now he seemed to be looking for ways to assure his people that he had not given away what in fact he had. Panama could reasonably be described as a dictatorship, but the people of Panama were going to be asked to vote on the treaties, and the results of that vote were far from certain. Still, everyone knew that, one way or another, Torrijos would win his referendum in Panama, while we had at best a close vote in the Senate. I called Ambassador Lewis in Washington ("This Escobar," he growled, "he's always talking"), and others made contact with senior members of the government in Panama.

For a while we hoped that Escobar's oratory, intended for domestic consumption, would remain within the borders of his little country. But his speech and the text of his press conference soon became available in the United States through the normal reporting processes of the State Department, and they were seized upon by American opponents of the treaties. On September 12 (when I spoke at lunch to a meeting at the Women's National Democratic Club), I taped an interview with Evans and Novak, who wanted to talk about almost nothing but Escobar. All I could say was that the text of the treaties would not support Escobar's interpretation, and that we had assurances that the government of Panama did not interpret the relevant clauses as Escobar did. Later, because I made it my business to talk with Foreign Minister González-Revilla, I was able to assure Senator Baker (who quoted the Escobar statements in the Foreign Relations Committee hearings) that I had been "told that we would not hear such statements in the future."

On September 16, CBS News got a scoop. The CIA, they reported, had bugged the Panamanian embassy, where some of the negotiating sessions had occurred. Panama, the network reported, had learned of the bugging and used its information to blackmail Bunker and me and get better terms in the treaties than we would otherwise have granted. It was true that *somebody* had bugged the embassy, crudely and in a way certain to be discovered. The U.S. intelligence community was as surprised as Bunker and I were. But the flap was real. Bunker and I, CIA Director Stansfield Turner, and National Security Agency Chief Robert Inman all testified, behind closed doors to the Senate Intelligence Committee. The committee chairman, Senator Daniel Inouye of Hawaii, certified that the bugging had not been the work of American intelligence, and that it could not have influenced the course of the negotiations because nobody had known about it until after the treaties were signed.

The Senate hearings on ratification began on September 26. The members of the Foreign Relations Committee were friendly but essentially noncommittal, with the exception of Michigan's Robert Griffin, who was distinctly opposed, and South Dakota's George McGovern, who was highly supportive (although I had to wince at his notion that it would help the cause if he could get Vance, Bunker, and me to admit that Panama had received a dirty deal over the years, and the new treaties were the least we could do in recompense). The hearings were televised live by the Public Broadcasting System and broadcast on National Public Radio. The next day, Secretary Brown, General Brown, and the military leaders testified firmly in support.

On September 28 I was at the White House for the third in the series of state-by-state briefings, this one for delegations from Arizona and Minnesota. The President spoke for forty minutes, and answered questions for an additional half an hour. I was impressed and moved by the depth of his commitment and understanding.

On Thursday, September 29, I went to a dinner of the Economics Club of New York, where Henry Kissinger and I spoke on the treaties to a black-tie audience of twelve hundred business and financial leaders. Then I was off to London for a week for a Pan Am board meeting and other work mostly related to the airline, but I remained in touch with Bunker and the White House. The news was not good. The Senators were asking, not unreasonably, how we and Escobar could be drawing such different conclusions from the text of the treaties. A roadblock was rising on the path to ratification, and we would need Panamanian help to clear it. I drew up a statement we might ask Torrijos to sign, acknowledging that ours was the correct interpretation of the language. On my return to Washington, Bunker and I went to the Panamanian embassy to give it to Lewis and ask his advice on the best way of communicating it to Torrijos, who was traveling in Europe and Israel on state visits.

While this statement was making the rounds of the Panamanian and U.S. governments, I went off to San Francisco to urge support of the treaties on the Commonwealth Club, the World Affairs Council, and the Pan American Society. On my return to Washington, I joined Bunker at a lunch of the International Committee of the Chamber of Commerce, which voted to endorse the treaties — subject to "clarification" of the points Escobar had put in dispute. By now Torrijos had agreed to stop off in Washington and meet with Carter on his way back to Panama, and on October 13 I was asked to make myself available for White House meetings the next day. We started at eight in the morning — Vance, Brzezinski, Hamilton Jordan, and myself, and a group of Panamanian representatives, including Escobar and Lewis. The President and Torrijos were meeting privately in the Oval Office. They joined us in the Cabinet room, and Carter reported that he and Torrijos had agreed that a statement on the apparently disputed issues would be necessary, but that Torrijos was unwilling to issue it until after the Panamanian plebiscite, which was scheduled for October 23.

The President then suggested that perhaps there could be some sort of secret understanding between him and Torrijos, which would be issued after the plebiscite. As he spoke I indicated my disagreement by shaking my head vigorously, and he stopped and asked me to explain my discomfort. I told him I thought it would be harmful to the chances for ratification if General Torrijos left Washington without some joint statement from the two national leaders. He would not necessarily have to make a public appearance in Washington in connection with the statement, and it might be phrased in a way that would not cause him problems when he returned home, but he had to agree to an affirmation of American security rights with relation to the canal. This was terribly difficult for Torrijos, personally as well as politically — to admit in public and in his own name that he had given the United States in effect the right to intervene in perpetuity on Panamanian soil to protect the neutrality of the canal. Escobar now redeemed himself by suggesting that he and I might be able to draft a joint statement, and we went to work in the Cabinet Room with an interpreter.

I asked Escobar to use as much as possible of the statement I had written originally, which Carter had already shown to a number of Senators. On the basis of the reaction of the Senators, which the President had reported to me, I proposed that the language be strengthened, especially with relation to the right of "expeditious passage" for U.S. Navy ships. Escobar heard me out, accepted the document as drafted, and then suggested the strongest possible formulation on the traffic problem — a statement that in an emergency U.S. (and Panamanian) naval vessels would "go to the head of the line" of ships awaiting entry to the canal. He then called Torrijos and secured approval of our document over the telephone. I took it to President Carter, who was meeting with Jordan and Press Secretary Jody Powell in his hideaway office. Carter was delighted, noting that in several aspects the statement was even stronger than what he had proposed to the Senators, and he called Senator Robert Byrd and asked if I could come over and informally present the amended wording to the Foreign Relations Committee.

Byrd received me in his office, looked at the statement, and seemed very pleased. Then I discussed the document at a meeting of the Foreign Relations Committee with Senators Sparkman, Baker, Pell, Glenn, Stone, Hollings, and Case, all of whom thought it would be helpful. Baker and Glenn remained concerned about the match between our commitment to respect the "territorial integrity" of Panama and our right to intervene militarily to protect the neutrality of the canal. When I returned to the White House there was a long discussion — broken by telephone calls to Ambassador Lewis — about whether we should seek a further amendment indicating that what we meant by respecting territorial integrity was that even if we had to intervene, it would never be with the *intent* to violate territorial integrity. We could not find any way to make this work, and I went out to the press room to read the statement Escobar and I had prepared as something that had been agreed upon by President Carter and General Torrijos. This was carried that evening by all the network news shows.

Torrijos went home to Panama, and I went back on the road — to Chicago for presentations to the Inland Press Association, the Mid-America Committee of business and financial leaders, and the Chicago Council on Foreign Relations; to Denver, where the President, Brzezinski, Harold Brown, George Brown, and I held the now well rehearsed dog-and-pony show for representatives of eight states (Colorado, New Mexico, Arizona, Nevada, Utah, Montana, Wyoming, and Oklahoma); to New Orleans for the meeting of the managing editors of the Associated Press; to Atlanta for a meeting of the American Jewish Committee. Everywhere I went I was interviewed on local radio and television shows. And in between the trips there were meetings with the Senate Foreign Relations Committee and the House International Relations Committee. There was another White House presentation for representatives of Rhode Island, Alaska, and Missouri. And the White House finally put together — somewhat belatedly — a National Citizens Committee for the Panama Canal Treaties, chaired by the venerable but enthusiastic Averell Harriman.

In November the Senators themselves began traveling to Panama for a firsthand look. Torrijos received them personally and graciously, and charmed most of them. The zonians, by contrast, tended to misbehave at meetings, reducing the effectiveness of their opposition. The Senators also saw how easy it would be for a single Panamanian National Guardsman with a bazooka to put the great locks out of commission for months: the problem of maintaining the security of the canal was more complicated and disturbing on the site than it seemed in Washington. General Brown had told the Senate Armed Services Committee, most of whom did not want to hear it, that assuring the security of the canal in the face of Panamanian hostility might require a hundred thousand American troops. For those who took a helicopter trip over the canal, it did not seem an unreasonable estimate.

Slowly but effectively, the executive branch organized for the coming struggle. Robert Beckel, who would later manage the Mondale campaign for the presidency, was designated by Congressional Liaison Director Frank Moore to handle the White House contacts with Senators. At the State Department, Deputy Secretary Warren Christopher was put in charge of treaty ratification matters, with Douglas Bennett, Assistant Secretary for Congressional Relations and a former Senate staff member, as point man. Bennett asked my former assistant Ambler Moss, who had remained at the Department, to organize a team that would do nothing but find answers to questions Senators raised in the debate. He established what came to be known as a Gang of Four — himself, Mike Kozak from the legal adviser's office, Colonel Larry Jackley from the Pentagon, who had actually commanded troops in the zone, and Betsy Frawley, who had recently moved from Senator Ted Kennedy's staff to the Department. Vice-President Mondale found space for them in his office, and they lived at the Senate through the months of the debate on the treaties.

I would be essentially an outside man — making speeches, giving interviews for print and broadcast, participating in media events (including a two-hour televised debate with Senator Goldwater, moderated by Dean Rusk, before a meeting of the Georgia Bar Association in Atlanta), and maintaining informal contacts with a number of Senators. Members of the cabinet would also travel around the country to give speeches in support of the treaties. The President would deliver one or more fireside chats on television, and as time passed he became increasingly involved in direct contact

with Senators, calling them at home during evenings and on weekends, inviting them for discussions in the Oval Office.

In the public fora, we were outspent and outmanned by a multi-
million-dollar direct-mail propaganda campaign and an outpouring
of rage from the right wing; but with the passage of time, depending
on which public-opinion polls you read, we seemed to be gaining
acceptance, if not support, of the treaties. When I talked with the
Senators privately, I found they were always balancing a number of
factors. First, they wanted to be sure the treaties did indeed meet
essential security concerns. They wanted confidence that the
United States was not being "taken," that we really had negotiated a
fair bargain. Second, they wanted assurance that it was in the best
long-range interests of the United States to enter into a treaty that
would involve Panama running "our" canal, that we could trust this
fellow Torrijos — and his successors — to live up to such obligations. And they wanted to know what would happen if the Senate
did *not* approve the treaties. What were the other Latins saying to
us? What sort of responsibility would lie on their shoulders if they
voted against the treaties? On the other side, there were always the
politics, the deluge of mail, the passion of the opposition, and the
"institutional imperative" of getting reelected. And, of course, we
needed two-thirds of the vote.

As 1977 ran out, our confidence grew. Early in the new year,
Byrd and Baker, the majority and minority leaders, announced
themselves in support. Then, for no apparent reason, we stalled. We
had sixty of the sixty-seven necessary votes, and our head counts
showed about a dozen undecided. On February 2, 1978, there was a
meeting at the White House to discuss the best approaches to this
group. The most likely candidates, our liaison people said, were
Quentin Burdick, Richard Schweiker, H. John Heinz, Zorinsky,
John Melcher, Jennings Randolph, Ted Stevens, Dennis DeConcini, Paul Hatfield, and Wendell Ford. I was assigned to keep in
touch with Heinz, Zorinsky, and Schweiker, and I spent the next
several days calling people in Pennsylvania and Nebraska who
might be assumed to have influence with their Senators. As it happened, Melcher called me, and in a very long telephone conversation
I was able to assure him that we could work out something with the
Panamanians that would give us a continuing background role in
preserving the efficient management of the canal after the year 2000.
I also spoke again with Goldwater; the White House had given up
on him, but I had not.

The Neutrality Treaty was called up for debate on February 8. It was the first time a Senate debate had been broadcast in full, live, by radio. There had been some hope that this public exposure would lead to a more dignified and direct discussion on the floor, but a number of the opponents of the treaty were seeking to create an emotional climate rather than to delineate a coherent argument. Their tactics were to interrupt the statements of supporters by questions and contradictory "facts," many of them only marginally germane. A few of them attacked me with assertions that I was on the one hand a supporter of Allende's Chile and on the other hand the tool of the big New York banks. They attacked Torrijos as a dictator with an "abysmal" human rights record, a friend of Fidel Castro, a drug addict who was likely to be overthrown any day, leaving the United States with a scrap of paper his successors could repudiate. In Panama, Torrijos was listening to the debate. Several times he called Carter to say he couldn't take it anymore, his manhood was involved; and Carter told him there was nothing any American President could do about this sort of thing, that the choice was to bear the personal attacks in silence or risk the violence and bloodshed that would follow the repudiation of the treaty. Torrijos kept silent.

To my sorrow, Senator Goldwater played shamelessly to the right-wing gallery. The treaty, he said, was a plot by the Trilateral Commission (a David Rockefeller–sponsored study group that brought together leading figures from the United States, Japan, and Western Europe): "Almost every member of the Carter Administration," he said, "including the negotiators, members of our Senate Foreign Relations Committee . . . are members of this organization. I believe that this is the reason we are getting all the pressure to push this treaty through. . . . I think our large banks and international banks have a lot more to do with this treaty than meets the eye. . . . The replacement value of canal operations, including armed forces facilities, totals $9.8 billion . . . so, when we hear from our President that this is not going to cost the taxpayers of this country anything, that is just plain wrong. . . . Militarily, arrangements in the proposed treaties are contrary to what most military experts say is in our best national interest. . . ."

Senator Robert Dole made alleged Panamanian involvement in the heroin trade the centerpiece of his opposition, stressing that Torrijos's brother, now Panama's ambassador to Spain, had been indicted by an American grand jury as the man behind a plot to smuggle $155 million worth of heroin into Kennedy Airport in New York. The fact was that nobody in our Drug Enforcement Agency (or in Panama) had taken this accusation seriously, but it was poison in the wells. Senator Strom Thurmond denounced "the abandonment of U.S. citizens and employees in the Panama Canal area to the laws of Panama." Senator Helms issued a blanket anathema: "The decision to give away the Panama Canal was based upon purely political pressures in total disregard of the defense and economic consequences of that decision." Senator Griffin raised the "question of whether this arbitrary and unnecessary six-month limit on the tenure of a chief negotiator may have led the U.S. to make hasty and unwise concessions under the pressure of an artificial deadline."

Against this sort of tirade, the defenders of the treaty seemed to have only plodding if truthful arguments. Every question of fact raised by the opponents was answered swiftly and accurately, thanks to the behind-the-scenes work of our Gang of Four, but the debate was not about questions of fact. After the first three days, the Senate recessed for the traditional Lincoln's Birthday–Washington's Birthday holiday week, and Senators went home to receive a barrage of complaints organized by the enemies of the treaties. When the debate resumed, it was again full of innuendo and invective — and we did not have sixty-seven votes.

The President and his aides decided it would be necessary to work out the problems of the handful of Senators whose support we still needed. The tactics employed included favors, flesh-pressing, and arm-twisting. The *New York Times* quoted an anonymous administration source as saying that "I hope the Panamanians will get as much out of these treaties as some Senators." Several pet projects the administration had opposed were now endorsed. The President spent hours calling Senators and meeting with them. In his memoirs, he reports that he took the time to read Hayakawa's textbook on semantics so he could discuss it with him as part of the campaign to gain his vote. Some of the Senators spent quarter-hours in the limelight of the morning and evening news shows, proclaiming that unless the treaty were amended in ways *they* thought necessary to assure American national security, they would vote against it and it would fail.

There was a fundamental unfairness here. Senators like Thomas McIntyre of New Hampshire, Robert Morgan of North Carolina, and Walter Huddleston of Kentucky had put their political futures on the line early in the campaign for ratification, and were now ignored; their reasons for approving the treaty were not newsworthy. Those who had hung on in an attitude of provisional disapproval became celebrities and beneficiaries of presidential attention. From the moment that Escobar's statements had become public knowledge in the United States, it was clear that *some* changes in the language of the treaties would be required to lock out the interpretations he had made. Byrd and Baker had demanded that the Torrijos-Carter declaration be written into the treaty in some form, and this we could do, for the Panamanians had known of that declaration before they voted in their own referendum. But lying on the table before the Senate were numerous amendments and "reservations" that made changes of such substance that Torrijos and his colleagues insisted they would have to take the treaties back for a new plebiscite, with unpredictable results. Several Panamanian political leaders who had supported the treaties before the referendum declared that they would oppose them if they were offered with the changes demanded by Senators whose votes we now felt we needed.

Two changes in particular had become critical, both to the vote and to the Panamanians. One was an amendment supported by Senators Sam Nunn and Herman Talmadge of Georgia and Russell Long of Louisiana, which would give the United States the right to continue to station troops in Panama after the second treaty expired in the year 2000. Intensive negotiations between the White House and the Senators produced a softening of this amendment to require only that the treaty leave open the possibility that prior to the year 2000 the United States and Panama might agree to a continuing U.S. military presence. The Panamanians didn't like it, but the language the Senators finally accepted didn't bind them to anything, and they decided they could live with it.

The second "reservation" was far more damaging. Introduced by Dennis DeConcini of Arizona, a first-term Senator who had not previously been an especially notable figure in the Senate, it gave the United States authority to intervene in Panama against *any* action that impeded the operations of the canal. As written — and intended — by DeConcini, this seemed to include, for example, a strike by Panamanian workers. Somehow this fell between the cracks at the State Department and in the White House, and the President permitted DeConcini to announce that his reservation had been accepted by Carter. It was now impossible to go back and DeConcini refused to entertain changes in his language. He talked at length to reporters, microphones, and cameras about how he was saving the country and the canal from what would otherwise be fatal mischief. The late Frank Church told a friend that he'd had a terrible nightmare in which he and DeConcini had been stuck together in a broken elevator in the Capitol, and he had to listen to DeConcini talk and talk and talk. We were all living some version of that nightmare.

Ambler Moss left his command post in the Capitol and went down to Panama to explain, cajole, and hold hands. Even with DeConcini triumphant and pledged to vote for the Neutrality Treaty that now contained his "reservation," we were not sure we could get sixty-seven votes. Torrijos scheduled a speech in which he planned to denounce the amendments, interpretations, and reservations that had been tacked onto the treaties, and was dissuaded only by a personal telephone call from Carter. The President pointed out that it might be possible to pull the sting out of some of these changes when the second treaty came up for a vote, and nothing could be gained by saying things that would ensure the defeat of the first treaty.

On the morning of March 16, with the vote scheduled for four o'clock that afternoon, the President told me Senator Baker was saying that his head count did not reach to sixty-seven, and he thought we had lost. At noon, the President heard from Senator Zorinsky of Nebraska, with whom I had been talking about the treaties for two months, and with whom the President had met one-on-one that morning; Zorinsky would vote against. Hamilton Jordan was still optimistic. He had in his pocket, he said, one crucial vote, that of West Virginia's Jennings Randolph. Randolph loved being in the Senate — he was seventy-six years old and he was running for reelection — and he thought an aye would jeopardize his seat. But he said that if his vote was the only way the first treaty would pass, we could have it. When Bunker and I went to the visitors' gallery to observe the vote, we didn't know whether we would leave it in pleasure or in despair. One by one, the Senators we had put in the leaning-against category came through for us — Edward Brooke of Massachusetts, Hayakawa of California, Bellmon of Oklahoma, Burdick of North Dakota, Howard Cannon of Nevada. In the end, we had sixty-eight votes, without Randolph, who then with great relief cast a no vote.

Bunker and I went to the White House to celebrate a little with a bone-tired President and his weary staff — but only a little, because there was a second treaty to be ratified, and no guarantee that our one-vote margin would hold. The President wrote in his diary that "the vote on the second treaty is going to be even more difficult." Senators went off for Easter recess, and the right wing worked them over yet again. I went to Africa and the Middle East on one of the "newstours" *Time* operates occasionally for business and civic leaders and political figures. We met the chiefs of state and the opinion molders in half a dozen countries. Almost without exception, they expressed amazement at the spectacle of the U.S. Senate spending so much time in forensics and pyrotechnics before taking an action the whole world knew should have been taken long since.

When I returned to Washington on April 1, I found the Citizens Committee not very active, the White House in unproductive turmoil, and the State Department paralyzed by the mounting anger reported from Panama by Ambassador Jorden and others. We had, in fact, broken our word: we had told the Panamanians that the White House would not consent to major changes in the treaties without consulting the government of Panama, and nobody had warned them about DeConcini.

During my absence, Royo had come to Washington and met with Christopher and Bunker to discuss what might be done to pull the fangs of the DeConcini reservation. He was told that the White House was looking for a way to add a statement to the second treaty reaffirming the limits on American rights to "intervene" in Panama. It was not enough. Panama's representative in the United Nations circulated a note indicating that Torrijos had written to the chiefs of state of every member nation setting forth his (and, incidentally, Senator Kennedy's) objections to the DeConcini language. The story was in the newspapers on April 5. DeConcini reacted by saying he would insist that Panama agree to accept his reservation before there could be a vote on the second treaty. Senator Baker warned us that even a "twitch from Panama might cause the treaties to go down the tube." Several Senators who had voted for the first treaty denounced Torrijos's letter and its implications.

I suggested that Royo return to Washington and work out with us a statement Carter could make at the exchange of instruments after the ratification, offering a strong reaffirmation of U.S. intentions never to intervene in the internal affairs of Panama. But passions were now too high in Panama to be soothed in that manner. Christopher, then Carter, met with DeConcini, seeking changes in his language that might assuage Panamanian fears. DeConcini told the news media that he was considering the President's requests, then announced he was rejecting them and proclaimed that he was perfectly willing to see the treaties go down if it meant that he had fought to preserve our national security. Ultimately, he went too far: his colleagues became embarrassed, and then angry. The first evidence of their displeasure was devastating to us. Senators McGovern and Daniel Moynihan announced that if the DeConcini reservation was inserted into the second treaty they would vote against it, because they thought it would be detrimental to long-term American interests for the United States to demand a document that countenanced intervention. Then the tide turned.

Senator Paul Sarbanes, who was chairman of the Subcommittee on Western Hemisphere Affairs and the floor manager for the treaties in the debates, called me at my home to say that he and Senators Byrd, Cranston, and Church wanted my views on a "reservation" they wished to put before the Senate. Their language was based on the Statement of Understanding that Escobar and I had drafted six months earlier for Carter and Torrijos, affirming that the United States accepted the territorial integrity of Panama and claiming no right to interfere in its internal affairs. They now believed, he said, that it would be better to have the treaty defeated on this principle than to put something through that would have to be rejected by Panama. As Church had said in a speech to the Senate, "Let us make clear to the world that we are not seeking for ourselves the kind of rights the Soviets claimed in Czechoslovakia in 1968." I agreed. I reported the conversation to Christopher, who informed Brzezinski.

The vote was scheduled for April 18. On April 13 I lunched with Brzezinski, who told me the President planned to make a statement insisting that the Senate insert a nonintervention reservation in the second treaty. In the afternoon, that signal was changed; the Senators involved wanted to do the job themselves. What they needed was an assurance that the language they were drafting would in fact be acceptable to Panama. Over the next few days, Mike Kozak in the State Department and the Senators wrote amendments that were shown to Ambassador Lewis, and by Lewis to Torrijos, in the last of the long series of give-and-take sessions between the United States and Panama. On Sunday morning, April 16, Ambassador Lewis went to Senator Church's office, and met there with Senators

Church, Byrd, and Sarbanes, and Warren Christopher from the State Department. Among them, they wrote a text proclaiming that nothing in the treaties should "have as its purpose or be interpreted as a right of intervention in the internal affairs of the Republic of Panama or interference with its political independence or sovereign integrity." Torrijos accepted it that night, and Byrd shepherded it through the Senate by a vote of seventy-three to twenty-seven.

The wording was unsatisfactory to DeConcini. Senator Byrd devoted most of April 17 to working on the junior Senator from Arizona. There were moments on that Monday when it scarcely seemed to matter. Hayakawa backed away because of his sleepless night. James Abourezk of South Dakota announced that because he disapproved of the way the administration was handling a pending gas decontrol bill, he was going to vote against the treaties. Cannon was reported leaning against. If we had lost DeConcini, we needed all three; even if we had kept DeConcini, we needed two.

The vote was scheduled for six o'clock Tuesday evening, April 18. Toni and I met Carol and Ellsworth Bunker at the Senate at five and sat in the gallery. Just before the vote Senator Abourezk was recognized to make a statement. He announced that the procedures the White House had agreed to follow in dealing with gas decontrol, while still insufficient to protect the public interest, were not so seriously insufficient that he would be compelled to vote against the Canal treaty. Then DeConcini voted aye, and Hayakawa, and Cannon, and we were home free. At sixty-eight to thirty-two, the vote was identical to that on the neutrality treaty.

We went to the White House, where Mrs. Carter greeted us wreathed in smiles. The President joined our little party, and took a call from Gabriel Lewis assuring him that Torrijos had accepted the treaties as passed by the Senate, with all the little amendments and reservations. The President then went before the television cameras to proclaim his gratification, and his conviction that the United States had acted with wisdom and in a manner to do us proud. From the White House, Bunker and I went on to a party at the Panamanian embassy, where we found Lewis on the phone with Torrijos, exchanging jubilant congratulations. Then Toni and I went on to the 1925 F Street Club for a dinner in honor of Andrew Heiskell, chairman of Time Inc. Among those present were Senators Long, Moynihan, and Dole, all of whom offered congratulations. I suggested to Senator Dole that it might be timely and useful for him as a leader of the opposition to the treaties to announce his recognition that the decision had now been taken through our constitutional process, and that the nation must unite in support of the new arrangements with Panama. He said he would do so the next day.

On April 19 I lunched with David McCullough, author of *The Path Between the Seas,* who had supported the treaties while they were pending before the Senate and had testified and lobbied for them. He said he believed that the Senate approval of the treaties would in fifty years rank as a "watershed" in American history, in many ways as important as the building of the canal itself. I like to believe that he was right.

Soon after the struggle had ended, I wrote for myself three pages of "Reflections on the Senate Vote." The experience, I thought, had not been all bad: "The vote reveals to the world that in our own fashion we are willing to match our words with our actions. For many years we have talked about our commitment to respect the rights of others and our concern that other nations — large or small — be entitled to fulfill their destiny in their own way and to be treated with fairness and magnanimity. After fourteen years of negotiation, we have finally approved a treaty arrangement with Panama, overcoming some virulent and widespread opposition and hostility. . . .

"The world today has a better understanding of our system of government — for good or for ill — and recognizes some of our weaknesses as well as our strengths better than it did before. Other nations . . . have watched with incredulity as we have gone through these strange shenanigans and these bewildering, sometimes troubling machinations. . . . The corollary is of course that the world saw us ultimately do the right thing against very heavy odds — and this is a very distinct plus both for the President and for the country. . . .

"William James once described our 'civic genius' as a people as the 'tried and disciplined good temper toward the other side when it fairly wins its inning.' Now that the inning has been fairly won, we will be tested to see whether we can really show that tried and disciplined good temper, and move forward to implement the Treaties in a way which will strengthen relationships in the Hemisphere and do us proud as a nation."

In the event, the passage of the implementation legislation proved as divisive and difficult as the ratification process, and the ideologues who opposed the new treaties retained their bad temper. One could no longer excuse their behavior as a misguided expression of patriotism, for at this stage rejection of the changes in our law necessary to meet our treaty obligations could accomplish nothing but mischief. I had hoped that — having achieved victory in the Panama Canal struggle — the President would build on the goodwill we had gained throughout Latin America, but the treaty fight had exhausted those who felt the administration could make Latin American relations a centerpiece of its foreign policy. Common wisdom in Washington held that Carter had dissipated his powers in a fight that was unworthy of the energy he had to expend and the political credit he had to consume.

I thought then and think now that the common wisdom was wrong. Victory does not diminish the stature of the victor. Having demonstrated that he could vanquish the public-opinion polls and beat emotion with reason, the President was in a uniquely strong position to move ahead. But one cannot live in the White House unmoved by the common wisdom of the capital. Later, in his memoirs, the President wrote that "if I could have foreseen early in 1977 the terrible battle we would face in Congress, it would have been a great temptation for me to avoid the issue. . . . The struggle left deep and serious political wounds that have never healed." Except for his passionate and continuing commitment to the morality of our relations with the Latin countries — his unswerving insistence that our attitudes toward the nations of this hemisphere would be determined by their willingness to honor the human rights of their inhabitants — the President put Latin American affairs behind him. The opportunity to create a new era of inter-American relations was lost.

The administration — and Washington in general — also failed to learn the other great lesson taught by the outcome of these less-than-great debates. In retrospect, it seems obvious that the President carried the treaties because some Senators who doubted the merits of the case were unwilling to take on their shoulders the bloody consequences of rejection. The conduct of foreign policy *is* lodged in the executive branch, however intrusive and demanding Congress may be. Apart from questions of war and peace, where the Constitution gives Congress a coeval role that a President denies at his peril, the Senate will not reject (although it may uncomfortably amend) a treaty on a subject of major importance that the chief magistrate insists is in the best interests of the United States. A number of political commentators have written that Jimmy Carter could not risk submitting the arms-control treaty he had negotiated with the Russians, because his enemies had made the ratification of the Panama treaties so difficult and painful. This is, I believe, a false perception. The same fear of the unknown that ultimately carried the votes in the Panama ratification would in my judgment have given the President a victory in Salt II. The tragedy is that he did not seek it.

And there is a tragic irony associated with our success in the negotiations for the new treaties and the fight for their ratification. For if Panama were still in turmoil, anguished by the dominating foreign presence in its midst, the risks involved in the hazardous course we have been following in Central America would be even more immediate and inhibiting than they are. It is precisely because Panama now regards the United States with friendship and trust — which friendship and trust the Panama Canal treaties did so much to earn — that an administration led by a President who opposed those treaties has been free to act as it has in Central America.

The irony speaks — perhaps cries out — for itself.

9

Carter, Sadat, and Begin

EVEN BEFORE WE HAD finished shepherding the Panama Canal treaties through the Senate, I had an inquiry from Cy Vance as to whether I might be interested in becoming the President's Special Representative in the Middle East. Anwar Sadat of Egypt had made his historic visit to Jerusalem while I was traveling the United States searching for public support for the treaties — but then everything had stalled. I told Vance I did not think a Special Representative could accomplish very much until the parties had reached some kind of agreement at the highest levels on their mutual objectives. Whether or not he agreed with this analysis, he kept within the State Department the task of representing the President of the United States in the linkage between Anwar Sadat and Menachem Begin, and assigned it to Alfred R. ("Roy") Atherton, who moved from Assistant Secretary for Near Eastern Affairs to ambassador-at-large. And then the President took these matters into his own hands. Like everyone else, I watched with concern and misgivings — and finally with exultation — as Jimmy Carter directed and stage-managed the unprecedented thirteen-day summit at Camp David in 1978 and then rescued the peace treaty between Israel and Egypt with his daring trip to the Middle East in early 1979.

Meanwhile, I labored for Jimmy Carter in a very different vineyard, as chairman of a Presidential Commission on World Hunger that was doubtless, as he assured me, near to his heart but inevitably far from his attention. (Urging me to undertake this task, he kept the possibility of a Middle Eastern mission in the background. I should be sure to choose a very capable vice-chairman, he said, to take over in case he needed me in the Middle East.) The commission was a highly diverse group, including academic nutritionists and political scientists (my vice-chairmen, as capable as anyone could wish, were Presidents Jean Mayer of Tufts University and Steven Muller of The Johns Hopkins University); agronomists such as Nobel Prize winner Norman Borlaug and politicians such as Senators Robert Dole and Patrick Leahy, business and religious leaders, and even pop singers John Denver and Harry Chapin. We met in public, and the sessions were difficult and often emotional as commissioners wrangled over what the real issues were. In due course it became clear that the problem is not that so many people are starving (although they are — tragically, many more now, in Africa, than then), but that great populations are undernourished; not that the world produces insufficient food, but that the food is badly distributed; not that the rich give too little to the poor (although they do), but that the poor are far less productive than they could be. This, it also became clear, is not the stuff of slogans.

We met and were told how important our work would be: at the first two-day meeting in June 1978 we were addressed by Cy Vance and Harold Brown, as proof that the cabinet took us seriously. We held hearings and visited strategic locations in the United States, and I spent a week at the headquarters of the bureaucratically self-centered Food and Agricultural Organization in Rome. The members of the commission were passionately committed and concerned. We argued endlessly over the documents prepared by our loyal and sometimes bewildered staff under our sensitive young executive director, Daniel Shaughnessy. Late in 1979 we produced a report. Its basic recommendation was "that the United States make the elimination of hunger the primary focus of its relationships with the developing countries, beginning with the decade of the 1980s." We believed the United States could contribute to this goal in various ways — narrowly, by directing aid programs to nutrition-related projects and by financing a larger grain reserve program to ensure supplies in crisis periods; more generally, by supporting the recently launched World Bank initiative for concentration on "basic human needs"; over time, by participating in programs to guarantee the prices of the commodities the developing countries produced and by removing tariff barriers to permit these countries to earn their way out of poverty by exporting their products.

I had insisted when the commission was established pursuant to a bipartisan resolution of Congress that its charter run for six months beyond the date of issuance of our report. This would ensure a center that could work toward the legislation necessary to implement our recommendations. By the time the report came out, however, the President was absorbed in Iran, I was engaged in the Middle East — and the reelection campaign had begun. We did not achieve unanimity on the commission, and the dissenter, Senator Dole, was among the most important actors on this stage politically. Legislation was introduced, and several House committees held hearings on our recommendations, but in the end no action was taken. I reflect with some bitterness that if that legislation we sought had passed, our aid to Africa would have been increased and redirected toward the improvement of agricultural production and distribution, and the current agony of that continent might have been substantially mitigated.

One bemusing moment associated with the Hunger Commission remains vivid in the memory. Mrs. Lillian Carter, the President's mother, was deeply interested in world hunger and eager to help. A thought was wafted by that she might become a commissioner, but I questioned the wisdom of that. I did meet with her, however, to gather her recollections of her extraordinary stint as a Peace Corps volunteer and her ideas on ways to remedy the poverty of rural Africa. This was a time when Billy Carter was making trouble for the President, lending his name to the promotion of a beer and acting as an agent for Qaddafi. Toward the end of our very pleasant conversation I felt emboldened to mention these matters to Mrs. Carter. I told her that I thought Billy's antics had become a more serious problem for the President than perhaps the family recognized, and asked whether she had thought of speaking with him to persuade him to moderate his behavior. "Me?" she said, somewhat startled. "Me tell Billy what to say and do? Why, I can't even tell *Jimmy* what to say and do."

I saw the President on many occasions during 1979, and we talked about a number of matters touching on foreign relations, and also about his tormenting, unsuccessful efforts to persuade Congress to adopt a rational energy policy. I was fascinated by the differences in our mind-sets. I live by general principles, which give order to the detailed information that comes to my attention. As a lawyer, I need the details, the facts of the case — for the case, for the moment. But I don't learn by accumulating details; I learn by discovering the right focus on the subject. In conversation, Carter was always looking for the specific, for the precise — and he would remember it: if you gave him an answer on one occasion, it had better be the same answer when the question came up again. He learned by gathering details and putting them together, but there wasn't always time to learn that way.

Carter is a brilliant man, but he was inexperienced in a number of areas and unsophisticated in a number of fields. He lacked the sure-footedness he thought he should have, and he was uncomfortable about relying on others for things he thought he should know and be able to do himself. He had an unusually solid grasp on what he wanted to accomplish, and an uncertain hold on how to go about it. As a result, he had difficulty in fixing and keeping his relationships with those outside the circle he had brought with him from his Georgia days. Brzezinski once said to me that when he entered the President's office he had to decide which President he was talking to — the formal President, the conversational President, or the friend. I tried at all times to get my conversations with the President on the informal level. He knew I had a high regard for him, quite apart from my feelings for his office, and usually we could work together easily and as friends.

One of the most dramatic of these meetings was in July 1979, when the President held what became his famous retreat at Camp David, from which he would emerge with his speech about the national "malaise" and his reconstruction of his cabinet. I was in the first group he summoned to meet with him on the mountaintop. The others were Clark Clifford, Lane Kirkland of the AFL-CIO, Jesse Jackson, John Gardner of Common Cause, political consultant Robert Keefe, and Barbara Newell, the former president of Wellesley College. Although Carter's later speech proved politically unfortunate, and the cabinet changes were handled in a way that caused considerable damage, all of us at Camp David felt that his reaching out for advice was a sign of strength, not weakness. "Malaise" was not a bad word to describe the condition of the country in summer 1979. The problems the President faced were real and difficult, and the Camp David retreat was an indication that he was dealing with them, not trying to finesse them. Unfortunately, the speech did not convey this impression. Moreover, by requiring offers of resignation from the entire cabinet, Carter communicated a message not that he was in control but that his administration was in disarray.

Toward the end of the summer of 1979, Secretary of Commerce Juanita Kreps decided that her obligations to a seriously ill husband had to take priority over public service. An academic and a very able, thoughtful, and hard-working woman, she was one of the people in the administration with whom I lunched fairly often, to discuss a wide range of subjects, including the reactions of the business community to the administration and what the Commerce Secretary could do about them. Her resignation had been forecast, and I was not entirely surprised when she told me she had recommended me to the President as her successor. Vice-President Walter Mondale asked me to come to his office on October 9, and offered me the post on behalf of the President. I told him I was flattered but I did not think it was the right position for me. Commerce to me is a post for a businessman: and while I have been a businessman, I think of myself first as a lawyer. Moreover, I thought I could be of greater help to the President in a foreign-relations assignment.

Presently the Vice-President was on the phone again to tell me that the President was not taking no for an answer and wanted me to come to the White House to discuss it with him. The President and I talked for an hour. Someone had told Carter that I had turned down the Commerce post once before, in the Lyndon Johnson days, and he said he wanted to be sure I knew that Commerce had become much more important in his administration. Moreover, it was about to become more important still with the passage of legislation that would turn over to this department much of the foreign trade responsibility previously allocated to the State Department and the Office of the Special Trade Representative in the White House.

I asked for a weekend to think it over, and I thought hard. The fact was that I did not want to be Secretary of Commerce, and in questions relating to what I am to do with my time and energy, I trust my instincts. When I called the President early Monday morning — the best time to call him was always before eight — he clearly expected my acceptance. He said he was disappointed. I said I hoped I would have some other chance to serve his administration; and he told me he was sure he would be back to me. Less than three weeks later, he was.

* * *

The Egyptian-Israeli peace treaty signed in Washington on March 26, 1979 — and celebrated that evening with a gigantic White House party I attended with more than a thousand other guests — came into effect three months behind the schedule laid down at Camp David, and fulfilled only half the commitments entered into by the parties. Still, it was an immense accomplishment and, as is now forgotten, a great gesture of trust and faith by Israel. By the terms of the treaty, Israel gave up the Alma oil fields it had developed in the Sinai in the previous decade (which were pumping almost $1 billion worth of oil a year); abandoned the military base at Sharm-el-Sheikh that controlled access to the Gulf of Aqaba and the Israeli port of Eilat, the nation's window on Asia; dismantled the most productive and unthreatened of the settlements previous Labor and presumably more "peaceful" Israeli governments had implanted on the territory taken in 1967; and surrendered strong points that previous Egyptian governments had used as bases for terrorist attacks throughout southern Israel. The quid pro quo was certainly not trivial: peace with the largest and militarily most potent of the nation's former enemies, a "normalization of relations" that might have great economic as well as political and security values. But it was at bottom a piece of paper that might be repudiated by a successor government of Egypt.

In another sense, however, Sadat at Camp David had also accepted a piece of paper: an Israeli promise to negotiate the creation of "full autonomy" for the Palestinians in Gaza and on the West Bank of the Jordan River, which had come under Israeli control in the same war that produced the occupation of the Sinai. Between 1947 and 1967 the West Bank had been governed by Jordan, and both Sadat and Carter had hoped and expected that King Hussein of Jordan would participate in negotiations for Palestinian autonomy. When he did not, he left Sadat in the awkward position of negotiating on behalf of the Palestinians, who had never asked him to do so. Sadat was sensitive to the Arab League accusation that he had sold the Palestinians down the river to get the return of the Sinai to Egypt. He accepted the Israeli refusal to permit any role in the negotiations for the Palestine Liberation Organization, which had in its charter a demand for the liquidation of the Jewish state; and he had agreed at Camp David to a five-year period in which the autonomous entity (described in one of the clauses of the agreement, at

Begin's insistence, as an "Administrative Council") would be given only prearranged powers and responsibilities and essentially would have to rely on Israel for its external security. But Sadat believed Israel had committed itself to "full autonomy" for the Palestinians — a phrase that had first been proposed by Begin himself but was nowhere defined in the agreement. Before signing the peace treaty, Sadat exacted a pledge that arrangements for "full autonomy" on the West Bank and in the Gaza Strip would be completed by May 26, 1980, exactly fourteen months later.

The six months between the end of the Camp David sessions and the signature of the treaty had been a time of much agitation at the White House and the State Department. Vance, Brzezinski, and the President himself had all made trips to the Middle East in that period, to keep the Israelis and Egyptians talking with each other (which they found much easier to do when they had a senior American official as a go-between) and on occasion to propose draft agreements to resolve specific disputes. With the treaty in place, and the negotiations shifting from Egyptian to Palestinian concerns, the President himself could no longer be directly involved. The parties still needed American help, however, and the helper had to be someone who was sufficiently close to the President of the United States to ensure his access at will to the President of Egypt and the Prime Minister of Israel.

This time it was Brzezinski who inquired about my availability, and I discouraged him. In any event, Carter had someone else in mind: Robert Strauss, a Texas-born Washington lawyer who had served as chairman of the Democratic party. As Carter's Special Trade Representative, he had skillfully managed the American end of the Tokyo Round of negotiations to modify the General Agreement on Tariffs and Trade, and had brought home a treaty on schedule. In his memoirs, the President reports that Strauss at first protested that he was not the right man for this job — not only was he Jewish, he said, but he had never read the Bible, a comment Carter knew enough to relish as a revealing non sequitur. Strauss was also far from eager to become involved again with the State Department, which he thought had played a disruptive role in the trade negotiations. Carter responded by assuring Strauss that he would not go to the Middle East as part of the State Department; he would go as a representative of the President. Strauss then announced to the press that as Middle East negotiator he would be reporting directly to the President and would keep the Secretary of State "informed." In theory, he had an office both at the State Department and in the Executive Office Building adjacent to the White House, but he hardly ever visited the State Department.

The major accomplishment of Strauss's months as negotiator was an agreement by the Egyptians and Israelis (meeting with Strauss at Leeds Castle in England) that the Palestinians would elect the officers of their autonomous entity, and that the election would be supervised by some international agency. The nature of the body to be elected remained in dispute — the Israelis felt that "autonomy" was an administrative concept, and required no law-making body; the Egyptians felt that without a legislature to ensure popular participation in policy making, the inhabitants of the West Bank would not consider themselves in any important sense "self-governed." And the composition of the supervising international agency was left for future determination. To confront these uncertainties, the negotiating group had been broken in two — one half to deal with "Modalities," the other half with "Powers and Responsibilities." In the context of Israeli-Arab relations, agreement on *anything* was newsworthy, and this modest step had taken weeks of work, both behind the scenes and under what Walter Lippmann once called "the searchlight" of the press. As Bob Strauss would be quick to admit, patience is not his strong suit, and after six months he was becoming restless.

Meanwhile, the President had decided to run for reelection, and Senator Kennedy was fighting to deny him the nomination. Strauss had been chairman of the Democratic party and had run Carter's 1976 campaign. Carter now wanted him to return home and organize his reelection drive, both in the primaries and in the ultimate election. He needed a new Middle East negotiator, and now he believed it was definitely my turn. When he called on October 30, I told him that I seriously questioned whether I was the right person. I thought it might be unwise for the United States to be represented by a committed and involved Jew in an area where so many of the conflicts had a religious aspect. Carter pointed out that both Kissinger and Strauss were Jewish and had been able to operate in the Middle East. My situation, I said, was different, because my Jewish involvements were far deeper than theirs. I was chairman of the board of the Jewish Theological Seminary, had been chairman of the executive board of the American Jewish Committee, and had served in other Jewish leadership posts. When he insisted, I told him I would have to think it over, discuss it with Toni, and let him know. He said he was lunching with Strauss that day and wished to complete the political arrangements. He did not feel he could move Strauss until he had me as his replacement. And, he added, "I don't have any second choice."

Early the next morning, I went to New York for a board meeting of the Mutual Life Insurance Company of New York, and was summoned out of the meeting by a message that the President was calling. He had been trying to reach me, he said, since seven o'clock that morning; he'd thought I was avoiding him. He needed my decision. "You're not making my life any easier," I said. "No," he replied. "But I *am* making it more interesting and exciting — and uncertain." Tentatively, subject to the results of my own meeting with Strauss (which the President thereupon set up for the next day), I accepted. I wanted an appointment on the same terms as my Panama engagement — no compensation and no requirement that I drop my law practice or my boards — with one exception: I thought that this time I should be confirmed by the Senate, to avoid the 180-day restriction on my tenure and also some of the nastiness that had surfaced in the Panama treaty debates. The President agreed.

I met with Strauss, who suggested graciously that the President should have appointed me to begin with. With my background, he said, I would have been much better placed to get along with the State Department. He thought progress was possible in the autonomy negotiations, and in any event he believed that it was vital that they be continued, in the interest of the parties and of the President. Out of the blue, I received a phone call from Ashraf Ghorbal, the Egyptian ambassador in Washington, whom I knew casually (everyone in Washington knew Ghorbal, a most effective and attractive representative of his country and one of the most experienced diplomats in the capital; his problem was that Sadat often failed to keep him informed on the views and plans of his own country). He said he had heard I was under consideration as the President's representative to the Middle East negotiations, and that I was hesitating because I felt my Jewish faith and connections might cause problems with the Arab side. He wanted to assure me that he and his government had complete confidence in my sense of fairness, and would be delighted to receive me as the President's representative.

On a purely human basis, I could not have refused this request from this President. The Middle East was Jimmy Carter's great achievement. He thought that Camp David was what history would record in looking back on his administration. It was, in the deepest sense, his baby. He had astounded his aides and advisers by going to the mountaintop and coming down with an agreement, and he remembered all the details. As I talked to him during the next year, I would find myself touching buttons, and calling forth exact recollections: on such-and-such a day, Sadat had said this, Begin had said that. At Camp David, Jimmy Carter had electrified the world; he had found the basis for Middle East peace — and now he saw it being frittered away. "What we're talking about," he said, "is the future of world peace. There is nothing more important I could ask you to do." Unlike other American ambassadors, I knew when I sent messages home that the President had an intense interest in the subject and would read my cables. When I returned from trips to the area, I almost invariably found a message waiting to come to the White House the next morning or even that day and meet with the President.

My appointment was announced on November 6, 1979, following a meeting of Carter, Strauss, and myself in the Oval Office. I made a point of telling the press that I would be reporting both to Carter and to Vance; Cy called that afternoon to express appreciation. But Israel and Egypt were not at the forefront of Carter's or Vance's attention that week. Two days earlier, the Iranian "students" had seized the American embassy in Tehran.

My fourteen months as "Personal Representative of the President for the Middle East Peace Negotiations" were, as the President had promised, the most interesting and exciting — and uncertain — of my life. They might also, I think, have been the most productive, if the incoming Reagan administration had built in early 1981 on the foundations we had laid for them. Even today, it is not understood how close Sadat and Begin came to an agreement in that difficult year, or how effective an Israeli-Egyptian agreement would have been in driving the West Bank and Gaza Palestinians to an acceptance of "full autonomy" under the Camp David accords. Despite their public denunciations of Camp David, the Palestinians knew this was the best they could get for the time being, and that from the institutions of autonomy they might generate the essentials of self-governance. Autonomy under Israeli control, after all, was not to be an end point: within three years of the establishment of the autonomous entity, there were to be negotiations to determine the "final status" of this territory, and in those negotiations the Self-Governing Authority of the Palestinians would be an equal party with Israel, Egypt, and Jordan.

I believe that an autonomy agreement for the Palestinians could have been achieved in 1981, and for the simplest of reasons — the leaders were Anwar Sadat and Menachem Begin. They knew and respected each other, and understood each other's political bases, strengths, and weaknesses. Sadat referred to Begin as "my cousin Menachem," and once said to me that he and Begin had told each other "things we have never told anyone else, including our wives." Each for his own reasons needed a successful conclusion to the process Sadat had set in motion in 1977. Begin was facing an election, and the polls showed his coalition well behind the Labor party; he could have used an opportunity to prove he was truly a peacemaker. Neither man was a free agent or could ignore the great political, religious, and economic forces that play for eternity in this cockpit of the world. But both were men of force and strength who could use reality to change reality. Coming to office with a clean slate in January 1981, Ronald Reagan and Alexander Haig could, I think, have brought them together and shielded them with American power and prestige while they did what had to be done. This is what I told Haig soon after he took office: that he and the President should declare their sense of the urgency of a successful conclusion of the Egypt-Israel autonomy negotiations, and appoint as my successor someone known to have the ear, the confidence, and the trust of the President. But they had other priorities.

I have, admittedly an optimistic temperament. Negotiators, almost by definition, have to be optimists; too often, we must try to fashion an acceptable agreement out of unworkable materials. When I took the Middle East assignment, I decorated the wall of my White House office with a framed statement of Casey Stengel's: "They say you can't do it, but sometimes that doesn't always work." At the beginning, however, I had no reason to disagree with the general assessment around the White House that the primary reason for keeping the negotiations going was less the hope for a resolution of the conflict than the fear of what might happen if they collapsed. Certainly, the time I spent at the State Department between my appointment and my confirmation, studying twenty years of cables and reports, gave little support for optimism.

The Department had been taken aback by Sadat's original initia-

218 The Making of a Public Man

tive, and not everyone in it shared the President's enthusiasm for the Camp David accords. A large number of the people in the Near East Bureau were diplomats who had learned Arabic and studied Arab culture and psychology, and their perspective on the world was understandably tilted by their backgrounds. They saw the interests of the United States as tied to the friendship of the Gulf nations, with their oil resources, their involvement with Palestinian refugees, and their view of Israel as an intrusion in the region. Finding this "professional" advice ignored at the White House, these diplomats saw their own government as unduly influenced by a "Jewish vote" in American elections. They lived in hope of finding a President who would "restore a balance" in American views of the Arab-Israeli conflict. They were supported, moreover, by many in the International Organizations Bureau, where senior diplomats felt we were sacrificing our influence at the United Nations by our refusal to accept the condemnations of Israel that flowed in a steady stream from the General Assembly and the UN affiliates. In both bureaus, the central attitude was that progress could not be made toward resolution of the tensions in the Middle East until the United States was willing to lean on the Israelis to make concessions. It was not the only attitude: the excellent and open-minded staff assigned to me by the State Department was also drawn primarily from the Near East Bureau. But a weary resentment of Israel's insistence on taking care of Israeli interests was something I came to expect in a great many of my contacts with the State Department.

My confirmation hearings were easy, especially by comparison with the great nuisance of pulling together the financial statements the White House felt the Foreign Relations Committee would require. Senator Edmund Muskie claimed the privilege of introducing me as an old friend from our Cornell Law School days, and the members of the committee were kind in their praise of my work on the canal treaties. The only opposition was from Senator Jesse Helms, and even he insisted that his major reason for objecting to the appointment was his disapproval of the idea of a part-time Presidential representative who continued to maintain his private associations. When I returned to my office after the hearings, I called him to inquire what additional information I could give him that might be helpful to him. He said there was no specific remedy I could offer, his objection was to the principle of the thing; but I should know he thought I was "behaving like a gentleman." He voted against the nomination in the committee and on the floor.

The day after the Senate vote, December 5, I met with President Carter, who handed over to me a massive loose-leaf book of handwritten and typed pages, his personal diaries of the thirteen days on Camp David, telling me not to let anyone else see them and to return them the next day. He said that no one else had ever read them — "not even Rosalynn." Reading the President's contemporaneous notes was immensely useful and revealing. Among other things, it gave me an understanding of why Carter's relations with Begin had deteriorated. I have no doubt that Carter fully believed that at Camp David, Begin had promised no further Israeli settlements on the West Bank during the autonomy negotiations — or that Begin believed he had promised to suspend his government's settlements program only for the supposed three months of the treaty negotiations with Egypt.

There is some evidence that Sadat himself, although deeply troubled by the spread of Israeli settlements, may not have shared Carter's understanding as to Begin's commitment at Camp David. In a press conference shortly after Camp David, Sadat referred to an Israeli commitment not to start new settlements "during the period of the negotiations on the peace treaty," not to a commitment that would run for the period of the negotiations over autonomy. But Carter had told the Arab states that one of the important accomplishments of Camp David was the long-term freeze. Vance and Assistant Secretary Harold Saunders, visiting Jordan and the Gulf states, had stressed Carter's achievement in persuading Begin to stop the settlements program. When it turned out that there were going to be more settlements after all, the President lost credibility with the Jordanians and the Saudis, who were reinforced in their beliefs that the United States lacked either the means or the will to set limits on Israeli actions. For Carter, the settlements issue became the central test of Begin's willingness to live up to his undertakings.

Such differences in interpretation were almost inescapable in the later stages of the Camp David meetings, when everyone was searching for words that would permit differences to be skirted so that this extraordinary venture in trilateral diplomacy would not end in failure. And they were inevitably made worse by the fact that both the Egyptian and Israeli negotiators were working in a language not their own.

One of the most disappointing sessions I moderated in my time as negotiator was a brass-tacks discussion between Josef Burg for Israel and Mustafa Khalil for Egypt, on the question of the powers to be transferred from Israel to the autonomous entity on the West Bank. The two men seemed in all but complete agreement on scme vital points, and we were discussing what we should say to the press, when suddenly Khalil said, "I cannot go along with that." Khalil was extraordinarily knowledgeable in English — he has a Ph.D. from the University of Illinois — but it was not until he heard me read a proposed public statement that he realized he had been misled by his hopes.

We had known what day the Senate would vote on my confirmation, and it was clear that I would be approved, so plans were made for me to travel to the Middle East the next day. I met with the press for half an hour and said that I was not taking any proposals with me, and that the purpose of my trip was to meet the principals, hear what they had to say, and learn the situation firsthand. In fact, it was a holding action, because we had reason to believe Sadat planned to postpone the next meeting of the second-level negotiators, as a gesture of protest against what he regarded as Israeli failure to be forthcoming, and we hoped that the arrival of the new American representative would keep things on the existing rails. Before leaving, I had a talk with Ambassador Ghorbal of Egypt and with the Israel ambassador, Ephraim Evron, a wise man who was a steady source of advice and comfort in the difficult months ahead.

Toni and I crossed the Atlantic on one of the planes in the Presidential fleet, stopping in Spain for adjustment to time zone changes and a meeting with Spanish Foreign Ministry officials. With us were Ned Walker, my highly capable assistant at the State Department; Andrew Marks, a young, dedicated, and imaginative lawyer in charge of my office at the White House; David Korn, director of the Israel desk at the State Department; two security men; and several secretaries and technical advisers. Harold Saunders, Assistant Secretary for the Near East, and Bob Hunter of the National Security Council had been expected to make the trip, but Iranian matters had intervened. A few months later, Ambassador James Leonard, a former deputy U.S. Representative to the United Nations, became my deputy in the negotiations and spent months on the scene, meeting with Egyptian and Israeli groups.

In Egypt we were greeted at the airport by Ambassador Atherton, who took me back to the embassy for a meeting of all the U.S. ambassadors to the area — Egypt, Israel, Jordan, Syria, and Saudi Arabia (which I was also to visit on this trip). We met in a special, secured office, a large group clustered in a small area under a plastic "bubble" that guaranteed against eavesdropping. The meeting lasted more than two hours, and it was very unpleasant.

Our ambassadors to the area, other than those to Israel and Egypt, made clear that they regarded the peace between those countries and the autonomy negotiations as a wrongheaded sideshow that was distracting attention from the real drama and was in itself probably harmful. The heart of the Israeli-Arab dispute, they insisted, was the Palestinian problem, and both the Palestinians and the surrounding Arab states had decided that the only "legitimate" spokesman for the people involved was the Palestine Liberation Organization. If Carter wished to accomplish anything permanent in the region, he had to sit down with Arafat and the PLO. None of the Arab countries would ever accept an agreement negotiated between Israel and Egypt; supported by the rest of the Arabs, the Palestinians would never accept it, either. The continued spectacle of American involvement in these negotiations was hurting our relations throughout the area.

Finally, I had had enough. I told the ambassadors that, if they wished, I was willing to return to Washington immediately and tell the President that they believed that *his* mission to the Middle East, not to mention his past efforts to bring peace, was a foolish mistake that would damage the interests of the United States. This calmed them down considerably, and produced offers of assistance — limited, however, by a continuing insistence that the only fruitful policy the United States could adopt was one that began with recognition of the PLO. They also felt that the oil of the Gulf states was the real U.S. interest in the area, and that our support of Israel was a strategy with unacceptably high risks.

The next day I met Anwar Sadat, and moved into a different world. We met alone, as we would on a number of subsequent occasions, at his comfortable home in Barrages on the Nile. Sadat was a man of great, encompassing vision, informal in manner (although always impeccably tailored), profoundly convinced of the rightness of his own positions and contemptuous of those who disagreed. After the first five minutes of what turned into a two-and-a-half-hour discussion, he was calling me "Sol," and when he referred to me thereafter it was always as "my friend [or dear friend] Sol." ("He likes to use private names," Begin once told me with a shrug. "I do not like to use private names. So he calls me 'Menachem,' and

I call him, 'Mr. President.' ") A soldier, he had been a junior member of the military junta that deposed the Egyptian monarchy, and had been Nasser's unassertive vice-president.

Sadat's hold on his people derived in large part from the attack his forces had launched across the Suez Canal on Yom Kippur, the holiest of days in the Jewish religion, in 1973. The Egyptian armed forces then "regained their dignity" by winning the first half of the war, although before it was over the Western powers had to hold the Israelis back from administering terrible punishment. The Israelis remembered all of this, the Egyptians only half of it. The leader of the counteroffensive that blasted Egyptian hopes, incidentally, had been Ariel Sharon, who under Begin was in charge of the Israeli settlements on the West Bank and in the Sinai.

Sadat was a man who believed that leaders should settle large matters and force their subordinates to settle the details. His complaint against Begin was that through nit-picking and pettifoggery the Israeli had "stopped in the middle of the road." Once he said with great sadness, "My cousin Menachem is so afraid, he does not realize we can do great things together." He understood the limits on what Begin could concede, however. By the time I entered the negotiations, he was no longer demanding that all Israeli settlements on the West Bank be dismantled or that all Israeli troops be removed from the area, but he did insist upon Moslem control of the Moslem shrines on the Temple Mount in Jerusalem. He felt this personally as well as politically. He was a religious man, who prayed six times a day and had a callus on his forehead from hitting it to the ground during those prayers. Even here, though, he was not without sympathy for Begin. Asking me to convey his Jerusalem proposals on my next meeting with Begin, he added, "But do it very carefully because this is a very sensitive subject with him." And he insisted that the Israelis not use the five years of "full autonomy" on the West Bank as a time for expanding the presence of their settlements, displacing or appearing to displace the native population.

Sadat's stress on the larger issues — the need for peace in the region, security for Israel and her neighbors, self-government for the Palestinians — was a constant source of discomfort to his subordinates. They had the responsibility for working out the details, many of which would be anathema to the Arab states and to many Egyptians. On several occasions, senior members of the Egyptian govern-

ment spoke to me before a meeting with Sadat to ask me to protect
him from himself. Carter, who had a relationship of deep affection
with Sadat, was also concerned that in his eagerness to win agreement the Egyptian might make commitments he could not carry
out.

Sadat's attitude toward other Arab leaders was often contemptuous. He referred to Colonel Qaddafi repeatedly as a "lun-átic" and
spoke of the Saudi royal family as "dwarfs." Syria's Assad, he repeatedly assured me, would not survive in power another six
months. And Jordan's King Hussein, in his view, was a weak man
who had been "bought and paid for" by the Saudis and would take
orders from them when the time came. Among the Israelis, he was
most fond of Ezer Weizman (whom he long insisted on calling
Ezra), a buoyant and irrepressible *sabra*.

Hosni Mubarak, the Vice-President, attended many of my meetings with Sadat but remained silent, attentive to Sadat's wishes. He
was always the dutiful subaltern, biding his time, and was well prepared when, tragically, that time came. A number of those in
Sadat's inner circle were men of considerable distinction. I became
especially fond of Mustafa Khalil, Sadat's Prime Minister and the
chief negotiator until August 1980, when Sadat removed him from
power and took the title of Prime Minister himself. Khalil was a
man of large horizons. He was fascinated by the relationship of Hebrew culture to Islamic civilization, learned Hebrew, and became
learned in Judaism. Bhutros Ghali, the number-two man in the
Ministry of Foreign Affairs (he could never become Minister, I was
told, because he was a Coptic Christian and his wife was Jewish),
was a professorial figure, as pessimistic as Sadat was optimistic, who
became emotional when discussing the plight of the Palestinians.
Kamal Hassan Ali, the general who became Foreign Minister and
chief negotiator with the Israelis (and is now Prime Minister), was
far from the normal image of a military man, being warm, concilia-
tory, and open-minded. He was overshadowed by Osama el Baz, a
remote figure with a brilliant mind and a shrill voice, a graduate of
Harvard Law School who was Sadat's speechwriter and adviser.
Brooding by temperament, el Baz was distrustful of the Israelis in
general and Begin in particular.

Sadat knew that many in Egypt doubted the wisdom of his
course. In September 1980, when negotiations were in abeyance because it seemed to Sadat that he was countenancing the spread and

growth of Israeli settlements, I secured a promise from the Israelis limiting their number, worked out a statement calling for recommitment to the principles of Camp David, dedication to the improvement of trust between Israel and Egypt, and resumption of negotiations looking toward another summit meeting with President Carter. When I arrived from Israel with Begin's approval of the statement, Ambassador Atherton said I might as well try it out, but he did not believe Sadat could accept it. Instead, Sadat, puffing on his pipe, listened as I read the document and then uttered one word: "Excellent." I was amazed, but followed up immediately: "Then you agree with the statement as I read it?" He nodded and blinked, and replied, "With every word of it." I took the next step: "May we go out together then," I said, "and I will read it to the press?" As we walked to meet the massive press contingent gathered outside, Sadat said to me, "Everybody in my government will be against this, but I am doing it because I know it is right." The next day I had to explain to Hassan Ali and Bhutros Ghali what it was their President had agreed to, because Sadat did not even have a copy of the statement.

It is also the fact, however, that I had to telephone the White House with the language of the statement after the press conference, because I had not consulted with *my* government before it was issued: the modalities of my conduct of these negotiations were — with full permission of the President and the Secretary of State — freewheeling. Carter had been in a meeting with a labor group when the news flash from the press conference swept around the world, so he heard the story first from me. He was excited and enthusiastic.

As the negotiations lurched from crisis to crisis the number of doubters inevitably grew, both in Egypt and in the United States. Every time the Israelis moved to exploit their strength — threatening to annex the Golan Heights, threatening to annex East Jerusalem, announcing grandiose plans for increasing the number of Jewish settlements on the West Bank — Sadat reacted, most often by slowing the process of "normalization," the growth of trade and tourism and technical cooperation that was creating a foundation for a real, not just paper, peace between the two countries. Sometimes the only effective tool in his kit was the threat to suspend or even terminate the autonomy negotiations.

Much of the pressure to keep the process moving came from the United States, which in the Carter administration firmly held the

Israeli settlements to be "illegal" under the terms of the Geneva Convention governing the behavior of an occupying power.[1] When the Reagan administration failed to press forward in the autonomy negotiations or to appoint a successor to my post, and stopped describing the settlements as "illegal," Sadat's position at home was directly affected. Although no one who walked an Egyptian street with him and saw his people swarm to touch his uniform could doubt his dominance of his nation's political life, charisma in the absence of results easily turns sour and leads to repression. In the months before his assassination Sadat had to rely increasingly on force to still his opposition. He told me, dismissing the matter with a chuckle, that he had received many death threats; and Jihan Sadat is certain that when the gunmen ran toward her husband's box at the military review, he rose because he wanted to die on his feet. When I was working with him, however, his native optimism was still an expansive force not only in his own country but throughout the region and, indeed, the world.

The aspect of Menachem Begin that not many understood was that he had a sense of humor. I remember telling him that every time I went home people wanted the answer to three questions: Would there be peace in the Middle East? What was it like negotiating with the Israelis? Why did I like Menachem Begin? He asked what my answers were, and I said, "The third question is the really tough one" — and he laughed appreciatively. On one occasion in New York, in the Israeli apartment at the Waldorf Towers, he and I ran on beyond our appointed time and an assistant came in to remind him that a prominent Jewish donor and advice-giver was waiting to see the Prime Minister. Begin nodded, and said to me, "What do you think of him?" I replied, "I'll tell you later." Begin said, "I agree with you."

Begin's view of his own place in history was very different from what most people would expect. Once I asked him who his heroes were. He replied by asking me what I thought. On the walls of his

[1] The Israelis denied the illegality, and I believe had a stronger case in law than the United Nations or the State Department wished to admit. Jordan had not been recognized as sovereign over the West Bank prior to 1967, when the Israelis took possession, and the British had abandoned their mandate two decades before. For Geneva Convention purposes, it was not clear that Israel's rights on this land were inferior to Jordan's. I believed after studying the case that the settlements were unwise and a barrier to peace, but not that they were obviously illegal.

office — typically, one met Sadat at home and Begin at the office —
there were pictures of Theodor Herzl, founder of Zionism, and
Vladimir Jabotinsky, the aggressive promoter of a Jewish homeland
in all of Eretz Yisrael, so I mentioned those two names first. Begin
nodded. "Of course, they are my heroes," he said. "But my greatest
hero is neither of them. The greatest of them all is Garibaldi." I was
astonished, but after I read Trevelyan's biography of Garibaldi, to
which Begin referred me, I could understand: the radical, the violent
man (always denounced, as Begin pointed out, in the headlines of
the *Times* of London), who became the great unifier of his country
and his people.

Begin cherished his image as an unbending negotiator. When I
held a press conference after a meeting with him, I always had to be
very careful to avoid any implication that he had given ground, even
though sometimes he had, and announcing it would have been helpful to the world's perception of Israel and Begin. I said to him once
that he and Israel were losing support because Sadat had the art of
saying no and making it sound like yes, whereas Begin would say
yes and make it sound like no.

The great sticking point for Israel was, of course, security. Whatever interpretation might be put on Resolution 242 of the UN General Assembly, clearly Israel would never return to the pre-1967
situation, with hostile armies on the heights above the Sea of Gal-
ilee, around the road to Jerusalem, a dozen miles from the Mediter-
ranean at the nation's narrow waist. Obviously, however,
Palestinian autonomy would have little meaning if Israel could con-
tinuously redefine its security needs with reference to the land sup-
posedly under the self-governing Palestinian authority.

Among the Egyptian demands was an agreement specifying what
the Israelis could and could not do in the name of security in Gaza
and the West Bank. At first, Begin and his learned and witty chief
negotiator, Interior Minister Josef Burg, had angrily refused to negotiate on anything touching Israel's security — which was, Burg
said, "a matter for Israel's own determination, and not to be subject
to agreement." Later, at our meetings in The Hague in February
1980, they agreed to discuss security matters in a committee formed
by the staffs of both nations' armed forces. The quid pro quo was a
committee on water rights, which the Egyptians wished to leave for
future negotiations between Israel and the new Palestinian governing body but the Israelis wished to have spelled out in advance.

Begin grew emotional very easily on a number of subjects. He had lost his parents and his brother in the Holocaust, and he wept as he told me about it, movingly and at some length. Often, he responded to a negotiating point with the words, "This I cannot *consider*,"[2] and I would say, "Let's think about it overnight"; and the next day we would discuss it. He could make a show of being angry, and sometimes it was out of the kit bag of the canny negotiator, and he was never far from the substance of an issue. Yet that substance often presented itself to him in a rather abstract and theoretical way. Despite his legal training, he was more a Talmudic disputer than an advocate for a practical brief. Indeed, part of the problem with the concept of "full autonomy," which was his, was the fact that it was only a concept, a large and principled gesture that would have to be limited, of course, by the reality of Israeli interests. And the philosophical roots of the concept lay tangled in Begin's distinction between autonomy for the inhabitants of the land (which was what he claimed he meant) and autonomy on the land itself.

For Begin, all of Israel ("what other people call 'Palestine,' " he once wrote me scornfully) was Eretz Yisrael, and the borders drawn on the truce lines of 1948 were irrelevant. He did not speak of the West Bank, but of Judea and Samaria, the provinces into which the area had been divided in biblical times. Sadat suggested that Gaza be used as a laboratory for autonomy, because it was not part of historic Israel and there were no Israeli settlements there — an idea that intrigued Begin but eventually did not take.[3]

The idea of "dismantling" the Jewish settlements on the West Bank was anathema to Begin, for whom the eviction of the Jews from the Sinai as part of the treaty with Egypt was a painful memory forever being renewed by the nationalists who were and always had been his political base. He said Sadat wished the West Bank to be "Judenrein," free of any Jewish presence, the term the Nazis had used; he could not accept, he would repeat, the idea that there was

[2] Once Begin replied to a suggestion by Sadat with the story of a rabbi asked if he had ever thought of conversion to Christianity. The rabbi was horror-struck: "Even to *contemplate* such a thing," he said, "would be a sin." Sadat told me about it; Begin was impressed that Sadat had remembered.

[3] During the course of my efforts to explore autonomy in Gaza, I met with the mayor of Gaza, and was photographed with him leaving his office. When the PLO viciously criticized him for meeting with me, he publicly denied that he had done so. Among my souvenirs of the concept of "truth" in the Middle East is the deadpan presentation of this statement on Israeli television, which used the mayor's denial that he had ever met me as the soundtrack for the film of the two of us leaving his home together.

any part of the world where Jews would not be permitted to live. Even on this issue we made some progress in 1980, for there was an indication that after the establishment of the Self-Governing Authority Israel might consider an agreement that the creation of new settlements on the West Bank should be only with Palestinian approval — provided the other side agreed that such settlements of Palestinians could be established only with the approval of Israel.

Even on the emotional subject of Jerusalem, which always evoked lightning flashes and thunderclaps, I felt sunbeams of hope. In the original UN plan for the partition of Palestine — which the Jewish Agency, the predecessor to the Israeli government, had, however reluctantly, accepted — Jerusalem was to be a stateless city, a self-administered secular expression of the fact that the place was holy to three religions. As the result of the 1948 war, when the Arabs attacked to prevent the formation of a Jewish state, the city had been divided between Israel and Jordan, with most of the holy sites under Jordanian control and Israelis forbidden to visit them. After 1967, the city had been united. The Israelis had made the Temple Mount accessible to members of all the religions, and had given the Moslems control of their mosques, although under the watchful eye of Israeli security forces.

It was generally agreed among the United States, Israel, and Egypt that Jerusalem should remain undivided, but the United States had never accepted the idea of Israeli sovereignty over the city. The American embassy in Israel was located in Tel Aviv, as were nearly all other nations' embassies, although the Israeli government had its seat in Jerusalem. The post of U.S. Consul General in Jerusalem was an anomaly. The United States did not seek the consent of the Israeli or any other government for the operation of this office, and the Consul General had no official diplomatic status. (Among his functions, never openly admitted, was to maintain U.S. contact with the Palestinians living on the West Bank.)

For Begin, the issue was closed: Jerusalem, all of it, was the capital of Israel. Any change in the status of the city was, he said, one of those things it was impermissible even to contemplate. As a symbol of Israeli sovereignty over the entire city, he planned to move his office into the area formerly controlled by Jordan. He stopped when we informed him that it would derail the negotiations completely, and that the United States could not criticize any action Sadat might take in response. Begin furiously rejected our "intervention in internal Israeli affairs," but did not in fact move his office; there were problems, he indicated, in getting the right furniture for the new establishment. This was vintage Begin: he yielded, but denied he had done so.

Camp David had fudged the Jerusalem issue completely, leaving all consideration of the city for future negotiations. Sadat accepted that, but as a Moslem — and as a politician conscious of what would be required to gain even the most grudging acceptance of his peace with Israel elsewhere in the Arab world — he required some juridical statement of his religion's control over its holy places. He wanted a flag that was not an Israeli flag to fly over the sacred mosques. For Begin, flying the flag of any nation other than Israel in Jerusalem would be a denigration of Israeli sovereignty. I asked Sadat one day whether he would be satisfied with a Moslem flag, not the flag of any state, to express "religious sovereignty" over the Moslem holy places. He was intrigued, and tentatively agreed. When I proposed the idea to Begin, it piqued his curiosity as a lawyer. (He was proud of his legal training; sometimes, when I wished to make sure he carefully considered a proposal I was making, I would say I was suggesting it "as one lawyer to another.") "Religious sovereignty — what is that?" he asked, and I said, "Exactly." He took the idea under advisement, and although he eventually rejected it, I was (and remain) convinced that it could be revived and made workable.

Even the issue of the governance of Jerusalem was not beyond hope of resolution. Sadat could not ask its non-Jewish residents to abandon all hope of administering their own affairs while others in what had been Jordanian Palestine received "full autonomy," but it was not necessary to divide the city with barbed wire to provide for the legitimate rights of the non-Jewish inhabitants. There could be two levels of government — as there are, for example, in New York City and in London, where the boroughs continue to have significant functions. East Jerusalem and West Jerusalem could have separate councils dealing with local questions, joined at the top by a mayor responsible to both communities, although asserting Israeli sovereignty in his unique person.

The issue that dominated the context of the negotiations was, of course, the settlements, some of them agricultural plantations and some of them hilltop fortresses, that the Israeli government installed on the West Bank land captured from Jordan in the 1967 war. There were not as many of them as press reports indicated, because each settlement was announced four and five times in different fora. Even in 1984, after several years of aggressive settling, the total population of these West Bank establishments was still less than 40,000, compared to 750,000 Palestinians. But there were enough settlements — and the announced plans for the future were sufficiently extensive — to persuade Sadat that "full autonomy" for the Palestinians was threatened. In summer 1980, relations between the two countries degenerated into a campaign of vituperation and loud accusation, and all negotiations were stopped. By then, Carter had become extremely negative about Begin, and doubted that there was any point in my returning to the area to make one last attempt with the two leaders, but he accepted my judgment that I should try once more.

On August 31 I went to Israel and tried to impress on Begin the importance of a freeze on settlements if the negotiations were to be resumed. I told him he was paying a high price in the United States for his attitudes, not only with Carter but with the American public at large, and that he should consider carefully whether the values he found in new settlements were worth the defeat Israel would suffer in world opinion. He remained adamant. A meeting had been scheduled for me the next day with the full Israeli negotiating team, including Burg, Sharon, and Yitzhak Shamir, the personally likable but tough Foreign Minister. I decided to put the situation before them with utter frankness — referring specifically to the firmness of the Prime Minister on the settlements issue and my feelings about it.

First I called President Carter to tell him that my session with Begin had been discouraging, and that I was considering abandoning my trip and returning to Washington rather than going on to Egypt and Sadat with nothing to offer him on the settlements problem. Then I met with the full negotiating team, where my presentation was received courteously but coolly. Finally Sharon, who as Agricultural Minister was responsible for the settlements — and clearly the strong man of the cabinet, the one man whom I thought Begin feared — said that he thought too much was being made of the issue, because the government did not plan and would not build more than four additional settlements for the duration of its tenure in office.

I said, "Your Prime Minister didn't tell me that."

"But I'm telling you," said Sharon.

I asked whether I could convey such an assurance to Sadat, and Sharon said that of course I could. It seemed to me conceivable — not likely, but conceivable — that Sadat would be willing to put the negotiations on course again with such an assurance, but I would need it from Begin. When I returned to my hotel I had a message from Begin, assuring me that on this issue Sharon spoke for him, that I could take whatever Sharon had said as an undertaking by his government. And it was on that basis that I drew up the statement agreeing to resume negotiations, which Begin approved and which Sadat later accepted and allowed me to announce to the press.

Begin was precise and meticulous. At my first meeting with him, I found that he had all but memorized things I had said at my confirmation hearings, and I soon learned that anything I might say to a member of his cabinet would find its way to him and be revealed in our next conversation. When I met with Sadat, he would normally accept whatever agenda I brought; when I met with Begin, we were operating on Begin's agenda, to such an extent that I often had to interrupt him to ensure that the points I had come to make were in fact made. Yet there was a kindness and humanity to Begin that many missed. He understood the *amour propre* of others. When he learned that Prime Minister Khalil had been upset by his failure to go to the airport to greet him when he came to Israel, he made light of it, noting that Sadat and not Khalil was his true opposite number — but the next time Khalil arrived, he went to the airport.

Begin knew about people's personal lives, inquired after the grandchildren, spoke movingly of his own family, and was dependent on his wife to such an extent that observers trace his decline as a political leader to the moment of her death. He came to Sadat's funeral at great risk as a personal, not a political, expression — although once there he was unable to refrain from lecturing Giscard d'Estaing, whom he was meeting for the first time, on the history, rights, and aspirations of Israel. I stood beside him, and later I said to him, "You didn't give Giscard a chance to ask you a question." Begin replied, "Before he can ask, he has to know what to ask."

Some time after I was gone from office, Begin rejected with indignation President Reagan's promising Middle East initiative of September 1982. I spoke with him about it a few months later, and received a typically personalized explanation. "I got upset," he said. "I was off on a vacation, my first in years, I was settling down to read a novel, when I got a call from the U.S. ambassador, that he must see me immediately. I said, 'Sam, I'm on vacation.' But he drove here, he handed me this large plan about which we had never been consulted, it said many things they had never said to us before. I asked him to delay so I could consult with my cabinet, but he told me the President was afraid of a leak and was going to announce it the next day. So I rejected it. It was my darkest day as Prime Minister. The time will come to look at it again." But the time never came — and the fault was hardly Begin's alone.

In a speech in October 1984, U.S. Ambassador to Israel Sam Lewis described the Reagan initiative as "a genuine effort to recreate momentum, to relaunch the Camp David agreement, with some embellishments, but fundamentally on the same terms. The timing, unfortunately, was, in my judgment, abysmal; the tactics of its presentation, worse; and the outcome so far, nil."

My time as Middle East negotiator was a kaleidoscope. I met with Sadat at the Barrages, in Alexandria, in Ismailia, in Aswan, and in Washington. I saw Begin in Israel, and also in Washington. I met with the negotiating teams in Israel and in Egypt, and in England and in the Netherlands (in February 1980, incidentally, the Netherlands was the only country in Europe willing to be host to such meetings). I visited Prince Fahd in Saudi Arabia, and King Hassan of Morocco in his luxurious oasis in the middle of the country's best golf course. I soothed the hurt feelings of King Hussein of Jordan, carrying to him an official invitation to visit Washington that I had wrung from a reluctant Jimmy Carter, who still resented Hussein's failure to participate in the peace process begun at Camp David. I met with the Foreign Ministers of Britain, Germany, and France in an effort to deflect, or at least delay, the "European initiative" that gave the Saudis, Hussein, and the West Bank Palestinians additional reasons not to play in what was — and still is — the only game in town.

There were long sessions with the negotiating teams, when I practiced what the press called "elevator diplomacy," installing the two sides on different floors and shuttling between them with proposals, not permitting them to meet until there was a prospect that they would agree. I successfully suggested restricted access by the press, and tried to ensure meetings of working groups rather than full delegations, to minimize the posturing. From the beginning, I downplayed the "Modalities" group and stressed the need to make progress on "Powers and Responsibilities," proposing that no specific agreements on details be announced, that each individual compromise should be banked until there was an overall deal. Although the separate groups worked best when the senior negotiators — indeed, when Begin and Sadat — were pushing them, they always worked hard, and hopefully.

My worst moment was created by my own government. The Arab-Israeli dispute passes through the UN Security Council at irregular intervals like a rogue railway train with neither origin nor destination, and one of these passages occurred on March 1, 1980. The usual mischievous resolution was introduced and commanded the usual majority. It called on the Israelis to abandon all their settlements, which everyone knew they wouldn't do, and in addition contained language commanding the renewed partition of Jerusalem. I was in Europe, meeting with the parties, and a representative of the Near East Bureau called to discuss the matter. I said that I thought no purpose was served by calling for "dismantling" of the settlements, and that the references to Jerusalem were incendiary. I cabled my urgent advice to the President and the Secretary of State that the United States abstain on the resolution. (I learned later that the President never saw my cable.)

In response to White House insistence, Donald McHenry, our UN ambassador, negotiated the removal from the resolution of the paragraph on Jerusalem, but other references to the city and the language on settlements remained. Then the United States voted for the resolution in the Security Council, to the fury and outrage of the Israelis.

I arrived in Washington to find turmoil. The President felt he had been misled, that he had been assured that *all* references to Jerusalem had been deleted. I was summoned to a meeting in Mondale's office — the Vice-President, Vance, Christopher, McHenry, and me. The President wanted us to draft a statement saying that in voting in favor of the resolution, the United States had made a mistake, address the problem frontally and get rid of it. Mondale said he had urged Carter not to indicate that a mistake had been made, but the President was determined. As we discussed what was to be done, the President walked in, looking grim and harassed. "How are you coming on that statement?" he asked. He turned to McHenry, whom he was seeing for the first time since the vote. "If I had known what was in that resolution," he said, "I would never have approved it." McHenry replied, "Most of it is boilerplate." The President looked hard at him and said coldly, "I would never have approved any mention of Jerusalem," and he left. With Christopher doing most of the drafting, we prepared several statements that avoided acknowledging a mistake, and Mondale went in alone to show them to the President. He asked Vance if he would like to come along, and Vance said, "No." Mondale returned, and we drafted a statement that blamed the vote on a "failure to communicate" that "resulted in a vote in favor of the resolution rather than abstention." Critics of the administration — at home and abroad — had a field day, and the episode hovered over our negotiations.

In every aspect of the Egyptian-Israeli negotiations, we were walking on eggs. Yet by stepping carefully we were able to make very considerable progress. In a memorandum I gave to Carter on January 14, 1981, a week before he left office, I listed no fewer than twenty-five areas where Israel and Egypt had agreed on powers and responsibilities to be granted to the Palestinian Self-Governing Authority.

administration of justice	internal transportation
agriculture	labor
budget	local police and prisons
civil service	manpower
commerce	municipal affairs
culture	nature preserves and parks
ecology	public works
education	refugee rehabilitation
finance	religious affairs
health	social welfare
housing and construction	taxation
industry	tourism
internal communication and posts	

It was not a trivial collection. We were, I estimated, four-fifths of the way to an agreement, and the five major issues still on the table were all, I thought, capable of resolution.

Since 1981, unfortunately, the situation has deteriorated. There has been the horror of the war in Lebanon, which led to the withdrawal of the Egyptian ambassador from Tel Aviv. And all negotiations between Israel and Egypt on the future of the West Bank and Gaza have ceased.

But there is reason for some encouragement. In Shimon Peres, Israel has a sensitive and thoughtful Prime Minister who has long recognized the need to deal in a forthcoming manner with the problems of the West Bank and Gaza. The renewal of diplomatic relations between Egypt and Jordan and King Hussein's recent efforts to involve the Palestinians in the peace process may yet lead to resumption of autonomy negotiations. If so, then the solutions to the five unresolved autonomy issues that were available in 1981 are, I think, available still:

1. "Public lands" — that is, settlements, which Israel claims to have placed only on land that had no private owners. As proposed in President Reagan's September 1982 Peace Initiative, the existing settlements would remain in the West Bank and Gaza, but once the Self-Governing Authority came into existence, uses of unallocated public lands for settlements by either Israel or the Palestinians would be subject to the agreement of both the Authority and Israel.

2. "Water rights." The Authority would have to be given sufficient say in the distribution of this most scarce and valuable commodity to ensure that Palestinian farmers were not disadvantaged by comparison with Israeli farmers. On the other hand, the Israelis would need assurance that the Authority would not cut off supplies to the settlements or act to reduce the flow of water to Israel. A joint commission would be set up to ensure fair distribution of water resources, and eventually a regional body — also including Jordan — would be appointed to develop and allocate water resources in the region.

3. "Security." The Self-Governing Authority would have a strong local police force to assist in providing security in cooperation with Israeli security authorities. So long as necessary, Israel would be responsible for external security.

4. "Powers." The Self-Governing Authority would have all the powers necessary and appropriate to exercise its responsibilities in the agreed areas. These powers would not be designated as either "legislative" or "administrative."

5. "Palestinians in East Jerusalem." One proposal considered would be to permit Palestinians in East Jerusalem to have absentee

voting rights in the election of the Self-Governing Authority. They
would vote in such elections as though they were residents of the
West Bank.

To work out the details of such arrangements would of course be
a full-time job for negotiators working a number of months, constantly prodded by the leaders of their governments and by the
continued involvement of a high-level representative of the President of the United States. For the Palestinians on the West Bank
and Gaza, the choice between full autonomy and today's tight supervision by the Israelis would not, I think, be as difficult as so
many commentators seem to believe. And for all the bluster of some
in Israel, the deepest instincts of that country call for — cry out
for — peace.

In the spring of 1985 during a visit to Washington, King Hussein
offered some new promise of progress toward Middle East peace. By
the time these words are published, we shall know whether that
promise was realized. Certainly I do not wish to suggest that the
only right road to peace is the one I traveled. There are many ways
to get there if the will and the commitment are present. But I do believe that the peace process in being remains a great asset. It may be
dormant, but it is not dead.

It must be obvious to all in 1985 that Israel is not the sole or even
the dominant source of tension in the Middle East. Peace and goodwill between the Jordan River and the sea would not end the tensions between Libya and its neighbors, between Syria and Iraq or
Iraq and Iran, between the two Yemens, or among Sunni, Shiite,
Druse, and Christian in Lebanon. Our obligation to all the people
who live on the land the League of Nations defined as Palestine has
a long history and deep roots. The Carter administration sought
earnestly — and not ineffectively — to fulfill that obligation. Its
footsteps, while blurred, are not yet obliterated. I believe that even
now they may point the way to peace in the Holy Land.

10

Meanings and Missions

As an American, I accept entirely the founding belief that all men are created equal, which implies a preponderant role for circumstance in determining what people make of themselves. As a Jew, I know, as Albert Einstein once said, that God does not play dice with the universe. Things do not just *happen*. Physical forces change the shape of the earth; historic forces change societies. Every event has its antecedents and can be explained. As a lawyer, I believe that the world is and should be orderly, that our government is one of laws and not of men. Yet as an American, a Jew, and a lawyer, I believe also that man's will is free; that we are all responsible for our actions; that what we do as individuals makes a difference; that equality at birth gives every man and woman an equal right to excel, to plod, or to fail. It is in the denial of this right, in the constriction of opportunity, that we violate the great tenents of our polity and our faiths. It is in the individual achievement of our inequalities that we express its glories.

Man is the mystery. In 1974, at the request of the Jewish Theological Seminary, I did six "radio conversations" on NBC with leaders from different walks of life. One was with Isaac Stern, who marveled at the simplicity of the slow movement of Beethoven's Violin Concerto: "What he had to say distilled all the thoughts that you can put into the most profound prayer. But how did he discover this? This is the point. You can analyze it, you can explain it, but you can't find out how he divined this in his own conceptual process. All you can do is recognize it and try to get near it."

The philosophers of intellectual history say that literary, artistic, and social thought are creations, whereas scientific and political thought are only discoveries. Leaders do not create movements; movements find their leaders. Only Beethoven, they say, could have written Beethoven's Violin Concerto, but anyone could have found Planck's Constant: it was *there*. I disagree. I have seen firsthand what a man can do because he rather than someone else has the authority to act. Xerography resulted not from a time but from the combination of Chet Carlson and Joe Wilson. Anwar Sadat had imagination, commitment, and the courage to take risks. Menachem Begin was the only person who could have persuaded Israel to accept Camp David. If it had not been for that strange man Omar Torrijos and Jimmy Carter, the United States and Panama would still be at each other's throats over the Panama Canal issue, as Britain and Argentina are over the Falklands — or Malvinas. No one but a Lyndon Johnson could have taken the country to the Great Society. Only a Richard Nixon could have put a stop to our isolation of China.

At a luncheon in Buenos Aires recently, the destined victims of the Argentine junta tearfully told Jimmy Carter that they were still alive because he had been in the White House — and their gratitude was not misplaced. History, I believe, will see Carter in that perspective, will remember the man who with courage and vision settled the Panama Canal disputes, presided over Camp David, and fought for human rights.

Of course, Carter suffered failures of leadership, but his was a strange flaw. Every man in public life is vulnerable, and there are moments when he needs the loyalty of his followers to carry him over a defeat. Carter seemed unable to admit that vulnerability in public. He had to appear to be in control, even when in truth he was not. The Iranian hostage disaster might have destroyed any President, but it was especially damaging to Carter because he had never gained — had never sought — the country's *sympathy*.

Toni and I were with the President on his first visit to a public gathering after his defeat. He and Rosalyn invited us to join them for a concert at the Kennedy Center in honor of Aaron Copland's eightieth birthday. In the car from the White House, the President talked about his responsibility to make sure that he turned over the government to his successor in good shape, and it dawned on me that he and Mrs. Carter were very nervous about how they would be greeted when they entered the President's box in the Opera House. Tradition is that the President comes into the hall last, after all the doors are closed, just before the concert or the opera begins, so we waited in the anteroom behind the box, and drank a glass of wine, until the Secret Service said it was time. Carter insisted that all four of us go out together, and as he entered, the audience rose with thunderous applause. He began to weep, and so did his wife, and you could see the tension and nervousness drain from them. The couple that went back to the White House after the concert was very different from the couple that had left it. One aspect of Carter's tension was unchanged, however: he pointed out to me in the car that the watch on his left wrist was set to Teheran time.

There are few great leaders in the world today, people you can point to and say, "They can move nations." Anwar Sadat, Golda Meir, and Helmut Schmidt were perhaps the last of them. In our own country, we waste our leadership talent. Names of subjunctive Presidents come to mind — men who would have been, could have been, should have been President. Hubert Humphrey, for example, had so much more to contribute than we allowed him to give. Among the moments of my life I remember most vividly is the scene at the Cow Palace in San Francisco in 1964, when the Republican National Convention booed and hooted at Nelson Rockefeller, who could have been a great President: he had this mysterious ability to take contented people and get them moving. (It should be remembered that Rockefeller lost caucus votes, convention votes, and primaries, but he never in his life lost a general election.) And sometimes our leaders waste their gifts. Ronald Reagan has an extraordinary capacity to rouse public support and sympathy, if only he had and could set forth not just the attitudes he believes Americans should have but the goals he would wish them to seek.

I was made keenly aware of the vagaries of leadership when in October 1981 I flew on Air Force One to Cairo as a member of the official United States delegation to the funeral of Anwar Sadat. On the plane were the three living former Presidents of the United States — Richard Nixon, Gerald Ford, and Jimmy Carter — together for the first time. During that long night, I observed them, listened to them, and talked with them: Nixon — opinionated, seemingly assured yet transparently tense and anxious; Ford — relaxed, attentive, not trying to impress; Carter — uneasy, withdrawn, yet ever alert and watchful. As I studied them, I searched unsuccessfully for answers: what qualities of leadership had brought each of them to the presidency?

I have long believed that this nation's businessmen and professionals should offer the country more leadership. American companies have a great stake in an orderly society and a peaceful world, conditions that cannot be achieved without just and wise governance. The heads of the great corporations have the habits of leadership, and experience (some of it hard experience) in judging the implications for the future hidden in the thickets of argument over today's decisions. Of course they have a fiduciary duty to their stockholders, but they can also achieve the breadth of vision that sees the community of their employees and their customers as equally important beneficiaries of their concern. They can achieve it, that is, if they try; too often, unfortunately, they don't.

Of course, a business exists primarily to earn a profit. It was Samuel Gompers who said that the worst crime against the working man is a company that doesn't make money. But the significant profits are those earned over time: the price of the stock relates not to the current asset value of the enterprise but to the estimated cash flow the investment will earn in the future. That is a function of the quality of the enterprise as perceived by the public, which is much more than a matter of public relations, and also inevitably a function of the general level of prosperity in the country, which has to do with politics and government. As a collaborative enterprise, a company relates in many and varied ways to the community it employs and to the government that establishes the legal order within which the company operates.

One of the disturbing aspects of America today is the deteriorating relations between businessmen and their employees, which are becoming much more adversarial. I find in too many of the corporate executives and labor leaders I know a sense of gearing up for a fight rather than looking for opportunities, and planning to seize them, in ways that would be beneficial for both sides. Management is concerned about foreign competition, unions are worried about declining membership. They come together only in the worst place, in a shared desire for the shield of protectionism, at the expense of their customers.

The businessman as a matter of self-interest should seek a higher horizon. It is trite but true that you can't be an oasis of wealth in a desert of poverty, because you can't plan intelligently for a future always menaced by such disparities. Nor can one be sanguine about the prospects for the long-term profitability of a company where the work force feels itself unfairly treated. There is, moreover — and businessmen must accept it — a place for the government at the table. The business community has a stake in what happens to the country; the government has a stake in what happens to the business community.

I believe it would serve both the nation and the enterprise community well if more people in the private sector spent some part of their careers in government service. A businessman who has worked for the government and brings his understanding of that world back to the private sector makes a real contribution to his company. And while serving the government he can make a special contribution to his country, provided he remembers that he has moved into a different national subculture with different purposes. Unfortunately, we have made it difficult for a businessman or a lawyer to do this in mid-career, because we have written conflict-of-interest laws so extreme that they require short-term government employees to sever all their connections with their previous employer if that employer is a for-profit organization. We would be wiser to offer business and professional people the same courtesies now extended to college professors, who are permitted to work for the government while on leave from their universities. It would be no great trick to insulate the individual from decisions affecting his past and future employers if the arrangements were all open and aboveboard.

An interesting and little-publicized example of what businessmen can do is the International Executive Service Corps, which grew out of speeches made in 1964 in the same week — quite independently, on different coasts of the country — by David Rockefeller and myself. This was the heyday of the Peace Corps, and we both suggested that one of the truly grievous lacks in the less-developed countries was management talent. There was no shortage of entrepreneurs in these countries, but African, Asian, and Latin societies had not facilitated the step from proprietorship to company. An American businessman who took the time to become knowledgeable about local customs might be able to help small and medium-sized companies in developing countries in ways beyond the imaginings of the government-aid community. If he could go there, he could communicate the systems, the technology, the ethics of modern business in ways no textbook could rival. As I said in my speech, "The best way to send an idea around the world is to wrap it up in a person."

To its credit, the Agency for International Development seized on this idea, brought Rockefeller and me together, and organized a conference of several hundred people in Washington. Rockefeller became chairman of the group, I became chairman of its executive committee, and Frank Pace, who had been Secretary of the Army, head of the Bureau of the Budget, and chairman of General Dynamics, became its president and chief executive officer. Over the two decades, almost nine thousand businessmen — mostly retired, but some on sabbatical from active careers — have gone to these countries and made their expertise available in consultant and managerial roles, for periods of six months to two years. The overwhelming majority of them have been successful in helping their hosts; virtually all of them have had an unforgettable learning experience.

I feel so strongly that businessmen and professionals should make time to undertake government service because for me such service has been emotionally far more rewarding than anything I have done as a businessman or as a lawyer for private clients. One misses in government work the measurements of performance that provide the rewards of effort in private enterprise: the profit-and-loss figures, the share-of-market, the productivity statistics, the stock prices. It can be infuriating to force decisions through a bureaucracy that likes to look in all directions before it moves, and a businessman must keep reminding himself that a government agency has more constituencies to satisfy than any business. Bureaucrats work on an astonishingly ad hoc basis, without any sense of where you want the enterprise to be six months or a year or two from now. They don't delegate well, because they are so often jockeying for position. And, of course, they know that some day this politically appointed boss will pass, and another will take his place. But once the businessman learns how the system works, without reference to whether he thinks it could work better, he finds there are levers to pull that do produce action. And when you do it right in government, the beneficiary is your country.

The criteria by which an outsider judges what to do when he works for the government are, quite simply, less selfish than the criteria he would employ in the private sector — and perhaps less selfish also than the criteria habitually consulted by the bureaucrat. The businessman or lawyer temporarily in government can single-mindedly seek the decision, the program, and the personnel he believes will be best for the public. But the civil servant does not serve the *civis;* he works in the belly of the whale. Often he has to think about how this decision will affect his future career, which may be tied to his support for the interests of his sponsors and his acceptance of the attitudes of his superiors rather than to the quality of his judgment.

As against the professional politician, the great advantage of the outsider in government is that he does not think in electoral terms of winners and losers and zero-sum games. He knows that life goes on, that everyone will come to work again on Monday, that the best solutions are those everyone can live with. Twice in my life I was offered an opportunity to run for office: in the 1940s, to be the Congressman from Rochester; in the 1960s, to be Governor of New York. Both times I went to talk with the man I would run against, Ken Keating and Nelson Rockefeller; both times I decided I did not wish to be in a fight to the finish with someone I considered an admirable public servant with views not that much different from my own. I do not like these all-or-nothing contests, just as I do not like to squeeze the last ounce of advantage out of a bargain. I believe in negotiated solutions, where both sides have gained enough of what they need to defend the deal and live with it.

We have an adversarial system of justice, and any lawyer spends much of his life fighting for one side or the other in a dispute. Yet all lawyers know that their clients' interests are almost always best served if a matter can be kept out of litigation and resolved in a negotiation. And the obligation of the negotiator is to respect his opponent, to keep in mind not only what his side must have if there is to be a deal, but also what his adversary must have. This takes judgment, of course: the art of the negotiator is to put forward as convincingly as possible his principal's main demand, retreating slowly and only as necessary to the point where agreement can be reached. Exercising these powers of analysis and of judgment is a wonderful game and always exciting, whatever the issue between the parties. I must say, however, that orchestrating an agreement when the subject matter is the exact rights and privileges of a company licensing a xerography patent does not hold a candle to representing your country in the negotiations for a new Panama Canal treaty or in the effort to achieve Middle East peace.

* * *

Even if I did not find government service so exciting, I would feel a strong personal obligation to undertake it. The poet Archibald MacLeish once said that "America is promises," but these promises have not been kept equally to all. Those of us for whom the most extravagant promises of this land have become a reality are, I think, required to seek appropriate expressions of their gratitude.

I am the oldest of my parents' four sons (the other three spell our name "Linowes"). The one closest to me in age is David, who is three-and-a-half years my junior, a CPA, management consultant, and professor of political economy and public policy at the University of Illinois. Davis chaired the Federal Privacy Protection Commission for President Ford and was chairman of President Reagan's Commission on Fair Market Value for Federal Coal Leasing, the members of which were so infelicitously described by Interior Secretary James Watt. He has written several books and undertaken several governmental assignments abroad. My brother Bob, eight years younger than I am, followed me to Hamilton (where he also got an honorary doctorate) and took his law degree at Columbia under the GI Bill. He is a nationally recognized zoning and development lawyer, is active in a number of organizations, and, as noted earlier, has served as president of the Washington Board of Trade. My youngest brother, Harry, fourteen years my junior, has his own CPA firm in Washington, and among his community services is his chairmanship of the Washington Performing Arts Society, the leading sponsor of concerts in the area. Each of us is still married to his original wife; each of us has four children.

We all wound up in Washington (although Dave now lives in Scarsdale, New York, and Champaign, Illinois), and we consider ourselves close. Not long ago, we sat together over a drink and talked about our parents. Joseph and Rose Linowitz were not highly educated people; they had come across the ocean in early adolescence, bringing their hopes and little more. They met and married in America, and their life was a struggle. We were given to understand, however, that they expected a great deal of their sons (*of course* we would be omnivorous readers, and do well in school, and become professional men), but none of us remembers being lectured or told what he should do with his life

My mother was a worrier of a classic kind. She gave her sons care and love and close attention, and could not shake the fear that somehow it was not enough. But her approach was not without subtlety. From the age of eight or nine, I had violin lessons, which meant violin practice. Once I rebelled, and demanded the chance to go out and play with the other boys. She told me I didn't have to practice the violin if I didn't want to do it — and the next day when I came home from school the violin was missing from its usual place behind the piano. After ten days or so I missed it, and began rummaging through the closets. When I reached the locked steamer trunk in the attic, my mother, who I thought was out of the house, materialized behind me and said, "Now you can have it" — and I never complained again about the need to practice.

My father was a shy, modest, quiet man with a puckish sense of humor. He and his brothers had built a wholesale fruit business of some substance in the 1920s, only to see it wash away in the Depression. But he never complained, and he was never impressed by worldly goods. His question about anything we achieved — a prize, an appointment, a promotion — was, "What are you going to *do* with it?" He shared my mother's feeling that the most important legacy they could give us was education; and the hardest and most painful part for him was that he could not give us the financial help we needed. It was characteristic of him that when he suffered his first heart attack while still in his early fifties, he asked the doctor to keep word of the diagnosis from my mother — to avoid worrying her. On his deathbed he wanted to be assured, above all else, that she would be cared for.

Values were taught in our house by example, not rhetoric. We were not a synagogue-going family, but Jewishness was in the home, and we knew and honored its demands. We never stood as a unit against the community that lived around us; we were always a positive part of our society. In the childhood memories of all of us, times were hard. People helped each other. When my mother learned that neighbors needed something, she would see that they had it. My father wrote debts to him off the books when he found that people who owed him money couldn't pay. My parents most of all loved and trusted this country. During World War II there was a family occasion when we all made it back home, and my father — who had left Russia to escape military service for the Czar — glowed with pride to walk beside his three oldest sons in uniform: private Bob, Army lieutenant Dave, Navy lieutenant Sol.

We lived in a mixed neighborhood. There was an Italian family on one side of our house, and an Irish family on the other side. I was Salutatorian of my Trenton High School class; the Valedictorian was an Italian boy whom I recently encountered again, for the first time in decades: he had become the senior partner in the investment banking house of Morgan, Stanley. There were no Negro families on our block, but they were only a block or two away. One of my black friends in high school became principal of the school. My brothers and I all acquired a sense of a large American community — and we have all passed it on to our children.

Toni and I have four daughters. Anne, the oldest (and the mother of our two grandchildren, Judy and David), is a social worker in Ottawa, where her husband works for the Canadian government as a transportation expert. June is an artist, and worked for several years for the National Urban Coalition. Her husband is a consultant on computer services. Jan works with emotionally disturbed children and is taking a doctorate at Harvard; her husband is a psychologist. Ronni, our youngest, teaches art at the Sidwell Friends School in Washington. The girls are close, confide in one another, and share a sense of humor and a sense of concern about what happens to other human beings.

I carry in my wallet — I have carried it for years — a homily by Ralph Waldo Emerson: "To laugh often and love much; to win the respect and the affection of children; to earn the approbation of honest critics and endure the betrayal of false friends; to appreciate beauty; to find the best in others; to give one's self; to leave the world a bit better, whether by a healthy child, a garden patch or a redeemed social condition; to have played and laughed with enthusiasm and sung with exaltation; to know even one life has breathed easier because you have lived — *this is to have succeeded.*"

One needs stability at the center. Since we were married forty-six years ago, Toni has been for me an unfailing source of serenity, understanding, and wise and loving support. Without Toni and our four daughters, and the pride and joy they have brought me, I could never have maintained the level of concentration my work has required. The more intense the work, the more important the hours at home, when relaxation speaks of love. Some of that, too, I believe, my brothers and I learned from our parents.

The last few years have not been encouraging for people of my views. Domestically, we seem to have lost the path to social justice on which Lyndon Johnson so boldly planted our reluctant feet. In Central America, we seem to have forgotten the lessons of a generation, and we are again behaving as though our overwhelming strength gives us an equally dominating wisdom. In the Middle East and in Europe, we want our friends to subordinate what they perceive to be their own interests to our strategy for the containment of Soviet power. Once the United Nations was for us (as it still is for many of the world's smaller sovereignties) an expression of man's hopes for the end of war, the triumph of reason, the expansion of prosperity; now we scarcely trouble to conceal our view of it as an insignificant enemy. On their own terms, the Reagan administration's foreign policies can be considered a success: they have made our allies passive and our opponents fearful. Having achieved these objectives, we now come gradually to the realization that as a nation we have not envisioned the higher goals to which they could be stepping-stones.

But if it seems that we have lost our way, the greater truth is that we have not lost our opportunities. We have the resources — natural, human, institutional — to remedy many of the wrongs that press on the family of man. In the perspective of history, today's disillusionments may well appear as a necessary corrective to the naive hopes and overblown plans of our old optimism. Those who pick up the torch will build not only on the idealism of the Kennedy-Johnson years but also on the hard truths thrown in our path by the years that have followed. The difficult — the seemingly impossible — jobs are in the end the most interesting. I am still working at them myself, never despairing; and I am moved and uplifted by support from new hands reaching out to help.

Index